THE
TREE
BOOK

J. EDWARD MILNER

THE TREE BOOK

*The indispensable guide to tree
facts, crafts and lore*

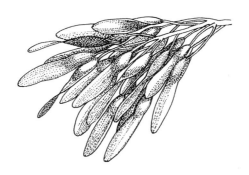

ACACIA Productions Ltd

COLLINS & BROWN

This book is in memory of my father, who knew of the project when he died but never saw any of it on screen or page. It is also for my dear wife Nikki, for my daughters Lisa and Yasmin, who already know the beauty and spirit of trees, and for my mother, to thank her for first kindling my interest in trees and in the rest of the natural world.

FRONTISPIECE A mature beech tree in the grounds of Cluny House, Aberfeldy, Perthshire.

First published in Great Britain in 1992
by Collins & Brown Limited
Mercury House
195 Knightsbridge
London SW7 1RE

British Library Cataloguing-in-Publication Data:
A catalogue record for this book is available from the British Library.

ISBN 1 85585 132 6 (hardback edition)
ISBN 1 85585 147 4 (paperback edition)

Conceived, edited and designed by Collins & Brown Limited
Editorial Director: Gabrielle Townsend
Editor: Colin Ziegler
Picture Consultant: Alan Watson
Picture Research: Amy Bradshaw
Art Director: Roger Bristow
Designer: Ruth Hope
Maps by Eugene Fleury
Illustrations on pages 3, 13, 17, 21, 25, 29, 33, 39, 43 by Eric Thomas
Filmset by Spectrum, London
Reproduction by J Film, Singapore
Printed and bound by New Interlitho, S.p.a., Milan, Italy
This book is printed on 135gsm Biomatt from Cartiera di Toscolano mill in Italy. The paper is chlorine free and over 50 per cent recycled.

Contents

Preface

THE IDEA for this book and the televison series called *Spirit of Trees* came in the aftermath of the Great Storm of October 1987, when millions of trees were blown down across southern England and bordering areas of continental Europe. I was already dissatisfied with the range of books available on the subject of trees, and when I observed people's reactions to the storm I saw that many felt a strong affinity with trees, an emotional pull, and that they really would like to know more about them; not necessarily about different and unusual trees, but about the familiar native trees of these islands.

Tree-books tend to be focused on one aspect of trees: identification, silviculture and forestry, history and some aspects of conservation are all extensively covered by a wide range of highly qualified writers. But folklore, traditional uses and even the ecology of trees all seem to be more or less neglected, and what has struck me is that it is really the interaction of these three aspects that is particularly intriguing. I am not a botanist, though I count myself as a scientist, but I am certainly a tree-enthusiast. There are so many different responses to trees; I have found that even scientists delight in the folklore and the history of trees and get emotionally involved in campaigns to protect them. As my friend Dick Warner, the presenter of the TV series *Spirit of Trees*, puts it at the start of the first programme, 'What is really fascinating is the complexity of the relationship between us human beings and these giant plants.'

So in the spirit of trees, if I can use that expression, what I have tried to do is to make a book which combines some of these different dimensions from the scientific to the cultural, and from the ecological to the spiritual.

I am extremely grateful to a number of different people whose brain I have unashamedly picked while researching and writing this book. Many of these people have given me constant help and encouragement; however any errors and omissions are mine. In particular I would like to thank John White, Rob Soutar, George Peterken, Donald Pigott, Oliver Rackham, David Bevan, Philip Grime, John Birks, Roy Vickery, Patricia Lysaght, Tony Miller, Ken Stott, Paul Hand, Alan Mitchell, Alan Watson, Gerwyn Lewis, Allen Meredith, Ted Green, Hazel Birch, Edgar Milne-Redhead, Dick Warner and many others who have all helped me enormously. I would also like to thank the staff of Acacia Productions, especially my researcher Amy Bradshaw, who has contributed substantially at every stage, Paola Zaccheroni and Trish Cann.

I have referred to several authors at regular intervals because they seem to me both authoritative and consistently interesting. Of these the most important are Nicholas Culpepper, the famous astrologer, physician and herbalist, and John Evelyn, the great English silviculturalist, both of the seventeenth century, and two twentieth-century writers, Geoffrey Grigson, the celebrated poet and countryman, and Oliver Rackham, the Cambridge don and authority on the history of our trees and countryside.

Introduction

MOST BOOKS on trees are written by foresters; this one is not. As a tree-lover I am delighted and fascinated by our own native trees, about which we still have so much to learn. So this book concentrates on trees in their natural state; I have emphasized our native trees, but I have also tried to give our tree flora some sort of global context by taking just a few examples of particularly interesting and notable trees — the biggest, the oldest, the strangest — in other parts of the world. It is a personal, some will say idiosyncratic, selection — there are many other trees and tree-topics I would love to have included.

The largest part of the book is the first one, 'The Trees of Britain and Ireland', which starts with portraits of eight major trees, including some botany, ecology, history and folklore about each one, and slightly shorter accounts of all the other native trees. Following chapters look at our trees from a number of aspects; the history of our trees from the pollen record, our ancient trees (limes and yews), two of our rarest trees (the Plymouth and Whitty pears) and their conservation and the interactions of our trees with other organisms. There are then accounts of the coppicing and pollarding of our woodland trees and the traditional management of willows and fruit trees.

'Trees and the Earth' broadens the perspective by discussing the role that trees play in the whole ecosphere, of which our islands and their trees are just one small part. Specific ecological strategies of different species are then discussed before some consideration of record trees, including the oldest (bristlecone pines) and the largest (redwoods), the living fossil tree and the strange trees of the island of Socotra. Folklore associated with trees is universal and Chapter 12 gives an introductory account of tree-lore in these islands.

Part 3 is concerned with the future of trees: there are many different voices entering the debates about trees, tree-conservation and tree-planting, so contributions have been included from some of the more thoughtful experts in this field. The role of the many tree groups and tree campaigns (most of them voluntary) is also vital and Chapter 15 surveys some of the most important ones.

Finally, 'Tree Information' includes a list of the main tree species with some comparative data about each, lists of famous trees and tree festivals to attend, suppliers of native trees, tree organizations and a list of references used in the book with suggestions for further reading.

Throughout the book, the dimensions of trees are often given simply as figures in brackets. In these cases the first figure is the tree's height in metres and the second figure, the tree's diameter in centimetres.

What is a Tree? Everyone knows a tree when they see one but to define the word precisely is not easy. What is the difference between a tree and a bush, or a large shrub? Is elder a tree; how small is a small tree?

Certain features are generally agreed; a tree is woody, more or less erect, at least in favourable circumstances, usually single-stemmed and for many authors 'able to exceed 6 metres (20 feet) in height' (Mitchell

1974). But some trees do not reach this height and yet are clearly trees, and perhaps the most important feature of a tree is that it looks like a tree! So an oak is a tree and heather is not a tree, but where is the dividing line?

This problem can be overcome if one defines a tree as a plant with a proportionally large main stem which is more or less rigid. When the wind blows across the scrubland, bushes bend and sway from the ground up; but the main trunk of a tree stays more or less rigid, though the branches may sway. I like this point because it seems to me there is a very interesting category of small, even minute trees right down to 'God's Bonsai', the tiny dwarf willow that grows on the tops of our mountains.

Whatever the definition that is accepted, there are always going to be borderline cases. I have already been taken to task by my colleague Dick Warner for excluding the elder.

The History and Biology of Trees Trees are very ancient in origin and have been on this planet longer than many animals. Their strategy of using their strong woody stems to hold up very large numbers of leaves to manufacture food on a large scale has clearly been a great success; they have dominated the vegetation of the planet since the Carboniferous period between 365 and 295 million years ago.

The first trees were cone-bearing (conifers), placed by plant taxonomists in the *Gymnospermae*, but within about 100 million years they had been overtaken and largely replaced by the so-called higher plants or Angiosperms.

Today there are about 700 conifer species left, many of them restricted to tropical mountains, having been replaced at lower altitudes by flowering trees, of which there are thought to be around 30-40,000 species today, out of a total of around 250,000 species of higher plants. The vast majority of tree species are in the tropical forests, but there is also a great diversity of temperate forest trees and new species are being found today in places like the Himalayas, China and the Amazon.

The life-cycle of trees is as diverse as in any other group of plants, but generally, after the germination of the seed, it takes a number of years for a tree to become mature and full-grown. Wind-pollinated trees, like other wind-pollinated plants, tend to have small, insignificant flowers, but most other trees have brightly coloured, often large flowers that attract pollinating animals by smell, appearance, or by secreting nectar.

Once the flowers have been pollinated, seeds and often the ovary and surrounding tissues all develop and grow into fruits. Sometimes, as in apple or cherry, these are attractive and tasty, leading to another relationship, that of trees with their dispersal agents. Once seeds reach the ground, either via an animal or bird, or by falling directly, germination does not always take place immediately.

Many tree seeds are tiny and must start to manufacture their own food by starting photosynthesis very quickly; within a day or two of germination. Others, like acorns, have large food reserves, allowing them to develop substantial roots to anchor them or to establish them in dense vegetation, before they begin to manufacture their own food. From that point on they usually begin to outgrow all other plants, gradually shading them out until they dominate their immediate environment.

PART ONE

THE TREES OF BRITAIN AND IRELAND

1

Portraits of Major Native Trees

HIS OPENING CHAPTER focuses on eight of the most widespread and characteristic native trees found in Britain and Ireland today. These are mostly our largest trees, and, in various combinations, make up most of the canopy of our natural woodlands and forests – except in some specialized habitats like wetlands, where other tree species, like alder and willow, take over.

Most of these trees are among the oldest members of our flora, though beech and, to a lesser extent, lime are more recent arrivals. (Indeed neither of these two species is truly native to Ireland, although beech is presently thriving there, having been introduced in the eighteenth century.) These portraits examine each tree's history, characteristics and life. Then they move on to look at the uses the trees have been put to by man over the centuries, and the folklore associated with each tree. There are also information boxes recording the average size and age of each species, and examples of record specimens.

The selection is inevitably an arbitrary one – elm would have been included if it had not been for its recent demise – but together, they are meant to comprise a representative group of the principal native trees found in Britain and Ireland today.

The trees featured in this chapter are the ash (*Fraxinus excelsior*), the beech (*Fagus sylvatica*), the birch (*Betula pendula* [silver] and *Betula pubescens* [downy]), the black poplar (*Populus nigra*), the lime (*Tilia cordata* [small-leaved] and *Tilia platyphyllos* [large-leaved]), the oak (*Quercus robur* [common] and *Quercus petraea* [sessile]), the Scots pine (*Pinus sylvestris*) and the yew (*Taxus baccata*).

THE ASH

Common Ash *Fraxinus excelsior* L.

The ash is a member of the family *Oleaceae*, which also includes the olive. The genus *Fraxinus* contains 65 species, one of which is native to Britain and Ireland. It is the most northerly member of the family and the only wind-pollinated species; the others are all insect-pollinated.

Other names Uinsinn (Gaelic), Uinnius (Old Irish), Fuinnseog (Irish), Ask (Norse). The name ash is thought to come from the Anglo-Saxon 'aesc', a poetic word for spear.

Some derivative place-names Ashford, Askrigg, Monyash, Aspatria; in Ireland, various including the River Funshion (Co. Cork).

Folklore Ash is the tree of Mercury and is represented by the letter N (neon) in the tree alphabet.

A Mature Ash
This ash (right), deep in a Highland glen near Inverfarigaig, Loch Ness, has a trunk covered with epiphytic mosses. Woods composed mainly of ash occur as far north as Rassall, near Loch Torridan.

An Ash Seedling
Growing alongside ferns, among lichen-covered boulders, this ash seedling's presence (below) indicates neutral or even alkaline soil conditions.

THE ASH IS ONE of the most characteristic and best-loved trees of British woodlands, where it is the fourth commonest tree species. It occurs as a dominant member of the main canopy in woodlands, on heavy or calcareous soils in many parts of the country. In the north-west of Scotland, for example, there is a small wood of almost pure ash on a limestone outcrop near Applecross, and the ash grows naturally throughout these islands as far as Shetland, though sparsely in the north. The tree is found almost to the Arctic Circle in Norway, and across Europe to Turkey. It can be found growing above 500m (1,640 ft) in suitable river valleys in the north and west (up to 1,600m (5,250 ft) in Europe), and often survives on poor soils where few other trees will grow. On moist, well-drained and sheltered lowland sites, the ash is fast growing, with the highest nutrient uptake of any native tree. It does, however, require full light to thrive, and finds it very difficult to recover from suppression under heavy shade in a wood.

'Oak before the ash there'll be a splash, Ash before the oak there'll be a soak.' In spite of the old rhyme, the ash is nearly always the last native tree to come into leaf, usually in May. According to an old folk tale, witches eat the buds on their way to Walpurgisnacht (May Eve) so that the trees do not come into leaf until St John's Eve (Midsummer Eve). In the autumn, ash is often the first tree to drop its leaves and, as its foliage is relatively sparse even in midsummer, a rich ground flora is able to grow up under native ash trees.

Ash trees are usually dioecious, but are sometimes polygamous. The clusters of male flowers are purplish and turn yellow when the pollen is shed; the female clusters are pale green. The flowers appear before the foliage and the tree is well adapted to a windy temperate climate, both pollination and seed dispersal being by wind. Up to 100,000 elongated winged fruits are borne on an individual tree, often staying there well into the following season. While a few seeds will germinate as soon as they fall, most of them will not germinate for at least two winters, during which time the embryos slowly develop. Nurserymen traditionally

'stratify' the seeds in wet sand for 6 or 18 months before sowing them. Under natural conditions, predation of the fruits by birds, small mammals and caterpillars can destroy most of the crop. When they are still green, some ash fruits are collected by country people and made into ash-key pickle.

According to Kennedy and Southwood, 68 species of phytophagous invertebrate are associated with ash, while 225 species of epiphytic lichens have been recorded from it: only the oak has more. The most characteristic insects are perhaps the ash bark beetle (*Leperisinus varius*), which makes a very complicated gallery pattern under the bark, and the dusky thorn moth (*Ennomos fuscantaria*), the small caterpillars of which feed on the leaves. The wood-boring caterpillars of the goat moth (*Cossus cossus*) also feed on ash. Three types of gall are common on ash, causing swellings and distortion of the foliage and flowers. Flower galling, which can affect whole trees, is caused by the tiny gall-mite, *Eriophyes fraxinivorus*. Various fungi are found on living and dead ash, but none appears to be particularly associated with the tree.

The Uses of Ash Ash is one of the most valuable native trees in Britain, its wood being very strong and flexible: indeed, laboratory tests show ash to have 'greater toughness [impact strength] than any other home-grown hardwood'. This has been recognized for a very long time; the Anglo-Saxons and others used ash wood to make spears, shield handles, etc. Ash is traditionally used for a wide variety of other products – tool handles, furniture, sports equipment, walking sticks, tent-pegs, oars, gates, wheel-rims, and the frames and shafts of diverse vehicles, from horse-carts to aircraft. Before the development of light alloys, ash wood was used for the construction of aircraft wings, including the famous Second World War de Havilland Mosquito.

Young shoots of coppiced ash have been used in the past for animal fodder, though this is sometimes held to be a cause of diminished milk yields. According to John Birkett, a farmer in Little Langdale, where there are numerous fine old ash (and sycamore) pollards, ash trees are still lopped during the winter in parts of the Lake District to provide winter fodder for sheep. Historically, ash has also had another link with sheep as, on account of its alleged health-giving properties, ash was considered the 'proper wood' for a shepherd's crook.

Among the historical eulogies of ash trees and ash-wood, John Evelyn's is perhaps the most famous:

'In short, so useful and profitable is this tree [next to the oak] that every prudent Lord of the manor should employ one acre of ground with Ash or Acorns to every twenty acres of other Land: since in as many years it would be worth more than the land itself.'

A number of varieties of ash are cultivated, perhaps the most celebrated being the weeping form, *pendula*, which may have originated from a tree found in the eighteenth century by the vicar of Gamlingay, near Wimpole in Cambridgeshire. Traditionally, ash has been coppiced on a 12- to 20-year rotation in Britain, and to a lesser extent grown as standards for timber. It is still coppiced at Bradfield Woods in Suffolk, where the ash poles are made into rake handles and steam-bent for scythes. Ash wood also burns well and makes very good charcoal.

Tree Lore and Folk Beliefs Known in Scandinavia as *yggdrasil*, the 'Tree of the World' and the 'Tree of Rebirth and Healing', the ash is thought to have healing and other restorative properties; ash leaves or keys bring good luck or divine true love and ward off witchcraft. Ash sap was believed to protect newborn babies and make them strong. Gilbert White, in *The Natural History of Selborne*, describes curing a child by passing it naked through the cleft trunk of a pollarded ash. Young children were thought to be cured of rickets by similar treatment. A famous shrew-ash (a tree in which a live shrew has been immolated) in Richmond Park was still used in this way until the late nineteenth century. Around the turn of the century, this ancient tree was replaced by another ash, which blew down in the 1987 storm; plans for a second replacement are being considered.

In Ireland, the ash frequently has a sacred significance which is thought to originate in the extensive Norse influence in that country. Tradition has it that three of the five 'legendary trees' of Ireland were ash trees. A count of trees associated with Irish holy wells confirmed that after hawthorn (whitethorn) it is the second most predominant tree 'as the companion of the holy well' and numerous great ash trees or their stumps can still be found at holy wells.

On the Isle of Man, ash trees are thought to safeguard the purity of springs, while in Hampshire and Sussex schoolchildren carried ash twigs in their pockets on Ash Wednesday – those arriving without them could expect to have their feet stamped on by all those with twigs.

Culpepper recommended ash leaves to cure an adder's bite, while decoctions of them in white wine 'helpeth to break the [gall] stone and expel it, and cure the jaundice.'

'The Ash, from the lightness of its foliage, the graceful sweep of its branches, and the silvery appearance of its stem, has been called the Venus of the Forest.' STRUTT, 1822

The Life Stages of the Ash
The fruits of the ash, known as ash-keys, are dispersed by the wind. Despite up to 100,000 being produced by each tree, predation by animals usually destroys most of the crop before it can grow into seedlings. Far more ash seedlings survive in urban situations, where predation of seeds is less.

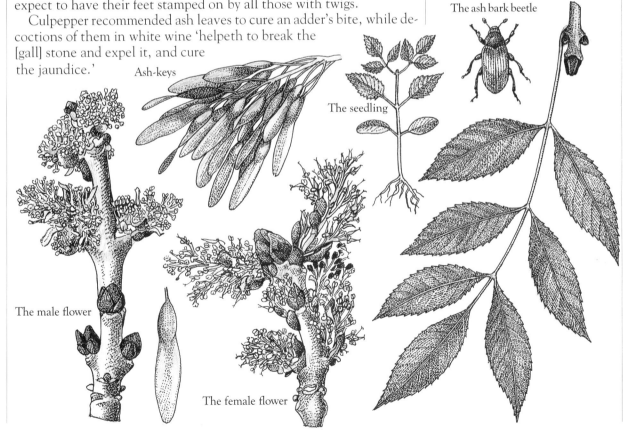

Ash-keys

The ash bark beetle

The seedling

The male flower

The female flower

THE BEECH

Common Beech *Fagus sylvatica* L.

The beech is of the family *Fagaceae*. The family's trees, which include oaks and chestnuts, comprise 8 genera and about 900 species worldwide, except parts of Africa, South America and Australia.

Other names Boc, Bece, Beace (Anglo-Saxon). The word 'book' is derived from the same root, probably because people in northern Europe used to write on blocks of beech.

Some derivative place-names Buckhurst Hill, Bechetts Green, Bookham.

Folklore Beech is the tree of Saturn and is not represented in the tree alphabet as the latter pre-dates the time when beech became widespread.

A Mature Beech

The smooth grey bark and deep shade cast by the dense foliage are characteristic features of this magnificent tree (right), which is typical of the Chiltern Hills of England.

JULIUS CAESAR WROTE THAT 'there are no beech trees in England', on the strength of which it was long assumed that the beech arrived with the Romans. It is now thought that he may have been referring to sweet chestnut trees as the pollen record has proved him wrong (see p. 75). Beech became established in England 3,000 years ago, though it was certainly much rarer in Caesar's time, and is now the third most common tree in British woodlands. It is often thought of as the dominant tree of the chalk hills of south-eastern England, but in fact it thrives on a variety of well-drained soils as long as it has sufficient moisture. It has been very widely planted and is a familiar tree throughout these islands, regenerating freely even north of Aberdeen. In continental Europe, it occurs naturally even further north, in both Norway and Sweden, while in Central Europe it ascends to an altitude of nearly 1,830m (6,000 ft). It is thought that but for human interference it would have continued to extend its range and frequency throughout these islands.

The magnificent beech trees found in woods and parks are characterized by smooth grey bark on a massive trunk, with dense green foliage which casts such a heavy shade that little else can grow beneath, leaving only the familiar carpet of beechmast and leaf-litter. Like oak, beech will grow on very poor, extremely acid, sandy soils as well as on shallow, chalky and even slightly alkaline soils, though it grows best on moderately acid soils. Beech trees have essential mycorrhizal associations and tend to be shallow-rooted, making them susceptible to storm winds – particularly when they are planted on shallow soils.

Beech trees can reach maturity and produce viable seed when only 28 years old, although 60 years seems more typical. They are monoecious and the diminutive green flowers appear in April – females first – at the same time as the leaves. Pollination is by wind, and the annual production of seed or beechmast is often low, with very heavy production in periodic 'mast years'.

Beech Roots

Despite their massive trunks, beeches tend to be shallow-rooted (below). This makes them susceptible to storm winds, especially when growing in shallow soils.

Size and Age

Beech trees will normally reach 30m (100 ft) when fully grown, but some are much taller. An individual has been recorded at Hallyburton House on Tayside at just over 46m (150 ft) and another at Tullynally Castle, Co. West Meath, at 40m (130 ft). The Great Beech Hedge at Meiklover in Perthshire is a quarter of a mile long and consists of around 600 trees nearly 30m (100 ft) high. It is said to originate from seedlings planted hurriedly when estate workers went off to war in 1746. The beech's normal life-span is taken to be 300 years, but some of the ancient pollards at Burnham Beeches, where there are about 500 very large old beech pollards, are known to be over 400 years old, while other 'hulks' at places like Windsor Forest and in the Wyre Forest area may be even older.

The seeds germinate the following spring. They are susceptible both to waterlogging and to drying, but after germinating are extremely shade-tolerant. A high proportion of beech seeds are eaten by mice, voles, squirrels and birds; John Evelyn recommended that one should 'sow them after January, or rather nearer the Spring, to preserve them from Vermin, which are very great Devourers of them'.

In Central Europe, beechmast is consumed by larger mammals, such as wild boar. In England the ancient tradition of 'pannage' rights, whereby domestic pigs were allowed into woods for a limited period in the autumn, used to be practised in some beech woods as well as in the more normal oak woods.

Kennedy and Southwood list 94 phytophagous insects and 4 mites which are known to be associated with beech, of which the barred hook-tip (*Drepana cultraria*) is perhaps the most characteristic, its caterpillars feeding on beech foliage. The strange caterpillar of the lobster moth (*Stauropus fagi*) is also found on beech and some other trees, while caterpillars of the beech seed moth (*Cydia fagiglandana*) are regarded by foresters as a major pest of beech seed. A leaf-mining weevil (*Rhynchaenus fagi*) is specifically associated with beech. Several types of galls occur on beech leaves, usually in the form of discoloration, leaf-roll or small extrusive pouch-galls which eventually fall to the ground. These last are caused by gall-midges such as *Hartigiola annulipes* and *Mikiola fagi*.

Many fungi are known to be associated with beech trees, in particular several edible species of *Boletus*, *Russula* and *Lactarius*, which also occur on oak. Beech woods are a good place to find the delicious wood blewit (*Lepista nuda*), while the spectacular *Ganoderma applanatum* grows on live trunks of beech.

If beech are allowed to live long enough — or if they have been pollarded — they eventually become hollow, providing a much richer environment for a wide range of wildlife — from woodpeckers and bats, to bracket fungi and wood-boring beetles. Once hollow, they can survive for decades — often centuries — being much better equipped to withstand strong winds. Even the great storm of 1987 failed to bring down any of the ancient hollow beeches or oaks in Windsor Park.

The Uses of Beech In his book, *Ancient Woodlands*, Oliver Rackham devotes a whole chapter to the history of beech. He points out that its ecology is perhaps better known than that of any other native tree. In southern England, it has been a valuable timber tree since the Bronze Age, and in the Middle Ages was pollarded in such places as Epping Forest and Burnham Beeches. At Burnham, the trees had been last pollarded 200 years ago, but this process was carefully restarted in 1990 under the management of the Corporation of London. Beech was also coppiced in some areas, such as the Chilterns, although it does not respond as well as many other trees to this treatment. As a standard tree in a coppice system it was unsatisfactory, casting too deep a shade for the coppice below, yet apparently it was nevertheless grown in this way in a few places.

Beech wood is white, or reddish if grown on very rich soils, and very heavy when newly felled. It is close-grained, hard and smooth, and is one of the strongest of native timbers, but tends to split and distort when dried, due to the considerable shrinkage it undergoes. It 'endures best under water or in waterlogged soil' according to Geoffrey Grigson, although this is rarely mentioned by modern authors. The piles under Winchester Cathedral and some of those under the old Waterloo Bridge were made of beech.

It is a very good wood for turning and steam-bending, and it is very popular for, among other things, furniture-making, tool handles, kitchen utensils and sports equipment. It burns well and is used in Scotland to smoke herrings. Charcoal made from beech is well suited for the manufacture of gunpowder.

The Latin word for beech, *fagus*, may be derived from the Greek *phagein* to eat, and in Europe beechmast was eaten in times of famine. In France, the nuts are still sometimes roasted as a coffee substitute and the ripe nuts yield an oil which can be used for cooking.

Tree Lore and Folk Beliefs Surprisingly for such a large and impressive tree, there seem to be hardly any folklore records associated with beech in England, apart from it being proof against lightning. In continental Europe it is much the same, as the only records of it having a cultural significance are prehistoric — the beech having been of considerable importance to the various Celtish groups who dominated Central Europe during the Iron Age.

Traditionally however, beech has long been considered to possess a number of medicinal properties. Culpepper, for example, recommends beech leaves as a cooling agent to alleviate swellings, and also advises boiling them to make a poultice.

Beech trees 'make spreading trees, and noble shades with their well-furnished and glittering leaves… the shade, unpropitious to corn and grass, but sweet and of all the rest most refreshing to the weary shepherd.' JOHN EVELYN 1729

The Life Stages of the Beech
The numbers of beechmast, the bristly fruit of the beech, produced each year vary enormously, very low some years and very high in periodic mast years. The beechmast contains the individual, ridged brown seeds, a high proportion of which are eaten by mice, voles, squirrels and birds before they have a chance to germinate.

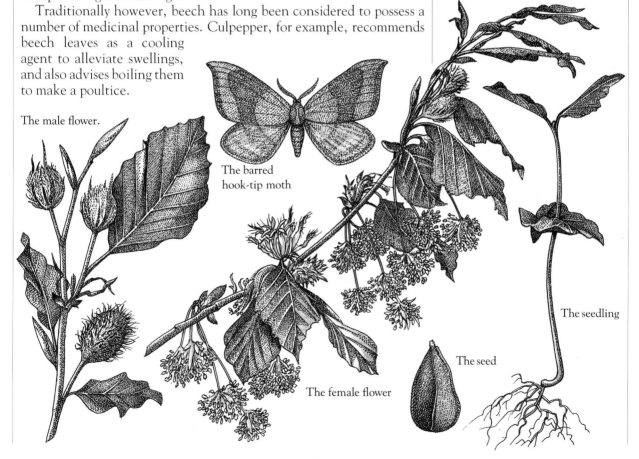

The male flower.

The barred hook-tip moth

The female flower

The seed

The seedling

THE BIRCH

Silver Birch	*Betula pendula* Roth
Downy Birch	*Betula pubescens* Ehrh.

The two species of birch trees found in these islands are of the family *Betulaceae*. A third species, *Betula nana* L., is a dwarf shrub which occurs in northern England and Scotland. There are two genera, the other being *Alnus* (alders). *Betula* has 60 species, which are native to temperate areas of the northern hemisphere, reaching as far north as the Arctic Circle.

Other names Beith (Gaelic and Old Irish), Begh (Irish), Paper Birch (Wiltshire), Ribbon Tree (Lincolnshire).

Some derivative place-names Birkenhead, Berkhamstead, etc. In Ireland, many names include 'beagh', 'behagh', etc., meaning birch land.

Folklore Birch is the tree of Venus, and is represented by the letter B (beth) in the tree alphabet.

A Birch Wood in Springtime
With their characteristic white bark and pale-green leaves (right), it is easy to see how birch trees have inspired painters, poets and writers alike through the centuries.

A Silver Birch in Autumn
Like all birches, the leaves of this tree in Glen Affric (below), in the Scottish Highlands, acquire a golden colour in the autumn.

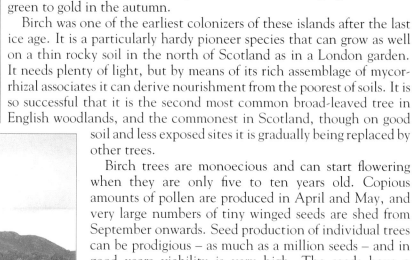

THE BIRCH IS A MOST GRACEFUL and attractive tree that has been an inspiration to poets and painters in every season, its myriad tiny leaves fluttering in the lightest breeze, and changing colour from green to gold in the autumn.

Birch was one of the earliest colonizers of these islands after the last ice age. It is a particularly hardy pioneer species that can grow as well on a thin rocky soil in the north of Scotland as in a London garden. It needs plenty of light, but by means of its rich assemblage of mycorrhizal associates it can derive nourishment from the poorest of soils. It is so successful that it is the second most common broad-leaved tree in English woodlands, and the commonest in Scotland, though on good soil and less exposed sites it is gradually being replaced by other trees.

Birch trees are monoecious and can start flowering when they are only five to ten years old. Copious amounts of pollen are produced in April and May, and very large numbers of tiny winged seeds are shed from September onwards. Seed production of individual trees can be prodigious – as much as a million seeds – and in good years viability is very high. The seeds have a chilling requirement before germination, yet are inhibited by heavy shade. This is confirmed by the observation that birch seedlings tend to grow on patches of bare soil, in gaps or clearings in the vegetation. Birch growing on poor soils is so dependent on its mycorrhiza that many seedlings die before fungal infection occurs. The roots are in any case very delicate and, as horticulturalists know, birch seedlings need very careful transplanting if they are to survive. Natural establishment on heavily grazed sites is poor and, while some seeds remain viable in the soil for a few seasons, birch does not build up a persistent seed bank.

The two species of birch support a highly diverse fauna of at least 334 phytophagous invertebrate species – more than any other native tree, apart from oak and willow.

An Ancient Birch

Birch grows more slowly and lives much longer in northern Scotland than further south. This lichen-encrusted birch tree at Glen Cannich, in the Scottish Highlands, is well over 100 years old.

Several species of moths are dependent on birch, including the spectacular Kentish glory moth (*Endromus versicolora*), unfortunately now thought to be extinct in many parts of Britain, and the winter moth (*Operophtera brumata*). Several species of leaf weevil (*Phyllobius* spp.) can also defoliate individual trees.

Birch trees are host to one of the most familiar types of plant-gall – the mass of small branches that sometimes look like birds' nests in the foliage – which are particularly visible in winter when the leaves have fallen. Known as witches' broom, it is caused by the fungus *Taphrina betulina* on *B. pubescens* and the closely related *Taphrina turgida* on *B. pendula*. The gall starts as a mass of buds crowded together, which gradually become a ball of tissue as it grows. A mature birch tree can have as many as a hundred witches' brooms and is also host to other smaller galls such as the small nodular leaf-gall caused by a gall-mite (*Eriophyes lionotus*). Nesting sparrows and other small birds commonly inherit old galls.

Birch is a very ancient member of the native tree flora and has a very wide array of fungi associated with it. Several of these are restricted to birch, including some which are the fruiting bodies of mycorrhizal species. Among the most characteristic are at least three species of *Russula*, including *Russula betularum*, *Cortinarius betuletorum*, *Lenzites betulina* and the large white polypore, *Piptoperus betulinus*, whose Latin names all suggest their habitual association with the tree.

The Uses of Birch Birch timber has been rather despised in these islands and is often said to be fit only for use in plywood, upholstery framing and a few domestic items like brooms. John Evelyn dismissed it as 'of all other the worst of timber', while claiming that a variety of uses had been found for it formerly, 'in the good old days of more simplicity, yet of better and truer hospitality.' Geoffrey Grigson claims that birch 'makes poor timber', but then admits that 'where other trees are scarce, the uses have been manifold, as in the Highlands.'

In fact, birch's toughness is comparable to that of ash, and it is a most attractive wood when turned. It was formerly used in large quantities to make hard-wearing bobbins, spools and reels for the Lancashire cotton industry, for which it was apparently admirably suited.

Perhaps the most familiar use of birch is in the making of traditional broomsticks or besoms, demand for which now far outstrips supply. Besoms are still made by woodsmen such as Bill Hogarth in Cumbria (see p. 97), who also supplies large amounts of birch brushwood to racecourses during the National Hunt season.

Less well known perhaps is the use of birch sap, tapped from the trunk in early April. In Eastern Europe, this is a major source of sugar and is also fermented to make beer and wine. In 1986, production in Russia, for example, amounted to 42,700 tons. Silver birch wine is also made commercially from local birch sap at Moniack Castle near Inverness, and in 1991 production amounted to 7,000 bottles.

Until recently birch was also used in a most unusual way in the copper refineries of South Wales. Green birch poles were employed to stir the molten copper; this prevented the formation of copper oxides in the melt, resulting in a purer copper being produced. Birch bark was used for tanning in the Highlands in the absence of oak, and a related species of birch is still in use today by indigenous tribes in Canada to make birch-bark canoes.

Today campaigners involved in the restoration of Scottish native birchwoods (see p. 166) emphasize that birch is excellent wood for making a variety of domestic items such as parquet tiles, panelling, and some types of furniture. Indeed, a new industry, making such items from local birch, is now planned and a breeding programme for birch has been belatedly started by the Forestry Commission.

Tree Lore and Folk Beliefs The folklore associated with birch is diverse: it is a protective tree against evil spirits and the evil eye, and symbolizes fertility and love. Birch kindling was used in Scotland to set alight a ritual fire at the rising of May's first sun, the traditional start to the warmer half of the year. The tree is believed to have life-giving properties and in different traditions these have been invoked in various ways. In some parts of Scotland birch branches were hung over doors on Midsummer Eve, and in houses and along streets on Rogation Day.

Then there is birch's less benign aspect. In medieval times, a bundle of birch rods was carried in front of the magistrate on his way to court, both as a symbol of his authority and as a means of correction. Its use as an instrument of punishment probably originates in the need to drive out evil spirits and it is still in use on the Isle of Man today.

Birch sap is recommended by Culpepper 'to break the stone in kidneys and bladder', and as a mouthwash. The only other medical use recorded seems to be the use of birch tar – when produced from fresh wood – in ointments for eczema and other skin ailments.

'Beneath you birch with silver bark
And boughs so pendulous and fair,
The brook falls scattered down
the rock:
And all is mossy there.'
S. T. COLERIDGE

The Life Stages of the Birch
The double-winged seeds of the birch are minute, only about 3mm (⅛in) long, but an individual tree can, in exceptional years, produce up to a million of them. The seeds are inhibited by heavy shade and therefore birch seedlings tend to grow on patches of bare soil, in gaps or clearings in the vegetation.

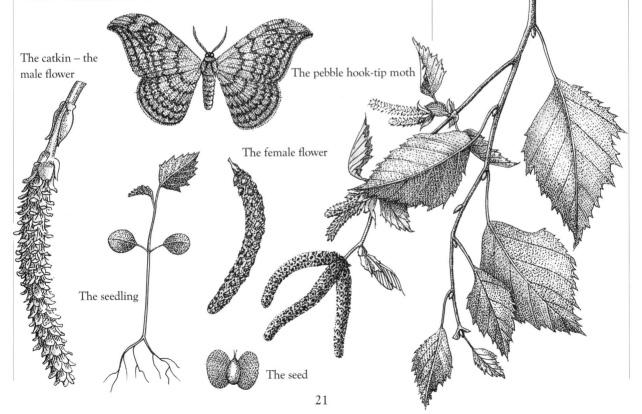

The catkin – the male flower

The pebble hook-tip moth

The female flower

The seedling

The seed

THE BLACK POPLAR

Black Poplar *Populus nigra* ssp. *betulifolia* (Pursh) Wettst

The black poplar is a member of the family *Salicaceae*, a large family of mainly fast-growing, marsh-loving trees with around 300 species worldwide, including willows. The genus *Populus* contains 35 species in the northern temperate zone, including the American cottonwoods. The native black poplar is the only indigenous *Populus* species apart from the aspen, *Populus tremula*.

Other names Willow Poplar, Cotton Tree, Water Poplar.

Derivative place-name Poplar (East London)

Folklore Black poplar does not feature in the tree alphabet, though the related aspen (*Populus tremula*) is denoted by the letter E (eadha) in the tree alphabet.

A Black Poplar in Flower
This full-grown male tree (right) is at Cotswold Water Park, near Cirencester. The way its branches curve down is a characteristic trait, while the red flowers (catkins) give a touch of colour for just one or two days in early April, before the leaves come out.

The Devil's Fingers
The fallen male catkins of black poplar (below) are known as the Devil's Fingers, and in many country areas it is thought to be unlucky to pick them up.

THE ORIGIN OF THE NAME POPLAR is the Greek *papaillo*, to shake, which is most appropriate, as the black poplar's flattened leaf stalks or petioles move very easily in the wind. The trunk is usually heavily burred and the bark deeply ridged and gnarled, appearing black at a distance.

The black poplar is a fine heavyweight tree, native to England and Wales as far north as a line from the Mersey to the Humber, with a few specimens occurring in south Yorkshire and as far north as the River Tees. Although it used to grow along the margins of rivers and streams, few can be found today in such habitats. Most occur as planted trees by ditches and ponds or in hedgerows on farmland. The native black poplar has also been planted in past years in urban areas, as it seems little affected by air pollution. Much planting has however been of European *P. nigra* stock, or of hybrid poplars with only some *P. nigra* ancestry.

Until recently, black poplar was not thought to be native to Ireland though it has been planted by farmers on their land since the last century. However, a recent study suggests that it is native to the Shannon river system and to some other rivers of the midlands of Ireland.

The black poplar is dioecious and its flowering and fruiting is spectacular, if short-lived. For one or two days in early April the scarlet male catkins create a wonderful impression on a full-grown tree, and, when fruiting, the female tree produces quantities of fluffy down, which drifts on the breeze like fragments of cotton-wool.

Despite the seed crop from an individual tree being prodigious and male and female poplars often growing near one another, natural regeneration of the native variety takes place only very rarely in England and Wales. For the seeds to germinate, they need to land on bare wet soil (eroded banks, or islands in rivers) at the end of June and the resulting seedling must be kept moist until the leaves fall in October. Both flooding and drought are fatal for the seedlings and they are unable to develop in a green sward or in competition with other vegetation.

Size and Age

The black poplar is a vigorous, fast-growing tree that often reaches a height of 30m (100 ft). Individual (planted) trees over 35m (115 ft) can be seen at Leighton Hall, Salop, while there is one at Longnor Hall, also in Salop, with a girth of 7m (23 ft). In the Vale of Aylesbury, it is the commonest tree in the landscape, there being hundreds of pollards but very few fully-grown trees. Pollards are also abundant in parts of Somerset, Oxfordshire, Hereford and Worcester and Derbyshire, and neglected pollards can still develop into most spectacular trees, as in the grounds of Christ College, Brecon.

A Black Poplar's Trunk

This trunk, with its gnarled bark and large, irregular bosses, is typical of the black poplar. At a distance, the amount of shadows these indentations create make the wood look darker than it really is – hence its name.

Modern changes to the landscape and, in particular, to the management of rivers and river banks have practically eliminated this habitat. This is unfortunate because, as Oliver Rackham explains 'our black poplars are evidently the last shadow of the vanished flood-plain wildwood.' However, the trees do sometimes regenerate vegetatively: fallen branches or trunks can take root in the mud and suckers can grow up from roots damaged by rivers in flood.

For the short time they are viable, the seeds of black poplar will produce a good crop of seedlings if kept in sufficiently wet conditions and protected from competition. However, like many willows (and unlike white or grey poplars) black poplars are very easy to propagate vegetatively, the traditional method being to take long cuttings or 'truncheons' about two- to two-and-a-half-metres long, point them and stick them firmly into moist ground where the new tree is wanted. Alternatively, straight shoots about half a metre long are cut from a pollard, or epicormic (from the main trunk) growth from a standard tree. Then they are set about half their length into damp soil in October or November and kept moist through the winter. By spring they will have rooted, but they should be kept in a nursery bed for a year before being planted out.

Black poplars are known for having very large root systems and can be a major threat to buildings and drains when planted inappropriately close to them.

Kennedy and Southwood list 189 species of phytophagous insects and mites associated with the poplar, of which the best known is the poplar hawk moth (*Laothoe populi*), though the hornet clearwing moth (*Sesia apiformis*) is perhaps the more spectacular. The tiny larvae of the poplar cambium fly (*Phytobia cambii*) make long tunnels which damage the wood for veneer use (it also attacks aspen and willow). Two types of leaf-galls are common on black poplar. The mid-rib is deformed by a reddish leaf-gall about 2cm long, which is caused by an aphid, *Pemphigius populinigrae*, that also attacks several other poplars and aspen. A second leaf-gall, known as gold leaf, is caused by the fungus *Ascomyces aureus* and is sometimes so abundant that it can give a single tree an almost golden appearance.

A number of fungi are found under and on poplars; the rare but edible *Krombholziella duriuscula* is apparently restricted to the genus *Populus*.

The Uses of Black Poplar Poplar timber is light but tough and it absorbs shock and resists splintering. It was traditionally used to make wooden shields and to line the bottom of carts. In more modern times, it has been used to make artificial limbs, packing cases (as in those for wine bottles), pallets, interior joinery such as shelving, toys, plywood, and light baskets such as those for soft fruit. A very pale, almost white wood, it is also used for veneers; it turns well and makes attractive bowls. Poplar wood has been used for the floors of oast houses where hops are dried and, since it burns very slowly, it is also a suitable wood for matches. Today *P. nigra* hybrids are being tested for biomass production on a short-rotation coppice, where they can produce up to 16 tonnes of timber per hectare every year. Poplar bark was also used in the past for tanning.

Tree Lore and Folk Beliefs According to Greek mythology, black poplar resulted from Phaeton's fatal attempt to drive Apollo's chariot. Phaeton's sisters made such a nuisance of themselves mourning his death that the gods on Mount Olympus decided to change them into black poplars.

In England, a famous black poplar in the village of Aston-on-Clun in south-west Shropshire is known as the Arbor Tree. Traditionally, this tree is dressed with flags attached to long larch poles, which are renewed every Oak Apple Day (29 May), when a carnival procession takes place. Local records show that the pageant used to be much more elaborate, with a historical sequence of characters including Diana, goddess of nature, St George of England and St George of Ethiopia, and ending with a wedding procession commemorating that of a certain squire John Marston and his bride, Mary Carter, in the 1780s. In Belgium, farmers used to plant 21 poplars when a daughter was born so that they could cut them as a dowry 21 years later!

John Evelyn recommends the use of black poplar leaves for winter cattle feed and claims that the juice of poplar leaves is an effective cure for earache, while the buds when crushed with honey are good for sore eyes. According to Geoffrey Grigson, an ointment was made in medieval times using poplar buds as the main ingredient. This was used for treating inflammation and bruises and must have been a stock-in-trade for the handlers of prize-fighters. Less sought-after were the fallen male catkins, which – according to Grigson – 'look like fat red grubs. Not surprisingly they have been called Devil's Fingers, and are supposed to bring ill-fortune if picked up.'

The Life Stages of the Black Poplar
Despite the prodigious amount of seeds produced by individual trees and the proximity in which male and female poplars are usually found, the black poplar regenerates naturally only very rarely. In order to germinate, the seed needs to fall on bare damp soil, and even in those conditions it succumbs to flooding, drought and competition from other vegetation.

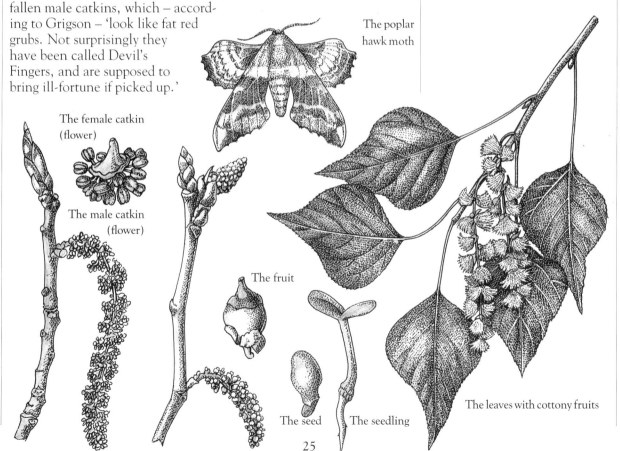

The poplar hawk moth

The female catkin (flower)

The male catkin (flower)

The fruit

The seed

The seedling

The leaves with cottony fruits

THE LIME

Small-leaved Lime *Tilia cordata* L.
Large-leaved Lime *Tilia platyphyllos* Scopoli
Common Lime *Tilia* x *vulgaris* (also known as x *europea*)
The two native species of lime found in these islands (the common lime is a hybrid of the other two) are of the family *Tiliaceae*, which contains about 300 species in 35 genera of trees, shrubs and herbs, widely distributed in both temperate and tropical regions.
Other names The name Lime, first used in the early seventeenth century, is an altered form of the earlier Lind. This itself has many forms: Linde, Linden, Lynde, Lynd, Lyne and Line, all of which relate to the German, Dutch, Norse and Old English names of the trees. The French name, *tilleul*, is derived from the Latin, *tilia*. The Welsh name, *llwyf*, means both lime and elm.
Some derivative place-names Lyndhurst, Linwood, etc.
Folklore Like oak, lime is a tree of Jupiter, but is not represented in the tree alphabet.

An Ancient Lime
Over 1,000 years old, this lime (right) is growing on the northern limit of its natural distribution, deep in the woods on the east side of Lake Coniston, Cumbria.

A Coppiced Lime
The many trunks of this old lime (below) in Silkwood, at Westonbirt Arboretum, Tetbury, Gloucestershire, are as a result of it having been coppiced and then neglected for several decades.

TWO SPECIES OF LIME, the small-leaved and large-leaved, are native in Britain, but the most familiar variety is their hybrid, the common lime. This too is native, occurring in a few places where both parent species grow together, but it has also been widely planted. The planted trees are derived from those originally imported from the Netherlands during and after the seventeenth century, when lime avenues in parks and towns became fashionable, sometimes as an ostentatious display of wealth. Spectacular lime avenues can still be seen at Hampton Court and in the grounds of various stately homes.

Native limes are now relatively rare in Britain. The large-leaved lime is found on neutral and alkaline soils; it survives here and there on steep slopes and cliffs, usually of limestone, in the Welsh Borders, Derbyshire and Yorkshire, and has recently been found on the Downs in Sussex. The small-leaved lime is the commoner species and can still be found throughout England and Wales on richer soils; but its occurrence is scattered and patchy, and it is often reduced from a noble tree to groups of old coppice stools, hidden away and largely overlooked.

The pollen record has much to tell us about the history of the two native limes (see p. 75). They spread into south-eastern England about 8,000 years ago, before the English Channel was flooded by the sea, and then spread northwards and westwards, stopping just short of the Scottish border and failing to cross to Ireland.

Pollen grains of the two species are distinct. The large-leaved lime was always rarer than the small-leaved, which was for over 2,000 years a dominant species in the primeval woodlands of the English lowlands, as it was across much of the Central European plain. Unfortunately, nothing remains today in England to give an idea of that vanished woodland in which the people of the Middle Stone Age hunted and fished: indeed, in all Europe only a few fragments of primeval

Size and Age

Lime trees can live longer than any other tree native to Britain, with the exception of the yew, and they also rate among our tallest trees. A very large coppice stool in the Silkwood at Westonbirt Arboretum is thought to be over 1,000 years old and this is not considered that exceptional, while when fully grown *T. cordata* reaches 38m (125 ft), *T. platyphyllos* 34m (110 ft) and the hybrid, *T. x vulgaris* 46m (150 ft). Champion trees listed are at Tottenham House, Wiltshire (40 x 117) and Forde Abbey (24 x 165) (both *T. cordata*), Scone Palace, Tayside (37 x 143) and Pitchford Hall, Shropshire (14 x 236) (both *T. platyphyllos*), Gatton Park, Surrey (44 x 159) and East Carlton Park, Northamptonshire (29 x 213) (both *T. x vulgaris*).

woodland remain, of which the most celebrated is the hunting forest of the Polish kings at Bialowieza. In its least disturbed central part, 300-year-old trees of small-leaved lime and common oak, with tall cylindrical trunks, form the upper canopy, about 30-35m above the ground. Beneath is a patchy canopy of hornbeams, and below this a tangle of young trees, many of them limes, struggling for light. It provides a glimpse of the woodland which covered the most fertile soils in the English lowlands before the first clearances began 5,000 years ago.

Lime trees are conspicuous among European forest trees for their heavy inflorescences, which are produced in high summer, the pollen being shed from late June to the end of July. The flowers are yellowish-white, the stamens exceeding the petals in *T. platyphyllos*, but only equalling them in *T. cordata*.

When limes are flowering, the emergent tops of the giant trees turn pale yellow and swarm with insects, especially bees and hoverflies. Limes are an important source of honey: this must have attracted the attention of prehistoric man, just as the sweet scent of limes attracts us now. Large populations of the lime aphid (*Eucallipterus tiliae*) build up on the foliage in summer and the drips of honeydew that they produce are the bane of motorists.

Altogether 53 phytophagous insects and 4 mites are recorded from *Tilia* species in these islands. Some of the characteristic insects are the lime hawk moth (*Mimas tiliae*), and the tiny lime mite (*Eotetranychus tiliarium*). The leaves of lime are very susceptible to attack by a number of gall-mites and gall-midges; one of the most characteristic is a nail gall, formed by the mite *Eriophyes tiliae*.

A number of fungi occur on lime trees, though none of them exclusively so; the spectacular *Ganoderma australe* can sometimes be found growing on the trunks of live lime trees.

The Uses of Lime Lime wood was used to make dug-out canoes and many household articles such as bowls, ladles and cups; and this was still the case in eastern Europe until well into this century. The strong fibre of the underbark, known as bast, was stripped by prehistoric people to make robes and nets, of which many examples have been preserved from as far back as the Middle Stone Age. This practice also continued into this century, especially in eastern Europe, where ropes, cloth and sandals were made from lime-bark. The sandals were bound to the legs with bast and were worn by the peasantry, especially during summer. Lime shoots were also used as tree-hay for winter fodder, a practice which survived in mountain regions into the present century.

Tree Lore and Folk Beliefs Throughout Europe, place names often refer to lime trees and many such names date from the early period of settlement in the Dark Ages. Sometimes they carry the memory of an earlier reverence for the tree, as, for example, in the Beauce, south of Paris at Tillay-le-Peneux – known to the Romans as Tigletus paganorum. Was this the lime tree or lime grove of pagan worship? In Estonia, ancient limes were reputed to have been worshipped by the Baltic people even after their late conversion to Christianity. Until recently, they were still the recipients of sacrifices; votive offerings were attached to their branches, especially by women in search of fertility.

The lime has long been regarded as an essentially female tree. For the early Germanic tribes, it was sacred to Frigga, the goddess of fertility. It seems fair to assume that this attribution was transferred to the early medieval poetic symbolism of the lime tree, as the trysting place of lovers, who lay on a bed of crushed, sweet-scented flowers.

It was also, perhaps not surprisingly, a tree to dance around, as shown in a delightful engraving by Hieronymus Bosch in the *Kreutterbuch of Strasbourg* (1577). This tradition continues in Germany today, where there are fine examples of *Tanzlinde*, with dance floors positioned under the spreading limbs of an ancient tree.

There was, however, a darker association of the village lime. Many were *Gerichtslinde*, beneath which the law court met – a function which is vividly recalled by an illustration in the *Luzerner Chronik* of 1513, showing red-robed lawyers beneath the tree, a prisoner kneeling and a guard bearing a fearsome club. It may well be that the female quality of the tree symbolized mercy.

In Switzerland and France, the lime tree was a symbol of liberty. The great lime in Fribourg was one of several planted in the fifteenth century to celebrate the battle of Morat (1476), when the northern Swiss cantons freed themselves from the domination of Burgundy. In France limes were planted – of which many still survive – to mark the end of the Wars of Religion and the granting of religious freedom by Henri IV under the Edict of Nantes (1598).

The lime is not a village tree in England, with the exception of the ancient tree at Dunham Town, near Altrincham in Cheshire; the hybrid has been widely planted in towns, but this is not universally popular.

'One found whatever one wished there: shade together with sunshine, lime-trees by the fountain, tender, gentle breezes…The delightful blossom on the trees smiled out at one so pleasantly that one's heart and all one's soul went out to it through eyes that shone, and gave back all its smiles.'

GOTFRIED VON STRASSBURG: Tristan

The Life Stages of the Lime
The characteristic heart-shaped leaves of the lime are usually sticky with honeydew, produced by aphids. When they are flowering, limes attract many pollinating insects, especially bees.

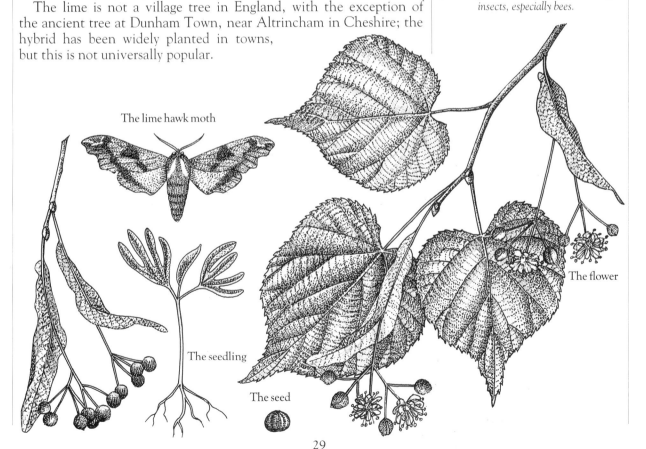

The lime hawk moth

The seedling

The seed

The flower

THE OAK

Common or Pedunculate Oak *Quercus robur* L.

Sessile or Durmast Oak *Quercus petraea* (Mattuschka) Leibl.

The two species of oak found in these islands are of the family *Fagaceae*, which also includes the beech. The genus *Quercus* includes over 600 species in the northern hemisphere, most of which are native to areas south of Britain where there is warm temperate or tropical montane climate.

Other names Darroch (Gaelic), Derry, Durr, Ral or Ralach (Irish), Daur (Old Irish).

Some derivative place-names Accrington, Akenside, Aysgarth and Matlock. In Ireland, Derry, Darrary and many others.

Folklore Oak is the tree of Jupiter and is represented by the letter D (duir) in the tree alphabet.

Oaks at Cawdor
These mature sessile oaks (right) are in open woodland in the grounds of Cawdor Castle, near Nairn, in the Scottish Highlands. The fissured bark often attracts the growth of epiphytes.

An Oak by Findhorn River
In order to gain more light this oak (below) has grown outwards over the river, where it does not have to compete with other trees.

THE OAK IS THE MAJOR TREE of the Atlantic deciduous forest, and is today the commonest tree of British broad-leaved woodlands. Since earliest times, it has also been the predominant timber tree throughout Europe. Indeed, the evidence of tree rings has shown that oak was in general use for construction as long as 9,000 years ago in Germany and 7,200 years ago in Ireland (see p. 77).

The two British species are closely related; *Q. robur* is more common in the south-east and central parts of England, while *Q. petraea* is more characteristic of the northern and western parts of these islands. Both species are found widely in Europe, although they do not occur naturally any further north than northern Scotland. Oak is a pioneer tree, doing particularly well on infertile and acidic soils, and natural pure oak forests are rare as oak appears to replace itself poorly. It is likely that, given time, oak will be replaced on fertile soil in England by a mixture of lime, elm and beech, and on calcareous soils almost exclusively by beech, though not on the poorer siliceous soils in the west.

The oak comes into leaf very late. Often it may not do so until mid-May and later there may be a second flush of leaves, known traditionally as the Lammas budding since it tends to coincide with the Celtic Lammas festival on 1 August.

The trees are monoecious, with unspectacular flowers, the male catkins and female spikes being each only about an inch long and pale green. The flowers open and release pollen in early May until late June. Some honeydew is produced by aphids, attracting bees, but pollination is by wind.

The fruit of the oak is the familiar acorn. Acorns are first produced after around 40 years, with seed production reaching a maximum between 80 and 120 years. Like beech, oaks tend to fruit very abundantly only in mast years, which occur every six to seven years, less frequently than in beech, the crop being largely determined

Size and Age

Under sheltered conditions on deep soil, oaks can grow into magnificent trees of 40m (130 ft) or more in height. The tallest oaks are not, however, particularly old – probably not more than about 300 years. Most really ancient oaks, which are invariably hollow, are not so tall; they occur in places that were ancient wood pastures, where the widely spaced trees were pollarded for centuries to provide timber and firewood. The massive hulks at Windsor Park and Moccas Park in Hereford and Worcester may be 800 years old. Even greater ages are ascribed to certain famous oak trees, but actual ring counts from cores and carbon dating have generally cast doubt on these claims. Indeed, the oldest living oak in Britain with complete tree rings was dated at 320 years. The largest examples of *Q. robur* to be listed are at Belvoir Castle, Leics (42 x 99), Abbotsbury, Dorset (42 x 147), and Bowthorpe, Lincs (25 x 318), and of *Q. petraea* at Whitfield House, Hereford and Worcs (43 x 148) and at Easthampton Farm, Shobdon, Hereford and Worcs (25 x 318).

An Ancient Oak Pollard

This scene (opposite) in Windsor Park is typical of a traditional wood pasture, with ancient trees surrounded by grazing land. In former times the trees were lopped for fodder and other uses at regular intervals. Today these ancient pollards represent one of the richest habitats for rare invertebrates, and are found in several old parks such as Hatfield Forest in Essex and Moccas Park in Hereford and Worcester.

by the climatic conditions of the previous year at the time when the flower buds first form. In other years, fewer acorns are produced, and in some none at all. Acorns are very susceptible to drying and can be killed by frost. Their dormancy is not deep: many begin to germinate by putting out a root very soon after falling, though a shoot is not produced until the spring. When they do germinate, the substantial food source available to the growing embryo allows the young seedlings to become established, even under shade or in closed grassland where there is no bare ground. In this the oak is unlike many other species of tree: as a result, oak seedlings tend to invade grassland unless they are subjected to considerable grazing pressure, or discouraged by man.

The seedlings develop a substantial tap-root which seems to be an adaptation to grazing as, like pine, they can survive the loss of some early shoots. They are less tolerant of shade if it is combined with other damaging influences such as caterpillar defoliation or attacks of the oak mildew fungus (*Microspaera alphitoides*). Oliver Rackham concludes that the natural regeneration of oak in England has diminished in many woods over the last 150 years due to a combination of factors, including additional grazing pressure by deer and the activities of grey squirrels, mildew and caterpillars – especially where coppicing has ceased, leaving most oaklings to struggle under heavy shade. In more natural woodland they would thrive in clearings caused by fallen trees.

Of all British trees, the oak supports the widest variety of insect and other invertebrate life. Some 500 phytophagous species of diverse habits are specifically associated with oak. Many of these are moths, including the lichen-mimicking merveille du jour, (*Dichonia aprilina*), the acorn moth (*Cydia splendana*) and destructive defoliating species such as the green oak tortrix (*Tortrix viridana*) and the winter moth (*Operophtera brumata*); as well as a wide variety of other insects including plant bugs, flies and beetles such as the weevils, *Curculio gladium* and *Rhynchaenus quercus*. The purple hairstreak (*Quercusia quercus*) is a most attractive butterfly, whose caterpillars feed on oak; the adults tend to fly in groups around the tops of oaks, both in woodland and above solitary trees.

Oak foliage is also known by arachnologists to be rich in small spiders, while dead and rotting oak wood, especially on ancient trees, is an entomological treasure house, with many very rare species dependent on the special habitats found only in these 'grandfather' oaks. Some nationally endangered species are known only from individual sites where ancient oak trees are to be found; for instance, the only present-day records for the chafer beetle, *Gnorimus variabilis*, and the click beetle, *Lacon quercus*, are from such trees in Windsor Park. Oak also forms many different types of galls, from the familiar oak-apple-gall, caused by a cynipid wasp (*Biorrhiza pallida*), to the more recently arrived knopper-gall, which is caused by another cynipid (*Andricus quercuscalicis*).

More fungi are associated with oak than with any other native tree and many species appear to be restricted to these trees, including numerous types of *Boletus*. The strange but edible Beefsteak Fungus (*Fistulina hepatica*) occurs on old living oaks and on dead oak stumps, as well as on sweet chestnut trees.

The Uses of Oak 'To enumerate now the incomparable uses of this wood...the land and the sea do sufficiently speak of this excellent material; houses and ships, Cities and Navies are built with it.' As John Evelyn's words suggest, the oak has been planted and cut for all major timber uses for many centuries, and the records of oak cultivation are extensive; in fact, as Oliver Rackham admits, there is 'an almost embarrassing wealth of historical information about oak.' But although oak timber was for some centuries the foundation of the Royal Navy, and the construction of large buildings has depended on oak beams since medieval times, it was the extensive use of oak bark for tanning that made oak woods such a valuable asset in former times. In the second decade of the nineteenth century, for example, it is estimated that 90,000 tons of oak bark were used per annum by the tanning industry, corresponding to around 500,000 tons of felled oak timber in a single year – perhaps twice as much as that used by the naval and merchant ship-building industries combined, at their maximum output.

The decline in English woodland industries was such that a century later oak bark was being imported from cheaper sources on the Continent. During the First World War, this reached nearly 45,000 tons per annum, though even then certain areas of England still produced bark in some quantity. Bill Hogarth, a coppice-wood merchant in the Lake District, continues this centuries-old tradition and reckons to spend three summer months a year cutting oak coppice and peeling the bark. Today oak bark is in short supply and worth several hundred pounds a ton to tanners of high-class leather, such as J. and F. J. Baker of Colyton, Devon. In former times, the peeled wood went for making oak-swill baskets; now much of it is used in the making of rustic garden furniture.

Oak is one of the most widely used hardwoods in Britain, especially for interior joinery work such as doors, windows and panelling, as well as for furniture. It is extremely durable and lower grade oak is used for fencing, mining timber, gates, etc. Since it also bends well and is impermeable, it is still used in boat-building. It is much used by wood sculptors and turners for its even grain and attractive appearance, which are well displayed in bowls and other turned items.

The oak's fruit, the acorn, has been used for food in times of famine and, though rather unpalatable, is still sometimes eaten, particularly in eastern Europe and Russia.

Tree Lore and Folk Beliefs The oak has been one of the most important elements of folklore throughout Europe since the earliest times; the name Druid means 'oak man'. According to Sir James Frazer's *The Golden Bough*, 'The worship of the oak tree or of the oak god appears to have been shared by all the branches of the Aryan stock in Europe.' The oak was sacred to many ancient peoples, including the ancient Greeks, the Norse and the Celts, who knew it as the tree of their most powerful gods – Zeus, Thor and Dagda (the elder Irish god) respectively. It is often split by lightning, possibly because it is frequently the tallest tree around and, as a result, it was often associated with the gods of thunder. Oak was also the sacred wood burnt by the Druids for the midsummer sacrifice, kindled by rubbing together two oak sticks.

An Oak Struck by Lightning
Often the largest tree in a particular area, the oak is frequently struck by lightning, which is probably why it is associated with the Gods of Thunder in many cultures. This oak is in Windsor Park, Berkshire.

It is said that Charles II hid from the Roundheads in an oak tree at Boscobel, since when children in various parts of the country wear oak leaves to commemorate Royal Oak Day (known as Oak-Apple Day) on 29 May: between 1660 and 1859 Charles II made it a national holiday to celebrate the restoration of the monarchy in England.

The centrality of oak to much European culture is revealed by many sayings and customs, where it is used to symbolize both outer and inner strength. The significance of 'mighty oaks from little acorns grow' is not simply one of size, and the symbol of oak leaves on military or civil honours is used in more than one country. Many people claim to feel the power of the tree just by standing close to a great oak and the benefits of such an effect should not be underestimated.

The medicinal significance of oak has historically been associated largely with the epiphytes that commonly grow on it – mistletoe and the polypody fern. However, Culpepper recommends various decoctions of leaves, inner bark and buds for 'staying all manner of fluxes [internal bleedings] in man or woman' and claims that powdered acorn taken in wine acts as a diuretic and 'resists the poison of venomous creatures.' The mystical strength of oak has long been employed in folk medicine: it is claimed, for instance, that rheumatism can be cured by walking round a large tree uttering appropriate incantations.

The Life Stages of the Oak
The oak's fruit, the familiar acorn, consists mainly of starch and acts as a food store for the developing seedling. This gives the seedling a better chance of survival, enabling it to put out a strong tap-root at an early stage in its development.

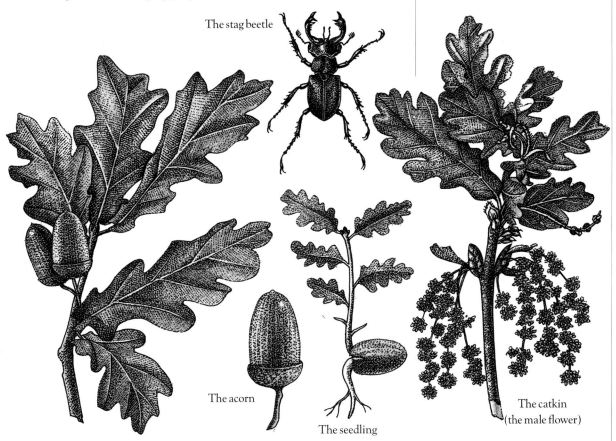

The stag beetle

The acorn

The seedling

The catkin (the male flower)

THE SCOTS PINE

Scots Pine *Pinus sylvestris* L.

The Scots pine is an evergreen coniferous tree of the family *Pinaceae*, which has 10 genera and 250 species of mainly northern temperate trees, and some shrubs. A few tropical species are restricted to mountains. *Pinus sylvestris* is the only native form and is sometimes distinguished as species *Scotica*.

Other names Scots Fir, Guithais/Guis (Gaelic), Ochtach (Old Irish), Giumais (Irish).

Derivative place-names Mountains in Scotland, such as Meall a Ghubiaj are named after the tree.

Folklore Pine is a tree of Mars and is one of the seven Chieftain trees of medieval Ireland.

The Traditional Scots Pine

The Scots pine is a very variable tree and forms like this one (right) in the ancient Caledonian forest of Glen Affric, in the Scottish Highlands, are becoming increasingly rare. Foresters have neglected them in favour of tall, straight forms that can be planted closer together, but raising seedlings from trees with all the different growth forms is essential if genetic diversity is to be maintained.

The Trunks of Scots Pine

A mature Scots pine has a very characteristic trunk. The fissures in the bark provide shelter for many small creatures such as spiders, woodlice and beetles.

THE CALEDONIAN PINE FOREST, in the Highlands of Scotland, is the only true native forest in Britain which survives in large tracts today, and the Scots pine is its dominant tree. Its characteristic features are the reddish or even orange colour of the bark on the upper part of the trunk, the paired blue-green leaves or needles and the resinous buds, the upper scales of which are free at the tips. In its Highland setting it is often a majestic tree, growing in a great variety of forms which may be genetically determined – various authors have described between 9 and 18 major types. Plantations are much more uniform, as foresters have selected seeds from the straightest and most upright trees to cultivate and have then planted the trees much closer together than they would grow naturally.

In England it has been present at different times according to the pollen record, but there is no conclusive evidence about its status in England or Ireland, and it may have been re-introduced after becoming extinct several thousand years ago. Whatever its origin, it now forms naturally regenerating woods in most parts of these islands. In the Cairngorms it ascends to around 900m (2,950 ft) and in southern Europe to over 2,200m (7,200 ft).

Elsewhere, *P. sylvestris* extends east across Asia in the temperate zone and southwards in mountains to southern Spain, Italy and Greece. The pine forests of Siberia are the largest stands of any individual tree species in the world.

Like all *Pinaceae*, *P. sylvestris* is monoecious and is well adapted to the exposed and windy habitats of the northern temperate zone. The male flowers are yellow and are borne in dense clusters at the base of young shoots. The pollen grains have two wings, expansions of the outer wall which probably serve to reduce the rate of fall and make for better wind dispersal. Pollen is produced abundantly in May and June; of native trees only the now scarce elm produces higher concentrations of airborne pollen. The female flowers are small cones, green at first and then gradually

turning brown; they mature over three seasons so that there are often three different ages of cone on the branches at the same time. The winged seeds are borne under the scales and, once released as a result of the alternate wetting and drying of the cones, they can travel considerable distances, especially during cold, dry and windy winter weather.

Sturdy and very frost-hardy, pine seedlings can survive some damage, but not the repeated grazing of their growing shoots by deer. As a result of greatly increased deer numbers in the Highlands in recent years, there is now little or no natural regeneration of pine in many unfenced parts of Scotland and the existing forest is dying.

Pine trees do not establish themselves well on peat, but thrive on bare mineral soil or sand, even when these are poor in nutrients. They are able to do this because they have a rich array of associated mycorrhizal fungi. These symbiotic relationships with various fungi in the soil provide the tree with essential nutrients and minerals, especially phosphorus, and may protect the roots from pathogens. The fungi gain sugars and other organic compounds that the trees manufacture during photosynthesis. In *P. sylvestris*, the mycorrhizal associations are essential and young trees need to become infected early or they do not survive; commercial potting compost is often sterile and therefore unsuitable for young pines.

P. sylvestris has 172 phytophagous insects and other invertebrates associated with it in these islands. Foliage-feeding caterpillars of both the pine looper moth (*Bupalus piniaria*) and the pine beauty moth (*Panolis flammea*) are considered serious pests of plantation-grown pine, though in natural woodland they rarely do more than occasionally defoliate single trees that are probably already under stress. Several insects, such as scolytid beetles, cause enough damage to timber to be regarded as economic pests. Pine twigs are sometimes deformed by the gall-mite, *Triseticus pini*.

Many of the mycorrhizal fungi produce attractive and often edible fruiting bodies and pine woods are rich in fungi of all kinds. Two of the most characteristic edible species associated with Scots pine are the large brown *Boletus pinophilus* and the pink *Russula cessans*.

The Uses of Scots Pine The timber of Scots pine is one of the strongest softwoods and is widely used for construction purposes and joinery. When treated with creosote, it can be successfully used outside for telegraph poles, pit props, gate posts, fencing, etc. Pine lasts very well in wet conditions and was formerly used for waterwheels and for building piles. In the Russian Arctic, pine trees are used to build roadways on soft, wet ground. In the eighteenth century, pine trunks were even bored to make water pipes. The Grants of Rothiemurchus set up a boring mill in 1770 and exported their pipes to London for several domestic water schemes.

Whole pine trees and pine stumps can still be found preserved under peat bogs all over these islands, mostly dating from the Boreal period, around 9,000 years ago, when a climatic change inundated the land, burying the trees. In some places, the remains of pine stumps can be found on the foreshore, where the sea level has risen and inundated the coastal forests.

The Male Flowers

During May and June each male cone looses clouds of pollen which are carried far and wide by the wind. The resulting seedlings are, however, popular with deer, whose numbers have greatly increased in the Highlands in recent times.

Like many pines, *P. sylvestris* can be tapped for resin, from which turpentine is produced. This is still practised commercially on the closely related Maritime pine (*P. pinaster*) in France and Portugal and, in the USA, the American Pitch pine (*P. palustris*) produces a large proportion of the world's supply of real turpentine. Other products from pine have included rope from the inner bark, tar from the roots and a reddish-yellow dye from the cones.

Medicinally, the steam from boiling fresh pine shoots is said to relieve bronchial congestion, and pine essence is used with bath salts to combat fatigue, sleeplessness, skin irritations and cuts. Historically, Scandinavian peasants used to grind up the inner bark to make bread, or to mix it with oats to make thin griddle cakes. Pouring boiling water on bruised fresh pine needles creates a medicinal tea.

Tree Lore and Folk Beliefs Aesthetically, the Scots pine is one of the most attractive of trees, not least because of the rocky places in which it often grows. Wordsworth extolled its virtues, especially in the winter or by moonlight. In Scotland, it has a history of spiritual and inspirational significance that can be traced back to pre-Christian Celtic and Pictish cultures. It is the clan totem of the Grants and the MacGregors. Elsewhere in these islands, there appears to be little folklore attached to pines, but Kenneth Watts has traced the planting of Scots pines along old droveways in the south of England during the eighteenth century, apparently as route-markers for snowy conditions.

The Life Stages of the Scots Pine
The complex root system of the seedling pictured below is particularly characteristic of the Scots pine, and essential to its survival. Many rootlets have a close relationship with various fungi in the soil, which provide the seedling with vital nutrients and minerals.

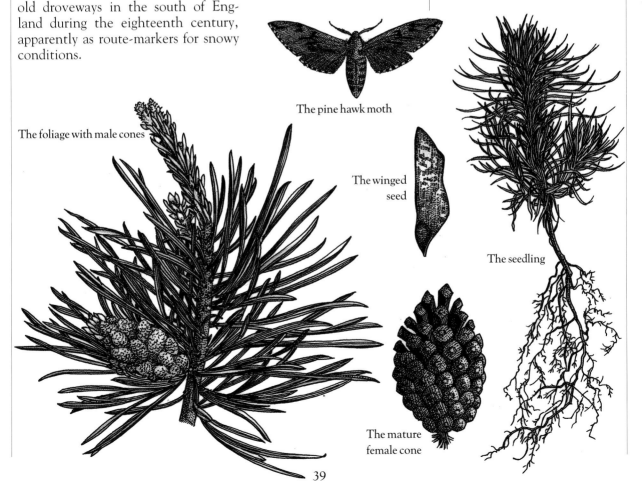

The pine hawk moth

The foliage with male cones

The winged seed

The seedling

The mature female cone

THE YEW

Yew *Taxus baccata* L.

The yew, of which several varieties are recognized – in particular *fastigiata*, the Irish yew – is of the family *Taxaceae*; this includes 5 genera and about 20 species of evergreen trees or shrubs in the north temperate zone and on mountains in New Caledonia. The genus *Taxus* includes about 10 northern species. *Taxus baccata* occurs from Ireland to the Caucasus, in the mountains of North Africa, northern Iran and in the western Himalayas.

Other names English Yew, Iubhar (Gaelic), Ibar (Old Irish), Iur (Irish), Ywen (Welsh), Palm Tree (Kent). The berries are known as snotty gogs or snottle berries in parts of England.

Derivative place-names Ilford, Ifield, Yeadon, Newry (and many others in Ireland).

Folklore Yew is the tree of death and, paradoxically, also the tree of immortality. It is represented by the letter I (idho) in the tree alphabet.

Ancient Yews

By the time yew trees reach a great age they are always hollow. The yew (right) is in the churchyard at Crowhurst, Surrey, and in the nineteenth century 12 people sat down to a cramped dinner inside the tree. Although yews are quite often found as single specimens and in small groves, yew woodland is very rare indeed today. The wood (below), at Muckross in Killarney National Park, south-west Ireland, is one of only three still in existence on the European continent.

THE YEW IS WITHOUT DOUBT our most mysterious and sacred tree. It grows to by far the greatest age of any native tree – indeed, the true age of many ancient yews is not known. Very old yew trees tend to create new trees where the main branches reach the ground and start to root. This property of layering can eventually result in the growth of a ring of trees growing after the original trunk has died.

Throughout these islands, yew occurs naturally in woods and on cliffs, including sea-cliffs, especially on neutral or alkaline soils. There is some doubt about its natural occurrence in Scotland, where some of the oldest trees were almost certainly introduced, but elsewhere it is probably native throughout, and even in the north of Scotland it occurs on remote sea-cliffs such as on the island of Bernara, where it could hardly have been planted.

Yews are slow-growing but are very shade- and salt-tolerant, and relatively immune to atmospheric pollution. They can be propagated from cuttings and layered branches, as well as from seed. On thin soil over limestone rock or chalk, yew can develop extensive pure stands, as few other tree seedlings can survive under the canopy, except some ash and holly; this may be due to the production of a toxin in the soil that discourages competitors, including yew seedlings. The most extensive yew woods are on a limestone pavement at Muckross in the Killarney National Park and on chalk at Kingley Vale on the South Downs near Chichester. In former times, it is thought that such woods were much more extensive. During earlier, inter-glacial periods, very large yew trees grew in many places; bog yews preserved in the peat have been dug up in places as far apart as East Anglia and the Bog of Allen.

The yew is an unusual tree in various respects. Its vegetative reproduction and layering are most unusual for a coniferous tree. The detailed structure of both male and female flowers, together with the unique fruit with its single seed surrounded by a red aril, are all features characteristic of the genus *Taxus*.

An Artichoke Gall
*This gall is quite common on yew and is caused by a small cecidomyiid fly, (*Taxomyia taxi*).*

Yew trees are normally dioecious, the male tree bearing small, yellow, pollen-bearing cones, and the female tree flowers that are simple, fleshy discs with a single ovule standing in the centre. Flowering is from February to April, when clouds of pollen are released by the slightest disturbance to the branches of the male trees. The female flowers are wind-pollinated, though honeybees have been observed visiting the flowers to collect yew pollen. Yew pollen is abundant, and, in spite of the relative rarity of the trees, the average pollen count for yew puts it in the top ten plants for atmospheric pollen abundance.

The familiar red berries, which take a year to ripen, are cup-shaped and sticky, and attractive to birds and some mammals. To humans they are edible if unappetising, but the seeds are generally considered poisonous. Snow and Snow have listed ten birds as feeding on the berries, of which two – the greenfinch and great tit – eat the seed.

Few phytophagous invertebrates are known to be associated specifically with yew, but a small cecidomyiid fly (*Taxomyia taxi*), is not uncommon, causing the growth of the artichoke-gall. A few fungi are found specifically under yew trees, including an inedible species of the glutinous, orange-brown toadstool, Slippery Jack (*Suillus tridentinus*).

The Uses of Yew Yew wood is heavy but very elastic and was traditionally used for longbows and spears; neolithic longbows have been found preserved in the peat in Somerset. The world's oldest artefact of wood was a yew spear around 150,000 years old, found near Clacton, and another, dating from about 90,000 years ago, was found in Germany between the ribs of a fossilized straight-tusked mastodon (*Hesperoloxodon antiquus*). Several English kings encouraged the military use of yew wood. Edward IV proclaimed that every Englishman should have a bow made of yew, ash or laburnum and Richard III decreed a general planting of yew for this purpose and the importation of foreign yew staves. Longbows appear to have been the key to military success, from Crecy in 1326 to the siege of Devizes in 1645.

The dark, reddish-brown colour of the wood and the irregularities of the ring structure result in most attractive surfaces on turned objects and veneers, though some of the colour soon fades. This use of yew wood dates from very ancient times; eighth-century Irish manuscripts refer to

VARIETIES OF YEW

The yew is famous for unusual variations of foliage and growth habit; horticulturalists such as Hillier (1990) recognize several of these as separate cultivars.

The Dovaston yew, var. *dovastioniana*, is an unusual weeping form, the original of which can be found at West Felton in Shropshire. It was planted in 1777 by a John Dovaston, who is said to have acquired it from a pedlar. The branches spread very wide, often almost horizontally, and the branchlets hang in curtains.

The Irish Yew, var. *fastigiata*, has an upright growth habit and is popularly grown in churchyards and cemeteries throughout these islands. It originates from an individual seedling found on the slopes of Cuilcagh Mountain, Co. Fermanagh, between about 1740 and 1760 by Mr George Willis, a tenant of the Earl of Enniskillen. It was transplanted to the nearby demesne at Florencecourt, where the tree can still be seen today. The variety was introduced into the horticultural trade by George Cunningham of Liverpool who received cuttings from Lord Enniskillen in about 1780. The original tree is female, but male *strobili* have been reported from the cuttings of offspring. The *fastigiata* form does not breed true, as the gene causing erect growth is apparently recessive.

its 'noble artifacts', domestic vessels being commonly made of yew at that time. The wood is also one of the densest coniferous woods and is popular with furniture-makers. Historically, yew wood was also used in dagger handles.

The timber is hard and is said to make fence posts that will 'outlive a post of iron'. The Vikings used yew wood for nails when building their ships, while John Evelyn recommended it for 'parquete-floors, cogs of mills, axles and wheels, the bodies of lutes, bowls, pins for pulleys, and for drinking tankards.' In Ireland a specialized art form has recently developed of turning and polishing carefully-dried, fossil bog yew.

Tree Lore and Folk Beliefs Yews are taken to be symbols of immortality in many traditions yet, at the same time, they have been seen as omens of impending doom. The leaves are poisonous to both man and beast, though it seems that domestic animals can gain immunity by frequently taking small amounts. For centuries yew branches were carried on Palm Sunday and at funerals in England; the custom still persists in parts of rural Ireland, where it was also said that yew was 'the coffin of the vine' as wine barrels were made of yew staves.

The spiritual significance of the yew was evidently very great in pre-Christian times and, while yew trees occur near churches throughout Britain and Ireland, in certain parts of the country some of these trees are truly ancient, pre-dating both existing churches and indeed Christianity itself (see also pp. 80-84).

Size and Age

Yew trees can grow to around 28m (92 ft) and often have multiple trunks, but it is their longevity which makes them so exceptional. As planting dates have been recorded and various subsequent measurements made, many yews are known to be well over 1,000 years old, while others are thought to be very much older (see p. 00). The following champions have been listed: Belvoir Castle, Leics (29 x 89), Ulcombe Church, Kent (13 x 334) and Defynnoc Church, Powys (9 x 342).

The Life Stages of the Yew
The familiar red berry has long been considered poisonous, but in fact many different birds and mammals feed on them and they are even edible, if unappetizing, for humans.

The foliage with male flowers

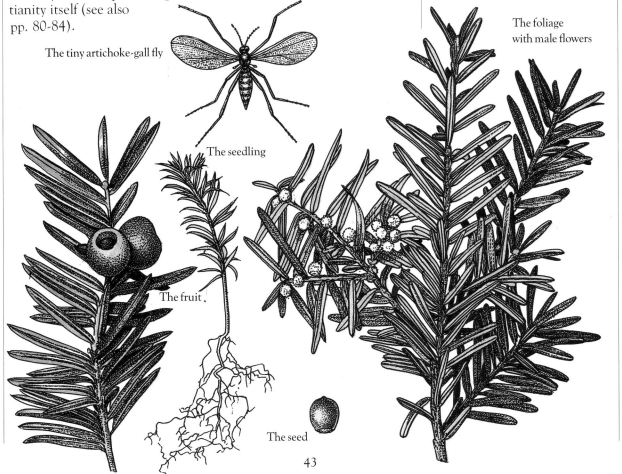

The tiny artichoke-gall fly

The seedling

The fruit

The seed

2

Portraits of Other Native Trees

The main trees featured in this chapter are the alder (*Alnus glutinosa*), the arbutus (*Arbutus unedo*), the aspen (*Populus tremula*), the box (*Buxus sempervirens*), the elm (*Ulmus minor* and *Ulmus glabra*), the field maple (*Acer campestre*), the hazel (*Coryllus avellana*) and hornbeam (*Carpinus betulus*), the holly (*Ilex aquifolium*), the juniper (*Juniperus communis*), the rosaceous trees – the cherry (*Prunus avium* [wild] and *Prunus padus* [bird]), the crab apple (*Malus sylvestris*), the hawthorn (*Crataegus monogyna* [common] and *Crataegus laevigata* [midland]), the wild pear (*Pyrus pyraster*), the rowan (*Sorbus aucuparia*), the whitebeam (*Sorbus aria*), the wild service (*Sorbus torminalis*) – the willow (*Salix*) and naturalized trees.

THE FIRST CHAPTER portrayed eight of the most characteristic native trees of these islands. Those described in this chapter are either more limited ecologically or geographically in their natural oc-curence – like alder, a tree of marshy ground and stream sides – or they are understorey trees, not generally a part of the main canopy of our woodland – like hazel or hawthorn.

The difference between dominant trees and understorey trees can be difficult to see and is somewhat arbitrary: several understorey trees will grow much taller in gardens or arboreta than they do in woodland and completely natural woodland, where understorey trees have never been cut, can no longer be found.

However, there are clear differences in habit between the two types and the distinction can be easily observed in, for instance, some of the many abandoned coppice woodlands that are to be found in and around large towns. In Coldfall Wood in North London, for example, where a derelict hornbeam coppice with oak standards has been neglected for about 50 years, the hornbeam stools and the oaks have now formed an almost continuous canopy at about 15m (50 ft). As a result, the trees in the wood have suffered mixed fortunes. Whereas birch – formerly grown as a standard in the wood – has kept pace and is still part of the canopy, lesser trees such as hawthorn, hazel and wild service now only survive either on the edges of the wood, or in one or two places where there are breaks in the canopy – for example, where large limbs of oak have fallen – letting in sufficient light. Several dead hawthorns, still standing deep in the wood, bear witness to the process, having apparently been shaded out. Holly, on the other hand, is very shade tolerant and has survived, albeit in a restricted form, as an understorey tree growing to a height of about 5m (16ft).

The portrait of each tree follows the same pattern as the previous chapter, with details of their uses and associations with folklore where appropriate.

A number of the more recent arrivals that have become fully natural-ized, like sycamore and sweet chestnut, are listed at the end of the chap-ter with approximate dates of their arrival here.

THE ALDER

WITH ITS DARK GREEN, rounded leaves borne on reddish stems and dark fissured bark, often covered in lichen, alder is a characteristic tree of wet places, marshes and stream-sides. *A. glutinosa* is native throughout these islands and in most of Europe as far as Siberia. Closely related species occur in similar habitats throughout the northern temperate zone and south to Assam, as well as in Indo-China and high in the Central Andes.

Like birch, alder is wind-pollinated, the attractive green catkins releasing pollen very early in the season, from late February to early April. The catkins become woody and black when ripe a year later, and drop their seed when shaken by the wind.

The seed is distributed by wind and by floating on water. Seedlings survive waterlogging, but require high levels of light, humidity and oxygen, which restricts natural establishment to river banks and mud, but mature alder woods do not seem to provide conditions suitable for successful regeneration. However, as alder seed does not develop a persistent seed bank, the precise role of alder in the marshland succession is not fully understood.

Alders can be grown easily from seed and also propagate well vegetatively; John Evelyn recommends taking 0.6–1m (2–3 ft) 'truncheons' in the autumn, 'binding them into faggots', and keeping them over winter with their ends in water before planting them in the spring.

All alders can fix atmospheric nitrogen by means of root nodules containing a bacterium, a species of *Frankia*. This gives the tree a great advantage for colonizing very poor soils and alders have been used to

Alder *Alnus glutinosa* L. Gaertner

The alder is of the family *Betulaceae*, which also includes the birch.

Other names Fern (Old Irish), Aller, Aller-Tree, Whistle-Wood (northern England), Irish Mahogany and many other local names.

Derivative place-names
Ollerenshaw, Ollerton.

The Alder

This site, on the bank of a river in Glen Affric, in the Scottish Highlands, is a typical habitat of the alder. The tree thrives in waterlogged conditions, its root nodules fixing atmospheric nitrogen.

reclaim spoil heaps and other industrial waste sites, where they add fertility to the soil, so allowing other species to become established.

Alders prevent erosion along the banks of rivers, particularly those flowing through soft rock or prone to torrential flow, and they have been widely planted for this purpose in the Highlands of Scotland.

Alder foliage is highly palatable to invertebrates, having 141 phytophagous species associated with it, including the alder kitten moth (*Furcula bicuspis*). Two sawflies that feed on the leaves of alder are considered pests by the Forestry Commission: *Nematus pavidus* and *Hemichroa crocea*. The so-called alder moth (*Acronicta alni*), the extraordinary caterpillar of which is one of our more bizarre insects, apparently prefers the foliage of other trees, while the so-called alder fly (*Sialis* species) has no connection with the tree at all, except that it can often be found alighting on it and hiding in crevices in the bark; its larvae are aquatic and carnivorous.

Several fungi seem to be specifically associated with alder, including various species of *Lactarius* and a large brown boletid, *Uloporus lividus*. Few if any of these species are edible.

The Uses of Alder Alder wood is light and soft but resilient. White when first cut, it rapidly turns reddish and, though this colour soon fades, the wood is much appreciated by wood-turners. Alder timber is very resistant to decay under water and, like elm and pine, it has been used for water pipes and for piles under bridges and houses; much of Venice is built on alder piles. It is still used for sluice-gates and other structures along water-courses.

Alder coppices well and the wood makes excellent charcoal; in the past, alder charcoal was much in demand for making gunpowder. It was also traditionally the best wood for making clogs, partly because it is a poor conductor of heat; most surviving alder coppices were formerly the haunt of the 'cloggers'. The catkins and bark give an inferior black colouring known in medieval times as 'a poor man's dye'.

Tree Lore and Folk Beliefs Medicinal uses of alder are few and far between – Grigson knows of none, though he goes on to say that 'early reference books say the whole plant is astringent, and in the last century it was used as a substitute for quinine in allaying fevers.' A decoction of the bark was said to have been used as a gargle and it is recorded as being used for treating burns in Norfolk, for piles and 'heart trouble' (nature unspecified) in Co. Cavan, and as an unsuccessful treatment for gout.

The alder is common in Ireland, as the predominance of the syllables 'fern' and 'farn' in place-names suggests. Traditionally, in Ireland it is unlucky to pass an alder on a journey, possibly because this would mean going through swampy land, where all kinds of misfortune might befall the traveller, but otherwise Grigson concludes that 'not much emotion has gathered around the alder.'

THE ARBUTUS

THE ARBUTUS OR STRAWBERRY TREE has been known in the Mediterranean region since ancient times. It was found flourishing in the humid south-west of Ireland in the mid-seventeenth century and is thought to have survived the last ice age in Ireland; once widespread, it has become

Arbutus or Strawberry Tree *Arbutus unedo* L.

Arbutus includes about twenty species in western North America and the Mediterranean south, to the Canaries. The arbutus is of the heather family, *Ericaceae*, a large family of about 50 genera (including *Rhododendron*, etc.) and 1,350 species, mostly shrubs with a few trees in arctic, temperate and tropical mountain habitats.

Other names Caithnei (Old Irish).

The Arbutus
The arbutus or strawberry tree is one of the few members of the heather family which grows as a tree. It is native to the Atlantic coast of Portugal and Spain, as well as here at Killarney in south-west Ireland, where it can grow to a height of 12m (40 ft).

scarce due to its being cut for charcoal. Today it is found in several places in western Ireland, including Killarney, where it grows up to an altitude of around 230m (750 ft), and near sea level in Sligo.

The leaves of the arbutus are elongated with a serrated edge; they are dark green and shiny above with dark reddish edges, but paler underneath. They do not fall for about 15 months, giving the tree an evergreen appearance. The bark is reddish-brown and fibrous.

The arbutus is unusual because it bears flowers and ripe fruit at the same time, in late summer and autumn. The flowers are white, urn-shaped and attractive to insects, though they are wind-pollinated. After fertilization, the globular fruits take a year to ripen. They look a little like a small round strawberry, but with a less interesting taste; the Latin name *unedo* means 'I eat one' (and no more!).

The seeds germinate the following spring, but the viability is low at around 50 per cent. The seedlings can thrive on a wide range of soils, but are extremely susceptible to shading and frost. As a result, they are largely restricted to rock crevices along the limestone shores of the Killarney lakes, where they naturally form more or less pure stands – though these have been disrupted by invasions of the alien *Rhododendron ponticum*, which has been planted in the area.

The tree is effectively very wind-resistant. Individual trees are frequently blown over, but new shoots appear with vigour all along the fallen stem and start again; as a result, it is a very long-lasting tree, although its precise age is difficult to determine.

The Size of Arbutus

Around the Mediterranean, *A. unedo* usually occurs as a large shrub, but specimens in Killarney National Park grow to 14m (46 ft). The champion trees recorded by Mitchell et al. are no larger; these are specimens at Selwood Park, Bedfordshire (4 x 11), and The Lodge, Sandy, Bedfordshire (2 x 26).

Aspen *Populus tremula* L.

The aspen is of the family *Salicaceae* which also includes the poplars and the willows.

Other names Aespe (Anglo-Saxon), Eadha (Old Irish), Creathach (Irish), Crithionn (Gaelic), Aps (south of England), Asp (various parts of the country and Ireland), Pipple (south-west England), Quakin' Ash (Scotland), Old Wives' Tongues (Scotland), Snapsen (Isle of Wight) and many others.

Derivative place-names Aspinwall, Aspley Guise.

The Aspen

Aspen tends to reproduce vegetatively, by means of suckers, and groups such as this one in Glen Cannich are quite common.

The Size of Aspen

Aspens reach a height of 20m (66 ft) on reasonably fertile soil and occasionally more when planted (25 x 38 at Munches, Dumfries & Galloway). The greatest girth recorded is also a tree at Munches (22 x 46). Fine specimen trees can be seen in many other botanical gardens.

No phytophagous insects are recorded from the strawberry tree in Ireland; however, all the European species so far investigated have endotrophic mycorrhiza, which probably explains why the tree is so successful at colonizing very poor and thin soils.

The Uses of Arbutus The fruits are edible, but are claimed to hurt the stomach and cause headaches. According to Grigson, 'a decoction of the leaves and flowers was considered an excellent antidote against the plague and for poisons' in the seventeenth century.

Tree Lore and Folk Beliefs There is little folklore associated with arbutus, although the tree is the first of seven shrub trees (less important than seven chieftain trees and seven peasant trees) of the medieval lores of Ireland.

THE ASPEN

ASPEN OCCURS NATURALLY all over these islands and is common in the north and west of Scotland, where it will grow at altitudes of up to 490m (1,600 ft) on mountains, even in the north, though it rarely reaches a height of more than 10m in such areas. It is the most widely distributed of the poplars, occurring as far north as the Arctic Circle in Scandinavia, south to the Mediterranean, and east across Europe and Asia to China and Japan.

The aspen is a fine, erect, fast-growing tree, with pale, yellowish bark; its trembling, round and bluntly serrated leaves make it an unmistakable sight, one much admired by artists and poets: Gerard Manley Hopkins wrote some famous lines in memory of the aspens at Binsey near Oxford after they had been cut down: 'My aspens dear, whose airy rages quelled,/ Quelled or quenched in leaves the leaping sun,/All felled, felled, all are felled.' The trembling of the leaves is caused by the flattened leaf stems as with the poplar.

Like the poplar, aspen trees are dioecious, that is either male or female, and the catkins appear well before the leaves. Aspen apparently sets seed only rarely in these islands, but reproduces vegetatively and with great vigour by means of suckers, often resulting in the growth of a small wood around a single parent tree. One such wood near Chepstow contains over 1,000 stems. It is a particularly attractive tree in autumn as the leaves turn a bright shade of yellow.

A number of phytophagous insects are known to be associated specifically with *P. tremula*, including the rare, light orange underwing moth (*Archiearis notha*). Two gall-midges – *Harmandia globuli* whose bright red, thimble-shaped gall can be seen on the upper side of the leaves in June and July, and *Syndiplosis petioli* – are restricted to aspen. However, there are many other insects which are associated with the *Populus* species in general and they are often seen on aspen.

A number of fungi are found specifically under aspen, including the large edible boletid, *Krombholziella aurantiaca*.

The Uses of Aspen Aspen wood, like poplar, is very light and has been used for veneer and plywood, for matches and light boxes for fruit and vegetables. It is widely used for pulp and paper in North America.

Tree Lore and Folk Beliefs In Wales, it was believed that the aspen could never rest because, as Grigson records, it was cursed as 'the tree on which Christ was crucified'. Many other traditions explain the trembling of the leaves in similar terms and, in the Christian tradition at least, it seems a universally unpopular tree. In Scotland, for example, aspen wood is little used because of the tree's folklore. Grigson, however, offers a rather cynical postscript: 'If the timber had been tougher, harder, more durable, and more valuable, perhaps the legends would have been different.'

THE BOX

BOX IS A SMALL TREE, but often grows as a dense evergreen shrub. It is very popular with gardeners for making hedges, and with small birds for nesting. Box occurs naturally on limestone and chalk, usually associated with beech, in the south of England; in other parts of these islands it has been much planted. At Boxwell in Gloucestershire there is naturally occurring box woodland, and at Box Hill in Surrey there are stands of box and yew together. Elsewhere, it is found further south in western Europe and in the mountains of North Africa.

The Uses of Box Box wood, as the name implies, makes excellent boxes and other small decorative objects. It is yellow, extremely hard and fine-grained; it is the best material for fine wood-engraving, for which it was much used in medieval times, and for several hundred years until the development of steel-engraving. It is also used for small, wood-turning products like chessmen, small pulley blocks and various moving parts in the textile industry. Its wood was so prized that, according to Grigson, it used to be much more common in the south of England before the box woods were decimated for the timber. This would seem to be confirmed by the frequency of 'box-' or 'bex-' in place-names. It has now become so scarce that the Society of Wood Engravers is considering planting box for use in the next century.

The buds of box are sometimes galled by a psyllid (*Homopteran Psylla buxi*) which causes the development of a small cabbage-shaped structure known unsurprisingly as the box cabbage-gall, which can be abundant on individual trees. Two other hemipteran bugs associated with box are the rare *Gonocerus acuteangulatus* and the predatory *Anthocoris buleri*.

Tree Lore and Folk Beliefs There is a tradition in some parts of England to use box sprigs in memory of the dead. In Lancashire, box sprigs are provided for mourners at a funeral, who then take them and drop them into the grave (Vickery 1984). Box is also used at the French Protestant church in Soho Square for decoration on Palm Sunday.

THE ELM

ULMUS GLABRA, THE WYCH ELM, is a native tree occurring in woods and beside streams mainly in the west and north of these islands, and especially in hilly districts. However, *U. minor*, the smooth-leaved elm, may not be native and is thought to have been introduced from southern Europe or North Africa. Elms are essentially trees of the lowlands, but wych elm reaches altitudes of 400m (1,300 ft) in Yorkshire, and English elm 460m (1,500 ft) in Derbyshire. Historically, elms were coppiced and pollarded and, in some places, enormous old pollards can still be seen, such as those at Knapwell, a few miles north-west of Cambridge.

Box *Buxus sempervirens* L.

Box is of the family *Buxaceae*, monoecious trees or shrubs, of which there are about 100 species in four genera, occurring in both temperate and tropical regions. *Buxus* has 70 species in the Americas, Europe, Madagascar, Socotra and eastern Asia.

Derivative place-names Box Hill, Bexley, Bexhill, Boscombe.

The Box
This full-grown box tree is at Boxhill, Surrey – one of the few places where woods of box still exist.

The Size of Box

Box trees can reach 10m (33 ft) in height. Champion trees are recorded at Birr Castle, Co. Offaly (12 x 19), and Gunnersbury Park (8 x 28).

The Wych Elm

Although elm is essentially a lowland tree, wych elm can be found at quite high altitudes and occurs widely as far north as Sutherland. This individual, photographed in the autumn, is in the woods at Cawdor Castle, near Nairn.

Smooth-Leaved Elm *Ulmus minor* Miller (this is taken to include *U. procera* Salisb., the 'English elm'.

Wych Elm *Ulmus glabra* Hudson

The elms are of the family *Ulmaceae*, which contains 15 genera and 200 species of tree, mostly in the northern temperate regions.

Other names Elem, Elven, Emmel, Holm, Wiltshire Weed, etc., and Lem (Old Irish), Leamhan (Irish), Wyce (Old English), Elm-Wych, Bough Elm, Wych-Hazel (south-west England), Wychwood and several others.

Derivative place-names Almsford and many others beginning with elm- such as Elmstead. In Ireland, Glenlevan, Drumleevan, and the River Laune in Killarney. In Scotland, the original name for the River Leven was Leamhain, i.e. the 'elm river'.

Elms are 'the most complex and difficult trees in western Europe, and the most intimately linked to human affairs', according to Oliver Rackham, who devotes a whole chapter to them in his book, *History of the Countryside*.

There is considerable disagreement about their classification, but according to Clapham et al. there are just two species of common elm, which can be distinguished by the size and roughness of their leaves: *U. minor* has smaller leaves (less than 7cm long), which are more or less smooth above, while *U. glabra* has larger (10–11cm) leaves, the upper surfaces of which are extremely rough to the touch. They also differ in that only *U. minor* produces suckers. Stace, however, separates the English elms from *U. minor* as a separate and 'probably native' species, *U. procera*.

Elm flowers are purplish-red, about 2cm long and appear in bunches in February or March, well before the leaves. The flowers have two awl-shaped styles surrounded by four or five stamens with purple anthers. The fruits are just over 2cm long, consisting of a single seed surrounded by a continuous membrane, making possible effective wind-dispersal. Heavy crops occur only every three years or so.

Elm is attractive to phytophagous insects; 113 species have been recorded from *Ulmus* species in these islands, together with 11 other

DUTCH ELM DISEASE

Elms were one of the most abundant and characteristic trees of the English countryside, especially in the Midlands, until the population was decimated in the 1970s by Dutch elm disease. This is caused by a pathogenic fungus (*Ceratocystis ulmi*), the spores of which are carried by various species of elm bark beetles (*Scolytus* species). Some large trees still survive, mostly in towns, and in many places, after *U. minor* or *U. procera* trees have died, vigorous regeneration from suckers has produced dense elm thickets. In London, these may be found in several places, such as Hampstead Heath, Barnes Common and Wandsworth Common. However, in the countryside so few mature elm trees remain that it cannot now be considered a component of the mature tree flora, except for odd places in Scotland and isolated parts of England.

Such a tragedy has happened before, and will no doubt happen again; indeed Oliver Rackham suggests that the Elm Decline which, according to the pollen records, occurred around 6,000 years ago, was most probably due to the disease, and that it may have spread very easily, partly as a result of the activities of neolithic man. At that time much of the wildwood, in which elm was a substantial component, was still standing: Rackham suggests that by killing a large proportion of elms, the disease may have significantly helped the process of clearing the lowland for agriculture.

Dead elms have become an all too familiar sight in England since the 1970s.

phytophagous invertebrates. With the decline in the elm population, many of these species have unfortunately been affected as well, in particular several large and attractive butterflies, such as the Camberwell beauty (*Nymphalis antiopa*), the white-letter hairstreak (*Strymon walbum*) and the large tortoiseshell (*Nymphalis polychloros*), all of which have become very scarce or extinct. Elm leaves are commonly galled by three species of aphid. One of these, *Eriosoma languinosa*, causes a spectacular pouch-gall to develop from a whole leaf; it turns grey at first, and then bright red or purple. Another, *Tetraneura ulmi*, produces a fig-gall; infestations may be so heavy as to result in thousands of these small growths on the foliage.

The Uses of Elm Soon after the Elm Decline of 6,000 years ago, the earliest neolithic trackways, such as the Sweet Track in Somerset, provide evidence of the early uses of elm wood as shaped beams. Since then, elms have been planted around settlements, felled for timber and coppiced for fodder throughout these islands.

Elm wood is of medium weight (that of *U. glabra* is more dense) and strength, but it distorts easily and has to be seasoned carefully. It bends well, and resists strains that split other timbers. Giraldus Cambrensis, a twelfth-century writer, claimed that the Welsh longbow was made of elm, instead of yew as in England.

Elm was formerly used a great deal for furniture, such as settee frames and Windsor chair seats, and in decorative turnery. Moreover, it was traditionally used for the hubs of cart-wheels, and for coffins. It is durable for exterior use, especially in wet conditions; before metal pipes were made, elm was one of the few timbers used for water-pipes since, according to Grigson, 'the portion in the well did not decay easily, the portion above the ground did not split when the water froze.' Many English towns had elm water mains, including Bristol, Reading, Exeter,

The Size of Elm

When full-grown, all these species are rounded, variably shaped trees, normally growing to around 30–35m. *U. glabra* is recorded as reaching 41m at Castle Howard, Yorkshire, and a diameter of 217cm at Braham House, Highland; *U. procera* reaches 32m at Belsay Castle in Northumberland, and a diameter of 199cm at Preston Park, Brighton.

Southampton, Liverpool and Hull. Some of these old mains survive and are occasionally disinterred during building works. Elm piles were laid under bridges and buildings, including some under the old Waterloo Bridge. When available, elm wood is still used in boat-building for keels, rudders and the bottoms of canal barges, and in the fishing industry for trawler boards and bobbins. The disadvantage of its use for furniture or joinery is that the wood is attacked by many destructive insects such as the death-watch beetle (*Xestobium rufovillosum*).

THE FIELD MAPLE OR ENGLISH MAPLE

FIELD MAPLE is a common tree in woodlands and hedgerows throughout England, particularly on neutral or alkaline soils, where it is often associated with ash and hazel. It is thought to be introduced in both Ireland and Scotland, where it is rare. Maple is shade-tolerant and often occurs as an understorey tree.

The paired leaves are five-lobed, downy when young and a dark green colour when mature. The flowers are small and pale in colour with five sepals and petals, and eight stamens, some trees having male flowers only. Field maple is pollinated by various small insects and the paired fruits are winged, similar to the more familiar sycamore keys, but smaller. As most do not germinate for 18 months, horticulturalists normally stratify the seed for that period.

Fifty-one phytophagous invertebrates are associated with field maple, of which the plumed prominent moth (*Ptilophora plumigera*) is one of the most characteristic. A number of gall-mites attack maple, as well as the related sycamore, including the densely gregarious *Eriophyes macrorhynchus* complex, the tiny red galls of which can sometimes be found in their hundreds, on the upper surface of a single leaf.

The Uses of Maple Field maple coppices well, and traditionally has been managed in this way. Rackham has found ancient stools 4.5m (15 ft) across, and in some places, such as Hatfield Forest, maple woods can

Field Maple, English Maple *Acer campestre* L.

The maple is of the family *Aceraceae*, which includes 200 species in three genera. These are mainly trees with some shrubs, they are generally temperate species, including the introduced sycamore (*A. pseudoplatanus*). *Acer* includes many attractive North American and Japanese varieties which are greatly prized by gardeners and landscape designers.

Other names Cat Oak, Dog Oak, Maplin Tree, Whistle-Wood, etc. The keys are known as Boots-and-Shoes (Somerset), Hasketts (Dorset), Kitty-Keys (Yorkshire) and Shacklers (Devon).

Derivative place-names Mappleton, Mapperley.

The Field Maple
Like other Acer *species from North America and Asia, our native maple turns a spectacular colour in autumn. This one is at Westonbirt Arboretum, Tetbury, Gloucestershire.*

be found. However, it was not always coppiced or pollarded, sometimes being grown as a standard tree for its timber. Unlike other species of *Acer* from Canada and Japan in particular, the foliage of field maple does not turn scarlet in the autumn, but a very attractive bright yellowish-green. As it resists pollution well, it is popular for planting in towns.

Maple wood is heavier than sycamore, fine-grained and brown, and much prized by wood-turners and cabinet-makers, especially for very fine articles, as it can be worked so thin as to be almost transparent. Since it takes a high polish, it is also an excellent veneer wood. In ancient times, it was used for making harps like those found in ancient Saxon barrows, including the Sutton Hoo ship treasure.

Like many members of the *Aceraceae*, maple trees produce sweet sap in the spring which can be used for making wine or maple syrup, and sugar can be extracted from the wood by boiling.

Tree Lore and Folk Beliefs Culpepper recommends decoctions of the leaves or the bark for 'strengthening the liver'.

THE HAZEL AND THE HORNBEAM

HAZEL WAS ONE of the first trees to grow widely in these islands, soon after the last glacial period, which it may possibly have survived in small refuges. It is normally found as the coppiced understorey in oak and ash woods. It grows at altitudes of up to 610m (2,000 ft), or alternatively forms a low scrub vegetation on exposed limestone, such as on the Burren in the west of Ireland and at Hutton-Roof in Lancashire.

Hornbeam is a relative newcomer, first appearing in the pollen records only 5,000 years ago, and its natural distribution is limited to the south-west of England. It has generally been managed for coppice wood and so is rarely seen as a full-sized tree.

Superficially, the hornbeam looks like beech, having similar grey bark, but the leaves are rougher to the touch, with more veins and a serrated edge. Moreover, the bole is rarely round and tends to have an oval shape, as if the trunk had been slightly compressed. Hazel leaves are quite similar in shape to those of the elm: they are even rougher to touch and are of squarer shape, but with a pronounced apical point. The leaves may be purplish when they first appear, but they then turn green and finally a bright yellow colour in the autumn, giving a hazel wood a spectacular appearance in October and November. Hornbeam leaves turn orange, giving an equally beautiful effect.

In hazel, the male flowers are catkins, known in country areas as lambs' tails. They are remarkable in that they start to appear before almost any other flowers and shed pollen as early as mid-February. As this is finished by mid-April, hazel flowering hardly overlaps with that of the hornbeam. The hazel's female flowers are very diminutive, with characteristic bright red threads that are the stigma and styles from a tiny group of flowers. Both hazel and hornbeam are wind-pollinated. Hazel fruits are the familiar hazel-nuts or cobs; hornbeam fruits have membranous wings and are found in untidy bunches.

Hazel and hornbeam have respectively 106 and 51 species of phytophagous insects and mites associated with them, though none of these is a spectacular species. The tiny caterpillars of several species of

---

The Size of Maple

Maple grows to between 9 and 15 metres (30–49 ft), but individual trees can reach nearly twice that height. Particularly fine specimens can be seen at Kinnettles Castle, Angus (27 x 81) and at Chilston Park, Kent (21 x 134).

Hazel *Corylus avellana* L.

Hornbeam *Carpinus betulus* L.

Both hazel and hornbeam are members of the family *Corylaceae*, monoecious trees or shrubs, the fruit of which are nuts surrounded by a ring of leaf-like bracts. There are four genera and about 52 species.

Hazel, one of around 15 species of the genus *Corylus*, is native to west Asia, north Africa and Europe. Hornbeam, one of about 35 species of the genus *Carpinus*, occurs naturally in the south of England and, though not native to Ireland, is found east to Iran and south to the Pyrenees.

Other names for hazel Coll (Ancient Irish), Cobbly-Cut, Filbeard, Nuttall, Victor-Nut, Wood-Nut.

Other names for hornbeam Horse Beech, Hurst Beech, White Beech.

Derivative place-names Cowdray Park, Hazel Grove, Haslingden, Heswall. In Ireland: Cullan, Collon, Colehill and Callowhill.

The Hazel

These fine hazel trees, at Muckross Peninsula in Killarney National Park, Ireland, are some of the few that have been allowed to grow naturally, hazel having been almost universally coppiced.

The Size of Hazel and Hornbeam

HAZEL On good soil Hazel will grow into a small but sturdy tree of 8–10m (24–30 ft) in height such as those in Killarney National Park, though this is not sufficient to attract the attention of Mitchell et al. HORNBEAM Hornbeam can reach a height of 33m (100 ft) on good, rather damp soil. The record trees listed are at Trebah, Cornwall (30 x 86) and Heron Court, Hampshire (20 x 146).

micro-Lepidoptera mine the leaves of both trees. Hazel is sometimes infested by a gall similar to big-bud in black-currants; this is caused by a gall-mite (*Eriophyes avellanae*). Hornbeam is affected by a species of witches broom (*Taphrina carpini*), and its leaves are galled by both gall-mites and gall-midges.

Several fungi are associated with either hazel or hornbeam or both, including the common edible boletid, *Krombholziella carpini*, and the beautiful, red – but inedible – *Russula lucteotacta*.

The Uses of Hazel and Hornbeam Hazel is a major coppice tree; its rods and sticks, being pliable and tough, are used for a wide variety of products. Coppice-wood merchants like Bill Hogarth (see pp. 96–98) produce around 20 different items from hazel, including thatching spars, net stakes and hurdles. Hornbeam wood is as hard as box and exceedingly tough and heavy, blunting saws more quickly than oak. The name hornbeam is derived from the ancient use of the wood for yokes – literally the beam between the horns. It is highly resistant to wear and is used for industrial flooring as an alternative to maple. It is also used for musical instruments, especially in pianos and harpsichords, as well as for cogs in machinery, and, historically, for pulleys, mallets, billiard cues, skittles and butchers' chopping blocks. According to John Evelyn, it burns 'like a candle' and was formerly coppiced a great deal for fuelwood and charcoal; old hornbeam coppices can be seen in many woods around London, whereas full-grown trees are almost completely absent.

Tree Lore and Folk Beliefs According to Grigson, the hazel is a magical tree in these islands and throughout most of Europe, and is protected like the rowan. A hazel rod protects against evil spirits and is the proper wood for a rod of power, as well as being the best for water-divining or making a wand, though rowan, birch or mistletoe could also be used for this. In Ireland, hazel was the Tree of Knowledge, while in medieval England it was a symbol of fertility. Hazel-nuts were carried as charms or

The Hornbeam
*This old hornbeam pollard, with witches'
broom in its upper branches, is in the
ancient wood pasture of Hatfield
Forest, Essex.*

to ward off rheumatism in some parts of England and the double nut (St John's Nut) was supposed to be particularly powerful. It was also a symbol of plenty; times of prosperity in Ireland were commonly referred to by old writers as times of abundant hazel-nuts.

THE HOLLY

HOLLY GENERALLY GROWS as a small understorey tree and is a frequent component of our oak woodland. It occurs less commonly in other types of woodland and can tolerate quite deep shade.

Holly occurs throughout these islands on most soils, but not in wet places; it grows to altitudes of about 550m (1,800 ft) in some mountain areas, where it is a common sight on hillsides. It extends north to Norway and east to Austria, its limit apparently being set by winter cold. It survives pollution well and is therefore much planted in towns.

Holly is dioecious, bearing insignificant white flowers in early summer that are pollinated by honey bees. The trees first flower after about 20 years, but maximum production of berries on the female trees is not until around 40 and then, as with many other trees, heavy fruiting only occurs in mast years. Though poisonous to man, the fruits are attractive to birds, especially in the winter when there is less other food around. For various reasons, they tend to stay on the tree longer than most other fruits: they do not fall off or go bad, even after frost, and individual holly bushes are frequently defended by pairs of mistle thrushes, probably in part because the fruits are such long-lasting food, surviving even very hard winters.

The seeds do not germinate in the first year and growers advise stratifying them in damp sand for 16–18 months before sowing.

In the wild, holly has proved a useful tree to peasants and farmers. In spite of its prickly leaves, it is grazed by deer, and the upper foliage of mature trees and the leaves of saplings provide nutritious and apparently

Holly *Ilex aquifolium* L.

Holly is of the family *Aquifoliaceae*. *Ilex* is a very large genus of nearly 400 species which occur all over the world, except in the Arctic.

Other names Bein-Viar (Norse), Cuillen (Old Irish), Helver, Berry Holm, Aunt Mary's Tree, Poisonberry, Christmas Tree, Christ's Thorn.

Derivative place-names Bainley Bank, Holdenhurst. In Ireland, many places that have 'cullen' in their name.

highly palatable fodder for domestic animals. Historically, it was coppiced and pollarded for this purpose; at Stiperstones in Shropshire there is a large grove of old holly pollards. Pollarding is still done in some places; in parts of the Lake District, upper branches are lopped for sheep and cows during conditions of freezing snow.

In gardens, it has been much planted, partly from interest in the range of variegated-leaf cultivars, and also because it can be tightly clipped, making it suitable for topiary work.

Holly is often found in old hedges dating back to before 1700. In Dungeness and Epping Forest, there are pure holly stands which are, according to Rackham, relics of the medieval holly woods once widespread in England, Ireland and Scotland. Such woods seem to have been restricted to these islands, so their relics are of particular conservation interest on account of their uniqueness.

Only ten phytophagous insects are recorded from holly though one, the holly leaf-miner (*Phytomyza ilicis*) is very common. The bright yellowish-green caterpillars of the holly blue butterfly (*Celastrina*

The Holly
Holly is particularly palatable to grazing animals – including cows and sheep – and in very hard winters the upper branches were lopped for fodder, a practice still continued in parts of the Lake District. This ancient holly pollard is in Windsor Park, Berkshire.

argiolus) feed on the flowers, buds and berries. Holly shoots are sometimes distorted by 'fasciation', a malformation caused by the bacterium *Corynebacterium fascians*.

The Uses of Holly Holly wood is white, heavy, very fine-grained and even, but it tends to distort when drying, so it is generally used in small pieces. It is dense, and freshly-cut wood sinks in water, as does box wood. Holly wood stains and polishes well and is prized for inlay work on decorated furniture. It can even be stained black and used as a substitute for ebony. Holly has often been used for making chessmen, the hammers in harpsichords and the butts for billiard cues. The fine grain makes it one of the few native woods that is acceptable to wood-engravers as a substitute for box. In medieval Ireland it was used for chariot shafts.

When boiled and fermented, the bark makes a sticky substance known as birdlime, which was formerly used to trap small birds.

Tree Lore and Folk Beliefs Young leaves when boiled have been recommended as a cure for colds, bronchitis and rheumatism, and a few berries can be taken as a purgative.

Holly is one of the ancient symbols of the midwinter festival and has been incorporated into Christmas celebrations; its scarlet berries are much admired, red being a colour to ward off evil. It is associated with many other country beliefs, partly because of its evergreen habit, as a result of which it remains 'fresh' throughout the winter. It is unlucky to cut down a holly tree, especially in Ireland where it is an abode of fairies; it should not be grown near the house and it can even be dangerous to sweep a chimney with a holly branch. In England it used to be planted near houses to ward off witches and lightning, as well as to repel poison. Inside the house, it would also ward off goblins, especially at Christmas. Alcohol was often sold at fairs and markets under holly trees: public houses called The Hollybush or The Bush may reflect these early licensing arrangements.

THE JUNIPER

AN ANCIENT SPECIES that arrived soon after the last glacial period, it can be found throughout these islands, extending as far north as the Orkneys and growing at altitudes of over 1,000m (3,300 ft); it often forms a dominant scrub on chalk, limestone and slate. In Ireland, a fastigiate form with dense foliage occurs mainly in the west. Elsewhere, it occurs throughout Europe, especially on mountains in the south, in North Africa, North America to Alaska and across northern Asia. In these islands, there is only one species, but two subspecies are recognized: the procumbent mountain form, *alpina*, and the erect or spreading lowland form, *communis*. There are about 60 other species of *Juniperus* which occur throughout the northern hemisphere from Mexico to the Himalayas and Taiwan, as well as on the mountains of East Africa.

As a member of the *Gymnospermae*, juniper has cones rather than flowers, which can be pollinated by wind or by insects. The fruits, which take two to three years to ripen, are rather dry, blue-black berries formed by the cone scales, which become fleshy and coalesce with up to six seeds inside. They are an important source of food for birds in some places. In the Chilterns, Snow and Snow found that although the

---

The Size of Holly

Given space and light, holly can grow into a fine tree and may reach 24–27m (80–90 ft) in favourable circumstances. At Staverton Park, Suffolk, holly trees, the tallest of which is 23m (74 ft), have overtopped and killed ancient oaks. A tree of over 27m (90 ft) has been recorded at Ashburnham Park, Sussex; another champion tree of 9 x 97 can be found at Castle Frazer, Grampian.

Juniper *Juniperus communis* L.

Juniper is of the family *Cupressaceae*, which includes cypress trees and the American western red cedar. It has 19 genera and 130 species, all evergreen trees or shrubs.

Other names Crann Fir (Old Irish), Aiten, Melmot, Horse-Saving, Bastard-Killer.

The Lowland Juniper

In the past, large areas of the Cumbrian hills were covered with juniper woods. Today, junipers are more often found singly, such as this one at Little Langdale.

The Size of Juniper

Juniper is usually considered as a shrub, though it can grow to a tree of about 10m (33 ft) in height. It is one of the slowest growing trees, with individuals living for centuries.

bushes are sometimes defended by mistle thrushes, juniper berries are apparently of little interest to other bird species. Elsewhere in Europe, fieldfares and waxwings in particular take a lot of juniper fruits, indeed the German name for fieldfare is *Wacholderdrossel* or 'juniper thrush'.

Phytophagous insects and mites are difficult to find on juniper, although 31 species are recorded as being associated with it (plus two other invertebrates), including the attractive juniper carpet moth (*Thera juniperata*) and the small juniper pug moth (*Eupithecia pusillata*). The caterpillars of the small juniper webber moth (*Dichomeris marginella*) cause sufficient damage to the needles and branches to be listed as a pest by the Forestry Commission. Juniper is sometimes infected by a rust-fungus (*Gymnosporangium* species), which galls the stem, and a gall-midge (*Oligotrophus juniperinus*) causes a bud swelling similar to the artichoke-gall on yew, known as the whooping-cough-gall after the medicinal use to which it has been put.

The Uses of Juniper It is said, that as dry juniper wood burns with almost no smoke, it was used in former times as the fuel for illicit distilling. This is meant to be the reason why juniper is less common in the Highlands of Scotland today, as so many trees were felled for this purpose. Juniper berries have a sharp tang and are used to make liqueurs and sauces and to give gin its flavour.

Early herbalists regarded juniper as a strong counter-poison with which to resist the plague. Culpepper recommends the berries for a very wide range of ailments, from the bites of venomous beasts to 'wind in any part of the body', and says that they should be taken to 'strengthen both the brain and the body'. The Somerset name, bastard-killer, derives from the swallowing of berries to procure an abortion. Today, oil of juniper is still available for use, as a cure to combat flatulence.

Tree Lore and Folk Beliefs In country areas of Scotland and continental Europe, Juniper is still considered to be a powerful agent against witches and devils; it is hung above doorways on the eve of May Day to keep away evil, and burnt on Hallowe'en to ward off evil spirits. According to Thistleton-Dyer, it is also supposed that 'juniper is potent in dreams' and that 'it is unlucky to dream of the tree itself, especially if a person be sick (already), in winter to dream of gathering the berries denotes prosperity, while the actual berries themselves signify either great honours or the birth of a male child.'

The Mountain Juniper
This can be found growing at 600m (2,000 ft) in harsh environments, such as here on Beinn Eighe, in the Scottish Highlands. Although juniper is generally a very slow-growing tree, it is extremely resistant to cold and wind, and this variety can survive prolonged periods of snow.

Rosaceous Trees

Several native trees are members of a very large worldwide family: the *Rosaceae*. This has about 100 genera and over 2,000 species, many of which are trees or shrubs. They have regular, usually hermaphrodite flowers, which are often scented, and they are characterized by their main parts, such as petals or sepals existing in groups of five. The fruits are often juicy and attractive to birds and mammals. In temperate zones, they tend to stay on the tree through the winter, providing an important food source for many birds and some other animals.

The early history of rosaceous trees in these islands is not well documented. Charcoal made from some of these trees has been identified at neolithic sites, but there are no good pollen records of them as, unlike many of the other native trees, they are insect-pollinated and produce much less abundant pollen.

The records of phytophagous insects for the trees in this family are not very complete. Kennedy and Southwood list 153 phytophagous invertebrates associated with blackthorn (*Prunus spinosa*, but give no figures for *P. avium* and *P. padua*), 209 from hawthorn (*Cretaegus monogyna*), and 118 from crab apple (*Malus sylvestris*), but only 58 from rowan (*Sorbus aucuparia*). The large majority of those listed are moths and butterflies, many of them relatively unspecific feeders.

A variety of galls are found on rosaceous trees, especially hawthorn. These include common leaf-roll galls caused by either a gall-mite (*Eriophyes typicus*) or an aphid (*Rhopalosiphum insertum*). Two insects are attributed pest status by the Forestry Commission: larvae of a gall-wasp (*Tirymus druparum*) damage the flowers and seed of many rosaceous trees (*Sorbus*, *Malus* and *Pyrus* species); and the wild-service aphid (*Dysaphis aucupariae*) attacks growing shoots and young leaves.

THE CHERRIES

P. AVIUM – the Latin name means bird's cherry – occurs commonly in most parts of these islands, extending as far north as Caithness and Sutherland, and is also found throughout most of Europe, North Africa, and Western Asia.

P. padus, confusingly known as the bird cherry in English, is a northern species in these islands, occurring naturally across Scotland, Ireland and northern England and ascending to about 600m (2,000 ft), often on

Wild Cherry or Gean
Prunus avium L.

Bird Cherry *Prunus padus* L.

Together with blackthorn (*P. spinosa*), these may be the only truly native species of *Prunus*, a very large genus of about 450 species, mostly found in the northern temperate zone, but also in tropical Asia and the Andes.

Other names The wild cherry is also called Idath (Old Irish), Crab Cherry, Hawkberry, Mazzard, Merry. Gean has the same origin as *guigne*, a French word for cherry; cherry and cerise have the same root. The bird cherry is also called Black Dogwood, Black Merry, Hagberry and many other local names.

The Wild Cherry
When covered with flowers, like this one at Box Hill, Surrey, wild cherries are a spectacular sight and attract many butterflies and other insects.

The Size of Cherry

P. avium is a tall, handsome deciduous tree that can grow to nearly 30m (100 ft) (Priors Mesne, Gloucestershire: 31 x 71) and a diameter of 170cm (Studley Royal, Yorkshire).
P. padus is a much smaller tree, rarely reaching a height of 12m (39 ft). Of the champion specimens, the tallest (14 x 33, at Old Kiln, Frensham, Surrey) is a planted tree outside its natural range, while that of greatest girth (11 x 55) is at Achnagarry in Highland.

---

poor soils. When flowering, it stands out clearly in ravines and gorges in mountain areas like the Peak District. In southern Britain, it is thought to be entirely introduced, but it does occur naturally across Europe to the Caucasus and through central Asia to the Himalayas.

The genus *Prunus* also includes various introduced species, such as *P. domestica*, the common plum tree, as well as hybrid varieties of plums and cherries.

There are relatively few insect-pollinated trees native to these islands, and both cherries are attractive and even spectacular sights in spring, when covered with a mass of white blossom – attracting butterflies and many other insects. The flowers appear blue-green to bees, which are particularly attracted to them, but they are pollinated by various insects including flies and butterflies. Some tits may also take the nectar from wild cherry flowers, according to Procter and Yeo (1973).

The fruit of *P. avium*, known variously as merries, mazzards and various other local names, is black or dark red with relatively little flesh around the stone. Although not as tasty as the cultivated cherry, it is still sweet and quite edible, unlike the smaller black fruit of *P. padus* which is too sour to eat. (The foliage of *P. padus* is also poisonous to stock, especially goats and, for this reason, is sometimes used for hedging.) The seeds of both do not germinate immediately, usually remaining dormant for at least a year.

Like the cultivated cherry, the *P. avium* produces abundant suckers and can develop into small groups of trees. *P. padus*, on the other hand, does not produce suckers and is nearly always solitary.

The Uses of Cherry Cherry wood is reddish-brown in colour and has a fine, attractive grain, which makes it much sought after for furniture, wood-carving and turning. It is traditionally used for smokers' pipes, especially in Europe.

The Bird Cherry
This flowering bird cherry in Glenn Morriston is a typical springtime sight in many northern and western mountains.

Tree Lore and Folk Beliefs There appears to be no historical record of folklore associated with wild cherry in this country, but in Japan a related species, known as *Sato zakura*, is the national tree, the blossom in particular being taken as a national symbol. Cherry trees are sometimes planted in Japan and in other countries in early August, in memory of those who died at Hiroshima and Nagasaki; such cherry trees have also been planted around the Peace Pagoda at Milton Keynes.

According to Geoffrey Grigson, cherry-tree gum is an old remedy for coughs and promotes a good complexion and good sight. In Europe, herbalists believe that it can help break up and expel gall-stones and kidney-stones if dissolved in wine. Culpepper recommends wild cherries for most urinary complaints.

THE CRAB APPLE

The CRAB APPLE usually occurs singly, scattered through almost all types of woodland in eastern England at roughly one tree for every ten acres, according to Oliver Rackham. Many small woods therefore have only a single individual (or none at all), although in the woodlands of the Lake District they are more frequent, often being found next to the sites of old charcoal-burning pitsteads. Crab apple also grows throughout Ireland, England and Wales, but is less common in Scotland. Elsewhere it occurs across Europe to south-west Asia.

Crab blossom is pinkish and first appears slightly later than that of wild cherry. It is lightly scented, attracting a variety of short-tongued flies, wasps and bees which pollinate the flowers.

The fruit is small, yellow to red and rather sharp. Crab apple perhaps derives its name from being crabbed, 'a tree of awkward character', which gives the wrong (i.e. sour) fruit.

The Uses of Crab Apple The timber of crab apple is of excellent quality; it is very uniform in texture and if dried very slowly is suitable for the most delicate woodworking, such as wood-engraving and fine carving. At one time it was used for making set squares and other drawing instruments. The fruit makes excellent jelly and wine. Geoffrey Grigson recommends that two or three crabs improve an apple tart. It appears to have been cultivated since ancient times; crabs were found in an oak coffin dating from the early Bronze Age.

Tree Lore and Folk Beliefs A variety of folklore is associated with apples, especially in England, mostly to do with determining true love and the suitability of marriage partners. A typical example is the throwing of apple pips into the fire while saying the name of your love; if the pip explodes then the love is true, if not, the pip will quietly burn away.

THE COMMON HAWTHORN, MAY, OR WHITETHORN

Hawthorn is one of the most common trees in these islands. Though a pioneer species that often invades grassland, it then continues to thrive as the woodland develops. It is slow-growing and has a characteristically dense, tangled crown, very popular with nesting birds from finches to

The Crab Apple
This crab apple in flower is near Enfield, Co. Meath, Ireland.

Crab Apple or Wild Apple *Malus sylvestris* Miller

The apple genus (*Malus*) has about 35 species in the north temperate regions and the crab apple is the only member native to Britain and Ireland.

Other names Aball (Old Irish), Gribble, Grindstone Apple, Bittersgall, Wilding Tree.

Derivative place-names Crabtree, Crabbet.

The Size of Crab Apple

M. sylvestris is a small tree in the wild, reaching a height of about 10m (33 ft), and it has smaller, more pointed glabrous leaves than the domestic apple (*M. domestica*), which is not native and is a hybrid of more than one European species.

The Hawthorn
Isolated trees such as this one growing on a limestone pavement near Kirby Stephen, Cumbria, are favoured by nesting hawks.

Common Hawthorn, May, Whitethorn
Crataegus monogyna Jacq.

Midland Hawthorn *Crataegus laevigata* (Poiret) DC

Crataegus is a large genus of at least 200 species (some authorities claim there are many more) of thorny trees and shrubs occurring throughout the northern temperate zone. *C. monogyna* and *C. laevigata* extend throughout much of Europe, and *C. monogyna* as far as Afghanistan. These two species hybridize freely and intermediate forms exist.

Other names Ske (Old Irish), Porn (Old Norse), Hag (Old English), Hagthorn, Quickthorn, May, Maytree, Bread & Cheese Tree, Azzy Tree, Holy Innocents' May and many others.

Derivative place-names
Hatherley, Hatherton, Thornton Heath. In Ireland, Skeagh, Skehanagh, etc.

Folklore Hawthorn is a tree of Mars and is represented by the letter H in the tree alphabet.

hawks. It often grows more as a bush to about 6m (20 ft) and is widely used for hedging. It does grow much taller under certain circumstances, such as when competing with taller species, and large old pollards have been recorded as reaching 16m (52 ft) in Hatfield Forest, and a similar height at Hall Place in Kent, with a diameter of 116cm (3 ft 9in).

A famous tree near Norwich, known as Hethel Old Thorn, is said to be the oldest hawthorn in England – reputed to have been planted in the reign of King John. It is protected as one of the smallest Sites of Special Scientific Interest in the country. Other ancient hawthorns, also probably pollards, are to be found at Castor Hanglands, three miles west of Peterborough, while there are many gnarled old trees in exposed places on limestone pavements near Kirby Stephen in Cumbria.

Hawthorn flowers appear in May and early June, with *C. laevigata* often preceding *C. monogyna* by about two weeks. In both cases, the flowers are abundant and heavily scented, attracting a wide variety of relatively unspecialized insect pollinators, especially flies, wasps and bees. The petals tend to be white to pale-pink in colour, although a number of cultivated varieties have entirely pink or even red flowers. The two species are distinguished largely by the structure of the flowers, *C. monogyna* having, as the name suggests, a single style, and *C. laevigata* (usually) having two styles.

The red fruits or haws ripen by late August or September and may stay on the branch until the following spring. Though haws may vary considerably in size, they are one of the most important bird fruits throughout these islands; they are particularly attractive to migrants such as redwings, fieldfares and hawfinches, as well as many resident species such as blackbirds, robins, thrushes and woodpigeons. Snow and Snow have recorded individual hawthorn trees being defended by mistle thrushes as the fruits are such a good source of late winter food. Haws are also eaten by small mammals such as voles, mice and squirrels.

The seeds are left undamaged after passing through the gut of most birds, which therefore act as excellent dispersal agents. The seeds require warm moist conditions to break their hard-coat dormancy, followed by chilling, and they do not germinate for 18 months. Horticulturalists therefore have to stratify the seeds in sand. No persistent seed bank has been reported.

The foliage is little grazed by other mammals, except deer, before the shoots have become woody. This is mainly because of the thorns, but perhaps also because the foliage is disliked and even toxic to stock. Hawthorn does, however, support a rich insect fauna; 209 phytophagous invertebrates of diverse habit are recorded from hawthorn in these islands, including several flies and beetles whose larvae develop inside the berries.

The Uses of Hawthorn The wood of hawthorn is hard and tough, the Latin name *Crataegus* being derived from *kratos*, the Greek for strength. Yellowish to pink in colour, it is used for fine work of various kinds, including veneer and cabinet work, and for making fine boxes, tool handles, mill-wheel teeth, mallets and the ribs of small boats. Because it is so fine-grained and even, it has been used for fine wood-engraving. It also makes excellent firewood and charcoal.

For centuries haws and hawthorn flowers have been used to make a variety of jellies, wines, liqueurs and ketchups.

Tree Lore and Folk Beliefs Hawthorn has perhaps more connections with ancient beliefs and traditions than almost any other tree. It is recognized as having a powerful supernatural force for good or evil in many cultures. The appearance of the blossom at the beginning of May in the Gregorian calendar (May Day was on what is now 12 May) signified the end of winter and the beginning of summer. The May Queen of pre-Christian Britain was crowned with may blossom, and traditions of putting up the may boughs and branches are still very much observed in parts of Ireland (see p. 143). It continues to be regarded as unlucky to bring may flowers into a house, and fairies or little people are said to live inside or under the trees.

As with other pre-Christian traditions, the widespread belief in the supernatural associations of hawthorn was sometimes strongly opposed by the Church, while at other times taken over and christianized. At Glastonbury, claims about the Holy Thorn were partly associated with ideas about hawthorn being the material of Christ's crown of thorns, even though C. monogyna does not occur naturally in Palestine. As a result, descendants of the hawthorn that is supposed to have grown from Joseph of Arimathea's stave are venerated.

Culpepper recommends pounded or bruised and boiled seeds as cures for various internal pains, probably because they and the dried flowers have the property of reducing blood pressure. A compote of fresh fruits is given as a cure for diarrhoea. 'Bread and cheese' is still eaten by children in several parts of England; the name apparently dates from a famine in 1752, when poor colliers in the Bristol area were said to have been reduced to eating hawthorn leaves and the fleshy part of haws from the hedgerows.

THE WILD PEAR

A RELATIVE of the familiar cultivated pear (*Pyrus communis*), wild pear is rather rare, and it is not universally accepted as a native species. Rackham, however, accepts it as such, partly because of its widespread occurrence as isolated trees in remote places, which does not suggest planting. Single old trees are also found in relics of ancient woodland such as Hayley Wood, Cambridgeshire, and Oxleas Wood, south-east London. Pear charcoal is widely reported from neolithic sites and is occasionally mentioned in medieval documents. These different records seem quite sufficient for wild pear to be accepted as a native species.

The white blossom first appears in early May and is visited by various flies, wasps and bees, many of which may be pollinating agents. A common gall known as black pear, which looks like a deformed fruit, is caused by a gall-midge, *Lestodiplosis pyri*.

The Uses of Wild Pear Pear wood is hard and fine-grained and is used for high-quality turnery when available. It is an acceptable substitute for box as a medium for wood-engraving and is used for making a wide range of musical instruments including clarinets, flutes, recorders and harpsichords, for the hammers of pianos and – when stained black – as a substitute for ebony for violin finger-boards.

The Size of Hawthorn

C. *monogyna* grows at altitudes of up to 550m (1,800 ft) and can be found thriving on very exposed cliffs, including sea-cliffs in the north and west. C. *laevigata* is a woodland tree, much more shade-tolerant than C. *monogyna*, though the hybrids are variable.

Wild Pear Flowers
The flowers are visited by many insects, several of which may be pollinating agents.

Wild Pear *Pyrus pyraster* Burgsd.

Pyrus is a genus of 30 species occurring in the northern temperate parts of Europe and Asia.

Other name Pirige (Old English).

Derivative place-names Perreton, Pyrton.

Folklore Pear is a tree of Venus.

The Size of Wild Pear

Wild pear is a pyramidal tree that grows to a height of 15m (50 ft) and sometimes has thorny branches. Record trees are at Markshall, near Chelmsford (26 x 124) and at Tickards Manor, near Guildford (21 x 73).

Rowan, Mountain Ash *Sorbus aucuparia* L.

Sorbus is a genus of about 100 northern temperate tree species. *S. aucuparia* occurs throughout Britain and Ireland, and stretches south to the mountains of Morocco, and east to the Caucasus and Turkey.

Other names Caerthann (Old Irish), Caorthann (Irish), Quicken, Quickbeam, Wicken, Witchwood and many others.

Derivative place-names Keeran and Drumkeeran in Ireland.

Tree Lore and Folk Beliefs According to Thistleton-Dyer, a pear tree appearing in a dream is a good omen. Culpepper claimed that wild pears are very effective if 'bound to green [i.e. fresh] wounds' preventing inflammation and effecting healing 'sooner…than others'.

THE ROWAN

THE ROWAN is a most attractive slender tree with greyish, silvery bark and serrated pinnate leaves, bearing dense white inflorescences. The autumnal foliage is orange or scarlet, giving a most striking effect, and the groups of orange berries after the leaves fall make this a tree that contributes spectacularly to the landscape in most seasons. It grows at heights of up to 975m (3,200 ft), a higher altitude than any other native tree apart from juniper and some small willows, and this factor, together with its spectacular appearance, seem to give it sufficient protection from any enemies (red being the best colour to combat evil).

The Rowan
The stunning autumn colours of this rowan in Glenn Cannoch (above) greatly contrast with the tree's appearance in early summer, when its white flowers make it an equally attractive sight.

The Whitebeam
The silvery foliage of the whitebeam (right) contrasts with its rather dark and smooth trunk. Like the rowan, it flowers spectacularly and produces reddish-orange berries.

The tree's heavily scented inflorescences are visited by a wide range of pollinating and nectar-collecting insects, including several families of beetles, flies and moths, and a variety of wasps and bees. The fruits are a major source of food for some birds such as blackbirds and bullfinches, and in Scotland for migratory redwings. In Scandinavia, rowan fruits are essential winter food for fieldfares and waxwings, the abundance of the crop being a major influence on migration behaviour. All these birds act as major dispersal agents for the tree.

As rowan occurs in woodland more frequently than in scrub, it is thought that the seedlings are shade-tolerant. The leaves are very palatable to the snail, *Helix aspersa*, and to grazing animals, but not to phytophagous insects, and very few are associated with it.

The Uses of Rowan As with other species of *Sorbus*, the wood is tough and strong, and is traditionally used for handles of tools, cart-wheels, and also – if large enough – for planks and beams.

Tree Lore and Folk Beliefs An old Celtic name for rowan is *fid na ndruad* or the wizard's tree (quoted in Lucas, 1962), and in Ireland it plays a significant role in popular magic. According to Lucas, 'it was hung in the house to prevent fire-charming, used to keep the dead from rising and tied as a collar on a hound to increase his speed.' It is planted near houses to protect them against spirits, especially of the dead; but above all it was regarded as the sovereign protector of milk, and was kept in the byre to protect the cows and put in the pail and around the churn to ensure that the 'profit' of the milk was not stolen or spoilt. As Lucas points out, this tradition could have originated in something much more matter of fact: in Norway, rowan bark shavings were frequently fed to cattle in winter, a tradition that is known to date back to iron age times, when winter feed could have been a critical problem. The only fault in this explanation is that this tradition of using rowan bark is unknown in Ireland; Lucas suggests that notions of its magical properties could have been introduced by Norse settlers. In Wales, rowan trees are often found planted in churchyards and people wear Easter crosses made of the wood.

THE WHITEBEAM

THOUGH A RATHER variable tree, the whitebeam is generally very distinctive and attractive, with a wide dense crown, upward-sloping branches and smooth, dark-grey bark. Its oval leaves are a silvery pale green when they first appear, contrasting well with the dark bark. Later, the green becomes brighter, although the undersides remain silvery due to an abundance of white hairs, and in autumn they turn gold or russet.

Whitebeam occurs commonly in woods and scrub on calcareous soils throughout southern England, and less frequently at scattered sites in northern England and Scotland. In Ireland, the same species can be found in Galway, but rarely elsewhere: it is thought by some authorities to be 'doubtfully native', there being another species, *S. hibernica*, which is endemic to Ireland, as well as two smaller shrubs, *S. rupicola* and *S. anglica*. In Europe, it is found as far east as the Carpathian Mountains but, as a result of its confusion with other species, the southern limits of its distribution are not known with any certainty.

The Size of Rowan

Rowan often grows singly, although in the north of Scotland there are naturally occurring pure rowan woods, such as that at Inverpolly National Nature Reserve. The trees rarely exceed 15m (50 ft) in height, though a record tree at Priestwood, Buckinghamshire measures 20 x 39 and another of record girth (14 x 63) is at Chilworth Botanic Garden, Hampshire.

Comments about rowan collected by Roy Vickery (1984)

'One must never transplant a rowan.'

'Some people won't have a rowan in the garden; I know a woman who refused to buy a house because it had two rowans.'

'A rowan is good to have growing in the garden or nearby, because it wards off the influence of witches.'

'It's unlucky to bring rowan cuttings into the house.'

'A rowan is the home of good fairies.'

Whitebeam *Sorbus aria* (L.) Crantz

The name whitebeam covers about nine species or microspecies of the genus *Sorbus* in Britain and Ireland, most of which are extremely localized in their distribution, and some of which, like *S. rupicola*, are sometimes confused with *S. aria*.

Other names Findcholl (Old Irish), Chess-Apple, Hen-Apple, Hoar Withy, Quickbeam, Whitten, Whip-Crop.

The Size of Whitebeam

Whitebeams do not grow to a great age, but their attractive appearance and ability to thrive in urban and even heavily polluted environments has led to them being widely planted in recent years. Whitebeams normally reach a height of 15m (50 ft) and the tallest recorded is in Battersea Park, London (20 x 61). The specimen with greatest recorded girth is at Megginch Castle, Tayside (12 x 83).

The Wild Service

The leaves of the wild service are unlike those of any other Sorbus and, for this reason, the tree can be easily mistaken for a maple. The flowers open in late May, as on this specimen in the Royal Botanic Gardens, Edinburgh.

Wild Service *Sorbus torminalis* (L.) Crantz

Wild service is a member of the genus *Sorbus* like hawthorn and rowan. It is found as far east as the Caucasus and as far south as Algeria.

Other names Chequers Tree, Lezzory, and, confusingly, Whitty Pear (a name also used for *S. domestica* in Worcestershire).

The white flowers of *S. aria* are small (1.5cm across) and are borne in attractive loose clusters. The fruits are round, bright red and very popular with birds and squirrels, having a better pulp/seed ratio than the otherwise similar rowan fruits, though they do not stay as long on the tree. In Lancashire and Cumbria, they are known as chess-apples like medlars and are edible when on the point of rotting.

The insect fauna specifically associated with whitebeam is limited, but perhaps the most characteristic species is a tiny moth, *Argyresthia sorbiella*, the caterpillars of which feed on the shoots and flower buds. Aphids also commonly attack the buds and young shoots.

The Uses of Whitebeam The wood is fine-grained, very hard and white, and excellent for wood-turning and fine joinery. In the past, it was an extremely important and valuable wood for making cog-wheels and other machine parts, though there seems to be no evidence of it having been planted or specially managed in England for this purpose.

Other Whitebeams A closely related endemic species, French Hales (*S. devoniensis*), is common in Devon, where its brown fruits have long been marketed and eaten by local people. Another closely related species, *S. rupicola*, is a small shrub found on limestone crags and rocks up to altitudes of 460m (1,500 ft) in scattered localities throughout these islands. The whitty pear (*S. domestica*) is a rarity only recorded from the Wyre Forest near Birmingham (see p. 86–87).

Several other close relatives of *S. aria* have been accorded species status and are found only in very limited areas. These include *S. hibernica*, *S. lancastriensis*, endemic to Lancashire and Westmorland, the Arran service tree (*S. pseudofennica*) and the Arran whitebeam (*S. arranensis*), both found only in Glen Catacol on the Isle of Arran. A number of other endemic species occur in very limited limestone areas in the south-west of England and south Wales. These are among the rarest trees in these islands.

THE WILD SERVICE

In England, wild service is generally a small- to medium-sized tree with a wide crown, leaves like the maple – but with more pointed lobes – and bark similar to that of wild cherry. Typically, cracks form in the bark, dividing it into small squares – hence the name chequers tree. An alternative explanation is that the foliage changes to autumn colours in patches, some branches being further advanced than others, making the trees stand out from late summer onwards. The small berries are brown and rather gritty to taste.

Wild service trees often grow in groups that have arisen from suckers. This is thought to be because it rarely sets fertile seed under present climatic conditions in these islands, though it sets abundant seed in France, where it often occurs in secondary woodland. In England, it is regarded as an indicator of ancient woodland, and it is thought that the average temperatures have dropped below the tree's optimum in the last few centuries.

The Uses of Wild Service As with other species of *Sorbus*, the wood is fine-grained and valuable. As John Evelyn put it, 'the timber of the sorb is useful for the joiner and of which I have seen a room curiously wainscotted; also for the engraver of wood-cuts, bows, pulleys, screws, mill-spindles, pistol and gun-stocks, and being of very delicate grain…looks beautifully and is almost everlasting.'

Tree Lore and Folk Beliefs Although there appears to be little folklore associated with wild service, it was thought to have certain health-giving properties – particularly its fruits. John Evelyn records that water distilled from the flower-stalks and leaves is recommended for various conditions: it 'is incomparable for consumptive and tabid bodies', and cures the 'green-sickness of virgins'.

THE WILLOW

MEIKLE AND STACE both list 21 species of willow, of which three are thought to be introduced. As they point out, the taxonomy of willows is very difficult, especially as the species are themselves variable; hybrids occur together with parent species and, for definite identification, material needs to be collected at different times of the year. As a result, few collections have sufficient comparative material upon which to rely. However, a further 11–26 recognizable hybrids are listed: some are combinations of three parent species and do not all occur here naturally.

In some lowland parts of these islands, the most characteristic tree in the landscape is undoubtedly the willow. Willows line the banks of rivers large and small, from the Thames to the Shannon, giving wonderful effects of light, especially late on winter afternoons. In many low-lying areas like the fens and the Somerset levels, old willow pollards also support the banks of drainage ditches and channels.

On the northern mountains above the tree-line and on offshore islands, there still linger remnants of an extensive willow-scrub zone, especially in Scotland; but these are different species, small trees, shrubs

---

The Willow
The Salix Fragilis, commonly known as the crack willow, usually grows in lines along river banks, such as here at Westonbirt, Gloucestershire. Twigs tend to snap off easily at the base when knocked, hence the name. This allows the tree to spread along a river, as the twigs root and form new plants when washed ashore.

Willow *Salix* spp.

All willows belong to the large genus *Salix*, which has around 350 (or, according to some authorities, up to 500) species, mainly northern temperate or arctic. The family *Salicaceae*, to which it belongs, also includes poplars and two other genera, *Chosenia* and *Toisusu*, each with a single species in north-east Asia.

Other names Saille (Old Irish), Salh, Wilig (Old English).

Derivative place-names Sale, Salcombe, Saughall, Salford, Withington, Widecombe, Willoughby.

and even miniature trees such as the dwarf willow (S. herbacea). Willows occupy these habitats as well as wetlands in temperate and colder regions throughout the northern hemisphere, while the mountain willows extend their range north into the tundra, where they can be found at sea level. They are some of the most hardy of plants, living in the extreme climate north of the Arctic Circle and extending further north than any other woody plant.

Willows, like the related poplars, are dioecious, catkin-bearing trees with simple, usually alternate leaves. Willows are distinguished from poplars by the single outer scale that encloses the winter bud, and the absence of a terminal bud on the branches. They are also largely insect-pollinated, whereas poplars are wind-pollinated. Willow catkins are also more erect and each flower bears one or two small nectaries which attract insects. The sprays of catkins are popular for decoration, especially the attractive pussy willow catkins, S. caprea and S. cinerea, which can appear as early as the beginning of March.

For successful germination, the delicate seeds of the willow, like those of the poplar, need fresh damp earth or mud in the weeks directly after maturing. This is now a rare habitat due to the increasingly managed nature of rivers and river banks. Most willows regenerate vegetatively with vigour and are therefore widely propagated from cuttings.

Willows are apparently extremely palatable to insects. Kennedy and Southwood list 450 phytophagous invertebrates associated with the genus Salix in these islands, more than any other tree. These include 162 different butterflies and moths and 104 bees and wasps. A number of attractive moths are typical, such as the puss moth (Cerura viminula), the lunar hornet clearwing moth (Sesia bembiciformis) on sallow, and the eyed hawkmoth (Smerinthus ocellata) on crack willow. The Forestry Commission lists a number of species as defoliating pests, including the puss moth, three sawflies, (Nematus species), at least seven species of crysomelid beetle and the spectacular poplar longhorn beetle (Saperda carcharias). Most of these are now controlled by willow-growers by using insecticides, but there remain some other more serious pests of osier beds, including a number of fungal rusts, especially Metelampsora amygdalinae (on S. triandra) and M. epitea (on S. viminalis) the button-top gall-midge (Rhabdophaga heterobia), as well as the osier weevil (Cryptorhynchus lapathi).

Salix is attacked by more different gall-forming parasites than any other mature tree except oak. These include gall-mites, gall-midges, aphids, fungi and beetles; one of the most spectacular is the timberman gall of the main stem tissues in goat willow, and also aspen. This is caused by a gall-forming longhorn beetle (Saperda populnea). The very common galls, which look like small witches brooms on some willows, are caused by the gall-mite Eriophyes triradiatus.

A number of fungi are associated specifically with willows, including the pale Lactarius aspideus which grows in muddy places under the trees, and the large cushion-like grey bracket fungus (Phellinus ignarius) on the tree-trunks.

The Uses of Willow Loudoun records that willow down, the feathery covering of the seeds, used to be collected for stuffing mattresses.

The Size of Willow Species

The main willow species native to these islands are as
follows, with their typical height in metres:

Bay Willow................S. *pentandra* L..........5–7m
Other names: Black Willow (Ireland), Sweet Willow
(Cumbria), Willow Bay (Staffordshire), French Sally
(Donegal).

Almond Willow............S. *trianda* L.........4–10m
Other names: French Willow (Sussex), Kit Willow (Northamptonshire), Snake-Skin Willow (Wiltshire).

Crack Willow...............S. *fragilis* L.........10–15m
Other names: Sail (Old Irish), Saileach (Irish), Cat's Tails
(Somerset), Snap Willow (Kent).

White Willow.................S. *alba* L...........10–25m
Other names: Saugh, Cricket-Bat Willow (var. *coerulea*).

Common Osier.............S. *viminalis* L...........3–6m

Goat Willow.................S. *caprea* L.........3–10m
Other names: Great Sallow, Sally, Black Sally (Wiltshire),
Palm Tree or Palm Willow, Pussy Willow (for its catkins).

Gray Willow.................S. *cinerea* L.........2–10m
Other names: Common Sallow, Pussy Willow (for its catkins).

Dark-Leaved Willow. . S. *myrsinifolia* Salisb. 1–3m

Eared Willow.................S. *aurita* L.........1–2.5m

Purple Willow...............S. *purpurea* L.......1.5–3m

Dwarf Willow...............S. *herbacea* L..........1–6m

Several other small creeping species also occur, but
never in a tree form.

(See also pp. 102–105)

Willow foliage has long been used as fodder, and even stored for this purpose for the winter months. In Scandinavia, willow bark was sometimes ground up and eaten mixed with oatmeal in times of famine. The crack willow, so called because its brittle branches very easily split from the trunk, has bright red roots from which a purplish-red dye can be extracted. The wood, too, becomes reddish or almost salmon-coloured when seasoned. Willows have been popular with beekeepers for centuries and in ancient times were planted to attract insects.

Light and rather soft, the wood is similar to that of poplar, but it is very variable and depends on the habit of the tree. Because of its lightness, it was used for making fast sailing boats, and coracles were sometimes made by covering willow rods with hides. Traditionally, willow is used to make cricket bats for which the best wood comes from a variety of *S. alba* called *coerulea*, which is fast-growing and straight-grained. Willow wood is also used for making artificial limbs and toys. In addition, the bark has been used for tanning. Nevertheless, the main economic use for willow is to make baskets.

Tree Lore and Folk Beliefs In early biblical times the willow was emblematic of rejoicing and celebration but, being bitter to the taste, it soon became associated with romantic sadness or even mourning. According to Thistleton-Dyer, 'it was customary for those who were forsaken in love to wear a garland made of willow'; willows frequently appear in poems of lost love and Ophelia drowned herself by a willow. Moreover, when the Israelites found themselves by the waters of Babylon they wept, remembered Zion, and hung their harps on willows. On the other hand, in temperate climates willow branches are also used instead of palms to celebrate Palm Sunday, and country people customarily wore sprigs of pussy willow in their lapels around the same time of year.

In Ireland the sally (*S. caprea*) has power against enchantment, and it is lucky to take a sally rod with you on a journey. A peeled sally rod placed round a milk churn will ensure good butter.

NATURALIZED TREES

Several very common trees that were introduced into these islands over the past few hundred years have since become naturalized. For instance, the sycamore (*Acer pseudoplatanus* L.), which originated in central Europe, is now one of our most common trees, invading much of our scrub and woodland and growing vigorously as far north as the Shetlands and at altitudes of up to 460m (1,500 ft) in mountain areas. It is also little affected by salt spray from the sea. The following is a list of the most common naturalized species, with their approximate dates of arrival:

Spruce............. *Picea abies* (L.) Karsten ....Native in inter-glacial period, reintroduced c. 1500
Sweet Chestnut.... *Castanea sativa* Miller ....Introduced c. 100
Sycamore........... *Acer pseudoplatanus* L..................Introduced c. 1250
Walnut................ *Juglans regia* L......................Introduced c. 1400
Plane................ *Platanus orientalis* L...................Introduced c. 1520
Holm Oak............. *Quercus ilex* L.......................Introduced c. 1580
Fir...................... *Abies* species.........Native in inter-glacial period, reintroduced c. 1600
Horse Chestnut... *Aesculus hippocastanum* L. ....Introduced c. 1600
False Acacia........ *Robinia pseudacacia* L..................Introduced c. 1601
European Larch..... *Larix decidua* Miller. ....Introduced c. 1629
White Poplar........... *Populus alba* L.......Date unknown when introduced
Grey Poplar.......... *Populus x canescens*....Date unknown when introduced (Aiton) Smith

The Horse Chestnut
Native to north Greece and Albania, the horse chestnut has long been cultivated in other parts of Europe and was first brought to the British Isles at the beginning of the seventeenth century as a spectacular flowering tree.

The Sycamore
Today this is one of the commonest naturalized trees found in the British Isles. Since being introduced over 850 years ago it has thrived, invading woodland and regenerating in hostile environments – on coasts and at high altitudes.

Detailed accounts of these trees is outside the scope of this book, but a list detailing some of the characteristics of common native trees is given on page 178.

3

The History of Our Native Trees

FROM THE AVAILABLE geological and other evidence it is clear that much of these islands was covered with ice for the 10,000 to 15,000 years up to the beginning of the present 'post-glacial' (or more probably inter-glacial) period known as the Holocene. Evidence of the tree flora since that time is derived mainly from pollen data which go back to the beginning of this period, around 10,000 years ago. Before that there were few trees in these islands; the climate for the immediately preceding millennia was probably too adverse for there to be more than a very patchy occurrence of birch and willow, with a little juniper. Some 10,000 years ago the climate began to warm, and trees to spread.

Pollen studies

The pollen of many plants, including trees, is well preserved in peat and in anaerobic lake sediments — so well preserved, in fact, that the patterns on the outer cover of the grains can be used to identify the species of plant from which the pollen comes. When lake and even pond deposits are sampled and a core obtained, analysis of the existence and relative abundance of different pollen types can be assessed.

One of the leading figures in this field is Professor H. J. B. Birks of the University of Bergen, and much of this chapter is based on his definitive paper on the patterns of tree-spreading in these islands over the past 10,000 years, based on pollen data. He amassed evidence from a large number of investigations (by many authors) of pollen samples from cores taken at a wide range of different places, from Kent to St Kilda and from Shetland to Killarney. Only those sites which also had 'satisfactory radiocarbon chronologies' were included; in other words those in which independent carbon dating of the levels from which pollen grains were analysed had been done. This gave him 135 acceptable sites. These were not evenly distributed, however, and since there were relatively few for south and east England, the data for this area are less detailed.

From the data collected, Birks was able to produce what he terms 'isochrone contour maps' for pollen distributions: maps in which places with similar pollen values at the same date are placed on the same line. What the data clearly show is the history of the spread of different tree species. Naturally these maps have their weaknesses: they are more accurate for those species which produce large amounts of pollen (especially wind-pollinated species), and are less satisfactory for rarer species or for those producing much less pollen (especially insect-pollinated species) such as varieties of *Tilia* and *Fagus*. Birks presented his data in species order, based on their arrival, and this will be followed here.

Birch Trees in Glen Affric
One of the earliest native trees to spread widely in these islands, birch was already well established 9,500 years ago.

Radiocarbon Dating

During the 1960s and 1970s the dating of organic remains became much more precise than before as a result of the introduction of radiocarbon dating, using radioactive isotopes of carbon: these isotopes are present in the atmosphere but then become 'trapped' in organic matter when a living organism dies and breaks down at a specific rate in the millennia that follow.

Isochrone Contour Maps

The maps below indicate the history of the spread of eight tree species throughout these islands. The information needed to create them has been amassed by Professor H.J.B. Birks of the University of Bergen, using pollen samples taken from cores which could be dated through radiocarbon dating. These particular eight have been chosen because they are the only ones whose pollen samples are present in a great enough strength for the resulting maps to be considered reliable. The only exception to this is

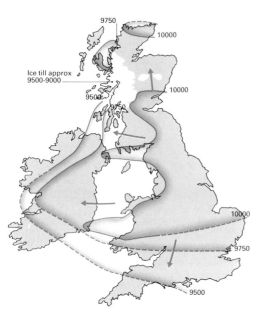

Birch (Betula pubescens and B. pendula)

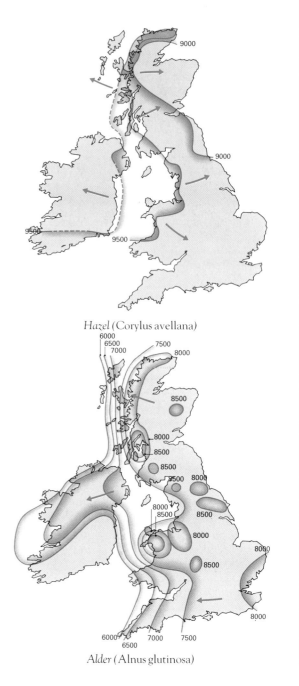

Hazel (Corylus avellana)

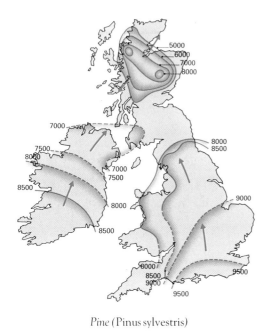

Pine (Pinus sylvestris)

Alder (Alnus glutinosa)

beech, which, despite having pollen grains in sufficient numbers, has been excluded on the grounds that it is thought to have reached these shores much more recently than the others, as the earliest reliable samples date its arrival to 3,000 years ago.

The lines represent the limit to which each species of tree had spread at the time (in years ago) indicated by the figure next to each line. The shading shows the side of the line to which the species had reached by each date, while the arrows are to give extra clarification of the direction in which the trees spread. A broken line is used when dates have had to be estimated due to a lack of proven information.

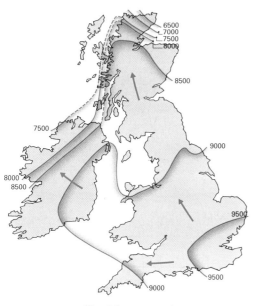

Elm (Ulmus *species*)

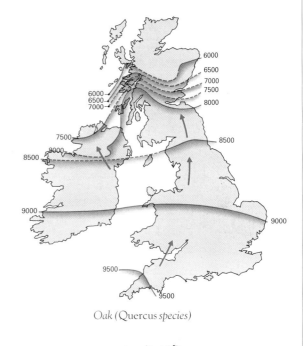

Oak (Quercus *species*)

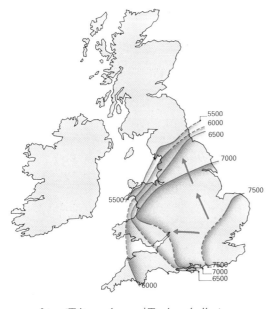

Lime (Tilia cordata *and* T. platyphyllos)

Ash (Fraxinus excelsior)

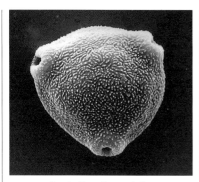

Birch (Betula pendula)

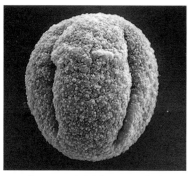

Common Oak (Quercus robur)

Birch Pollen of birch has been found in some places dating back 13,500 years, but it is thought to have become very rare or even extinct between 11,000 and 10,200 years ago. The subsequent pollen record suggests that *Betula* spread from the east, starting just over 10,000 years ago, across low-lying land now on the bed of the North Sea. *Betula* was already well established throughout much of these islands 9,500 years ago.

Hazel Hazel appears to have first become established around the shores of the Irish Sea over 9,000 years ago, though how this happened is not clear. It has been suggested that dispersal agents including birds, rodents and even humans may have been responsible for this pattern: however, fresh hazel nuts can float in fresh or seawater and retain viability for at least 30 days, suggesting that water currents may be more likely dispersal agents.

Elm Elm had reached southern England by 9,500 years ago, spreading quite rapidly west to Wales and eastern Ireland, and ultimately to the rest of Ireland and Scotland; its spread through Scotland was slow, probably because of the predominance of acidic soils, and a more unfavourable climate. It reached northernmost Scotland by 6,200 years ago, becoming a minor component of woodland and scrub in Caithness. There was a dramatic decline for a period between 5,500 and 5,000 years ago, but this did not affect its range within these islands, and the populations did recover later.

Oak Oak spread up the western seaboard of Europe from 10,500 years ago, reaching south-west England 1,000 years later and south-east Ireland 100 years after that. It then spread rapidly throughout these islands over the next 1,400 years, except for the north of Scotland; it then took another 2,000 years to reach its northern limit as an important component of Scottish forests.

Pine Pollen data show that pine was already present widely but locally in southern England over 9,000 years ago. In the next 500 years it spread north to the Lake District and the northern Pennines. It was already present in Ireland over 8,800 years ago, though not in Wales, suggesting that the Irish populations had an independent origin. Pine expanded in northern Scotland between 8,500 and 8,000 years ago in the Loch Maree area. There is a theory that Scots pine could have survived the last glacial period in small sheltered areas in north-west Scotland, and therefore had an independent origin from pines elsewhere in these islands. An alternative theory suggests that pine spread rapidly via Ireland up the west coast of Scotland more than 8,500 years ago, but that it was rare and restricted to marginal habitats.

Both the Irish and the western Scottish pine populations underwent massive declines around 4,000 years ago, leading to a major reduction in the range of pine in western Scotland and ultimately its presumed extinction in Ireland between 2,000 and 1,000 years ago. In both these areas pine forest was replaced by extensive blanket bogs, though the reasons for the decline in pine in these western forests is not clear.

Alder There are many very early records of alder: wood and catkins 10,500–9,500 years old have been found in Yorkshire, and it was present and locally abundant along the mid-Wales coast more than 8,900 years ago. Before that, alder may have been widely distributed throughout most of these islands, but its pollen occurs in small amounts at many sites and is only well recorded at a few sites. Alder fruits float and remain viable for over a year, which complicates the interpretations. Moreover, small amounts of pollen could be recorded at sites some way from an alder population. By 7,500 years ago alder had expanded inland in England and Wales, though in Ireland it was still confined to the north-east 7,000 years ago. It continued to spread, finally reaching the extreme north of Scotland by about 5,300 years ago. The pattern is erratic and later studies have suggested that the spread of alder was much more patchy, both in time and space, than that of other species. It is thought that this is due mainly to its very specific habitat requirement of damp conditions as a result of which its distribution is always likely to be patchy.

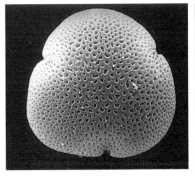

Small-leaved Lime (Tilia cordata)

Lime Lime was present in southern England 7,500 years ago and gradually spread into central England and other parts of Wales, becoming a major component of the forests, as in mainland Europe. Lime never reached the extreme south-west of England but reached its northernmost limits in the Lake District around 5,500 years ago; this coincides geographically with the residual native populations of *T. cordata* today in the Lake District and Upper Swaledale.

Ash Pollen records show that ash was present in southern and central England in low but consistent amounts between 7,000 and 6,000 years ago. It then spread slowly northwards to Scotland and westwards to Ireland where it probably replaced hazel on calcareous soils, and its pollen values also increased in England during the next 2,000 years.

Other species Various other species are present in some pollen samples but not enough to enable maps to be drawn — with the exception of beech which arrived much later (only 3,000 years ago). However the existence of several tree species can be traced in some places right back to the earliest birch dates — rowan, juniper, poplar and cherry among others. Yew and holly first appeared very soon afterwards, around 9,000 years ago. Hawthorn first appeared around 7,000 years ago. Hornbeam did not appear until the same time as beech around 3,000 years ago, and then only in very small numbers; it seems to have become common only 2,000 years later.

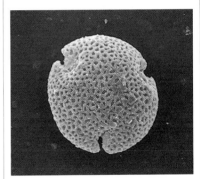

Ash (Fraxinus excelsior)

Interpretation The pollen data reveal differences in origin, directions of spread and timings of spread for the species studied. Assuming that the sites where the earliest expansions occurred indicate the areas of earliest establishment, the following conclusions can be drawn: birch arrived from the east, pine (partly), elm, alder (partly), lime, ash, beech (and presumably hornbeam) from the south-east, oak, alder (partly), pine (partly) and hazel from the south-west; and pine (partly) from the north-west. These conclusions fit in with present ideas of the presumed last-glacial refuges for these species in mainland Europe.

From the pollen data, some palaeobotanists, such as Dr K. D. Bennett at Cambridge, have tried to describe the general woodland composition at different times over the last 10,000 years. It is generally agreed that the peak development of forest in these islands before the clearances started by early humans, was around 5,000 years ago. The main river valleys and wetlands were dominated by alder woodland, and this may also have been the case on hillsides in north-west Scotland. On calcareous soils, in all probability, the major trees were ash with hazel, elm and maple, while, on lower-lying fertile soils throughout most of England, woodland was dominated by lime.

Most of central Ireland was dominated by hazel, while the more acidic and less fertile soils of the west of England and Wales, the east of Ireland and much of the lower-lying land in Scotland were dominated by oak. Pine was extensive in western and northern Ireland, and further up the mountains in England, Wales and Scotland, though by 5,000 years ago it had still to spread to the extreme north of Scotland and the Hebrides. Birch dominated the extreme fringes of woodland growth in the north and west, and was present everywhere, though with its low shade-tolerance it is not thought to have been able to form woodland except in marginal areas.

Some high mountains and some of the central parts of Ireland, which had extensive blanket bog even at this time, were probably not wooded. In parts of Wales and northern England it may have been possible to notice an altitudinal variation from lime (or alder in the river valleys), through oak to pine and then birch and juniper, with bare ground at the highest altitudes.

One of the results of pollen analysis is the discovery of how the flora of particular areas has become extinct; new species have arrived and established themselves, but at the same time other species have been squeezed ecologically, eventually losing out and disappearing from particular areas; in many cases this was partly due to the effects of man and his animals. For instance, by Loch Lang, in South Uist, the whole woodland cover declined from about 4,000 years ago, to be replaced by blanket bog. Oak, alder and elm had been present before then; they are all now extinct throughout the Western Isles.

Dendrochronology

Dendrochronology is the science of precise dating, using the accurate counting of tree growth-rings which first provided an accurate and generally agreed calibration of carbon dating.

By counting every tree-ring back from the present on very old trees, an American botanist, Douglass, established as long ago as 1929 a pine chronology for the American south-west that went back to AD 701. The patterns of rings differ every year, depending on the growing conditions at the time. In this way they are a treasure house of information about the ecological history of trees, and indeed the general climatic history of the sites. Douglass's work was followed by other researchers in the USA, who established much longer chronologies, back to about 7,200 years ago, by examining the very ancient bristlecone pines in the White Mountains of California. These counts were used to check radiocarbon dates, so that correlation tables could be drawn up.

The application of this technique in Europe proved much more difficult. There are no long-lived trees like the bristlecone pines that can be counted; yew trunks may be as long-lived, but the heartwood of yew rots long before the tree dies and continuous ring counts are impossible to obtain for more than a few hundred years. The tree rings on yew are

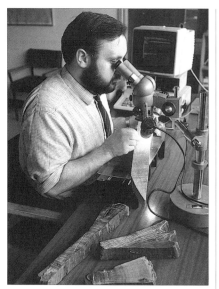

Tree-ring Counting
In the palaeo-ecology unit at Queen's University, Belfast, tree rings of ancient oaks (below) are counted and checked (above). A tree-ring history, going back 7,000 years, has now been completed and used to calibrate radiocarbon dating.

Bog Oaks
These semi-fossilized oak tree trunks were preserved over the centuries under peat in central Ireland.

also extremely variable and irregular. The technique was then applied to oak, an approach made possible by obtaining large numbers of very ancient semi-fossil 'bog-oaks' in Ireland, and computerizing the records. This made it easy to compare complex sequences of rings (years). While individual oak logs were rarely more than about 300 years old, a long series of overlapping records was put together, reaching back 7,200 years, confirming a similar series worked out in Germany.

The team specializing in this work is based at the Palaeo-ecology Centre in Queen's University, Belfast, under Professor Mike Baillie. By the mid-1980s, a complete chronology was in place, based on Irish oak. As a result the team have been able to date precisely oak logs, building timbers and other oak relics. The oak timbers of an Irish archaeological site, the Corles 1 track, were constructed of timbers felled in late 148 BC or early 147 BC; however the timbers used to construct an ancient roadway known as the English Sweet Track on the Somerset Levels near Glastonbury were felled very much earlier, in late 3807 BC or early 3806 BC.

TREE RINGS AND VOLCANOES

The tree-ring data also provide very precise information about environmental events — including atmospheric dust-veils, thought to have been caused by major volcanic eruptions. Several periods of extremely narrow growth rings have been found, some of which coincide with acidic horizons in the Greenland ice cap. Six such periods have been identified between 4370 BC and AD536. At least two of these dates are known from historical evidence to have been traumatic periods for the human populations involved.

The period that started in 208 BC was apparently caused by a major volcanic dust-veil which led to famine and massive loss of life in China. Downturns in oak growth in Irish (207 BC), German (208-204 BC), and American (206 BC) trees show that this was obviously a disaster on a global scale. A similar event, in 1628 BC, was the massive Bronze Age eruption on the island of Santorini in the Aegean, which led to famine and social disruption throughout the Mediterranean region and northern Europe.

The dendrochronological research for America, Ireland and Germany has stimulated similar work in other places, such as the Middle East and the Aegean; trees will provide an enormous store of information about recent prehistory, the applications of which have yet to be fully understood or appreciated.

WOODLAND HISTORY: THE NEW FOREST

by Dr George Peterken, Joint Nature Conservation Committee, Peterborough.

All woodlands contain a multitude of clues about their immediate history. At its simplest and most obvious, woodland composed of just one species growing as equal-sized trees in straight lines all the same distance apart is clearly a plantation, and it will still be detectable as such a hundred years after being planted. Less obvious is the wood that was treated as a coppice (see pp 94–98), though these invariably continue to show thickets of multi-stemmed trees long after the last woodman has laid down his billhook.

The New Forest may look like an exception, but it is in fact a special and complex case of a forest which tells its own story. Scattered throughout the open wood-lands are giant beeches and oaks which have short, thick trunks and heads of large branches, fanning out from a height of 2–3m (7–10 ft). These are the trees which were pollarded every few years to provide a crop of leaves for browse and sticks for fuel. In the New Forest, this practice was made illegal in 1698, so, allowing for the independent spirit of New Forest commoners, we can say that most old pollard trees are at least 300 years old.

But many of the large trees have single stems. They grow between the pollards, some bending aside to give themselves more room to grow. They must have grown up after pollarding stopped, suggesting that somehow the effects of deer, horses and cattle were controlled during the eighteenth century. Most date from before 1750, by which time there would have been little space in which more trees could grow.

Grazing and browsing was heavy for many decades, but in 1851 an Act of Parliament was passed which provided for the removal of deer from the forest so that timber could be grown properly in the plantations. Out-side, in the open woods, this allowed more trees to grow up. In some woods there was a great deal of space, per-haps because big trees had been felled, or had simply died as they stood. Here more oak and beech were able to spring up in the gaps, eventually growing as slender, tall trees which joined the older trees and pollards. In other woods there was less space: beech and oak could not thrive, and instead thickets of holly grew beneath the shade of the older trees. Either way, the woods be-came so dense in the latter part of the nineteenth cen-tury that new regeneration was again discouraged.

By the twentieth century the pollards and some of their immediate successors were dying on their feet or breaking up in winter gales. As they became older and less vigorous they were killed by combinations of drought, waterlogging and fungal attacks. When the numbers of deer, horses and cattle were again reduced during both World Wars there were gaps into which new trees could grow: once again, where these were large enough oak and beech grew tall, but where there were few gaps more holly grew as underwood.

Since the Second World War, the numbers of animals have greatly increased, with the result that the New Forest is once again heavily grazed. Even though the drought of 1976, the gales of 1987 and old age have brought down more of the large old trees, saplings have not been able to fill the gaps. Indeed, many of the holly bushes that grew up a few decades before have been browsed so heavily that they have died. The woods are becoming more open with each passing year, but if the number of grazing animals is ever reduced, they will rapidly fill again.

This is an unusually complicated history, but it can all be read in the size and shape of present-day trees. In fact, close attention to detail shows that each wood tells its own variant on this general story. Even now, although the great majority of saplings in the New Forest are eaten by deer and horses, some buck the trend by surviving in thickets of gorse or ungrazed corners.

The short, thick trunk of the beech on the left shows that it was once pollarded, a practice outlawed in the New Forest in 1698.

4

Our Ancient Trees: Limes and Yews

AT LEAST TWO SPECIES of native trees in these islands — lime and yew — can live naturally to an immense age. Other species, like oak and beech, may also reach a great age, but only as pollards. Ancient lime trees may not be very familiar, but research by Donald Pigott, Director of the Cambridge University Botanic Garden, has shown that the ancient lime trees in the north-west of England have a very interesting history and are probably well over a thousand years old. Ancient yew trees are more familiar in several parts of the country, notably Wales and the Welsh Borders, Cheshire, the south-west of England, Surrey and Sussex. Allen Meredith's research has revealed an enormous amount of new information about their significance in human affairs, and has led to rethinking about their extraordinary age.

An Ancient Lime

Today, many ancient limes are found in particularly inaccessible locations, which is probably why they have survived the various forest clearances of the past. The Lake District, where this lime is growing, is now known to be the northernmost limit of the tree's natural distribution.

Ancient Lime Trees

From observed field distributions of certain native trees and shrubs, Donald Pigott confirmed that the latitude of the English Lake District was probably the northern limit of several species, including the small-leaved lime (*Tilia cordata*); while from the pollen record it is clear that over most of lowland England the lime was a major component, even the dominant tree species, in the forests of England at their maximum extent around 5,500 years ago. The area in which high frequencies of *Tilia* pollen occurred, when the forest cover was at its greatest, coincides almost exactly with the apparent natural distribution of the tree today. In other words, it was never naturally present further north, and the northern limits are still the same as they were at the greatest expansion of forests since the last glacial period. Since then the mean summer temperatures in north-west Europe have decreased by about 2°C, and other species have retreated further south.

Further study by Pigott and Jaqueline Huntley revealed that both the development of the ovules and the growth of the pollen tube following pollination — which normally leads to fertilization — were very temperature-dependent. In the northern populations he found that though fertile ovules were produced, after pollination there was usually insufficient growth of the pollen-tubes for fertilisation to occur. This contrasted with continental lime trees; French samples of pollen had germinated on all receptive stigmas, and numerous pollen-tubes had reached the ovary within two days of pollination.

Lime started to decline shortly after the major decline in elm, which began about 5,100 years ago, and is thought to have been associated with forest clearance and other human activities, such as the possible

79

The Regeneration of Lime

Donald Pigott mapped the occurrence of *T. cordata* in the north-west of England around Morecambe Bay and into the Lake District and North Yorkshire. He found that most populations were small, sometimes amounting to a single tree; that in all but a few localities every tree was very old; and that there was apparently no production of new seedlings. Seeds collected from these populations were almost entirely infertile, contrasting with 30-50 per cent fertility of seeds from trees in Worcestershire and Northamptonshire. In the exceptionally hot summer of 1976 the maximum fertility level increased to around 10 per cent, from which it was concluded that the primary cause of the failure to regenerate was climatic compounded by, for instance, predation by animals.

The Fortingall Yew

Although this engraving dates from the nineteenth century, it shows the tree as it was in 1736.

introduction of domestic grazing animals — lime seedlings are particularly palatable. Pigott concluded that while forest clearance would have adversely affected lime, restricting it to cliffs, inaccessible ravines and steep slopes — where it is characteristically found today — its failure to produce seedlings precluded its survival in all but the most unfavourable sites. In this lime contrasts with elm which, though it declined markedly and must have been greatly affected by woodland clearance, is still widespread in the north-west today, reproducing freely by seed.

Pigott's conclusion was that the aged trees that can be found today in the ravines of the southern Lake District and Upper Swaledale could have hung on without successfully reproducing themselves for a very long time. He made estimates of their age by several different methods. The simplest was by measuring lime trees of known age elsewhere, both out in the open and in plantations, and comparing their girths with those of the aged trees he had found. He also discovered that many of the trees that appear to be old pollards, standing up from the rock or soil in which they are anchored, with their branches appearing some feet up, are in fact old coppice stools which have gradually had their surrounding soil eroded away. On some steep slopes in the area the rate of this erosion can be calculated by measuring the average loss around single-stemmed, uncoppiced trees such as oaks growing together with the limes, and finding out the age of the trees by taking a core and counting the rings. Assuming this erosion rate to be more or less constant, it was applied to measurements taken from ancient limes, some of which had lost over a metre of soil around them. These various methods indicated that the most ancient limes were well over 1,000 years old. At one of the sites, Linsty Wood, the limes were apparently 'a conspicuous feature in the tenth century, as the name contains the Norse elements "lind" and "stigr", meaning a path where the lime-trees grow.'

In some recent warm summers good numbers of lime seed were set and seedlings produced, but their survival was very poor and all of them disappeared within two years, largely as a result of predation by small mammals and possibly deer. This suggests that it is not enough to produce some viable seed; sufficient numbers have to be produced on a regular basis to overcome predation, and this is clearly not happening. It is known that there was a warmer period between AD 1300 and 1500, when presumably large enough numbers of viable seedlings were produced to create the ancient lime trees of today.

Ancient Yew Trees

The village of Fortingall, in Glen Lyon, Perthshire, is at the geographical centre of Scotland. There are groups of ancient 'druid' stones, and a twentieth-century stone church that was built to replace a much older pre-Reformation building. But in a corner of the churchyard is something much older than the church, and possibly older than the druid circles — a living yew tree. No one knows exactly how old this tree is; what is certain is that in 1769 it was measured and had a circumference of 52ft (16m). An engraving that hangs in the vestry may be fanciful, but it shows a gigantic tree of comparable dimensions. Local tradition

GAZETTEER OF ANCIENT YEWS

No	Location	Approx girth in feet	Comments and position of yew in relation to church
1	Ankerwycke* (nr Wraysbury), Bucks.	31	In ruins of a nunnery. **N**
2	Ashbrittle, Som.	(25+)	On possible Bronze-Age mound. **SE**
3	Bettws Newydd, Gwent.	32	Hollow with internal stem. **W**
4	Broadwell GM, Glos.	25	Tree of life on ancient stone in porch. **S**
5	Buckland, Kent	23	**W**
6	Buxted, Sussex	30	**E**
7	Claverley, Shrops.	28	Church on ancient burial mound. **E**
8	Clun, Shrops.	33	**N**
9	Cold Waltham, Sussex	33	**N**
10	Crowhurst, Surrey	32	Once had a table inside hollow trunk. **S**
11	Crowhurst, Sussex	28	Iron railings surround the tree. **S**
12	Cudham, Kent	28	**S**
13	Darley Dale, Derby.	33	**S**
14	Defynnog, Powys	35	Pre-Christian stone on site. **N**
15	Dinder, Som.	31	Same girth in 1890. **SE**
16	Discoed, Powys	37	**N**
17	Doveridge GM, Derby.	22	**S**
18	Druids Grove* (Norbury Park, Mickleham), Surrey	24	Remains of ancient yew wood.
19	Eastham, Ches.	17	**E**
20	Eastling, Kent	30	**W**
21	Farringdon, Hants.	30	A huge hollow shell. **W**
22	Fountains Abbey*, Yorks.	22	—
23	Fortingall, Tayside	52	Separated ruin of tree. **NW**
24	Gwytherin, Clwyd	28	Pre-Christian stones on site. **E**
25	Hambledon, Surrey	35	**S**
26	South Hayling, Hants.	33	Iron railings surround the tree. **S**
27	Helmdon, Northants.	28	**E**
28	Hope Bagot, Shrops.	23	Holy well underneath the tree. **N**
29	Keffolds Farm* (nr Haslemere), Surrey	28	—
30	Kenn, Devon	30	**E**
31	Kennington, Kent	31	Large portion of tree missing. **W**
32	Kentchurch*, Herts. and Worcs.	31	Many large yews in deer park.
33	Knowlton*, Dorset	(25+)	Ancient yew on Pre-Christian site with ruined Norman church.
34	Leeds, Kent	30	**W**
35	Linton, Herts. and Worcs.	33	Internal stem. **NW**
36	Llanddeiniolen, Gwynedd	28	**E**
37	Llanfaredd, Powys	36	**W**
38	Llanfeugan, Powys	32	Circle of old yews. **E**
39	Llanfihangel-nant-melan, Powys	30	Circle of ancient yews, some damaged. **SW**
40	Llangernyw, Clwyd	(25+)	Old tank inside old yew. **N**
41	Loose, Kent	33	**SW**
42	Lorton*, Cumbria	(25+)	27ft in 1806
43	Loughton, Shrops.	33	**E**
44	Mallwyd, Gwynedd	31	**E**
45	Mamhilad, Gwent	31	Split yew with internal stem. **S**
46	Middleton Scriven*, Shrops.	29	Largest of two yews and hollow. **S**
47	Much Marcle, Herts. and Worcs.	30	Round seat inside hollow yew. **S**
48	Newlands Corner* (nr Guildford), Surrey	24	Remnants of ancient yew wood.
49	Norbury, Shrops.	33	**S**
50	Pennant Melangell, Gwynedd	27	**E**
51	Selborne, Hants.	26	Blown down in storm of January 1990. Later replanted. **SW**
53	Staunton, Glos.	31	**W**
54	Stedham, Sussex	30	**W**
55	Strata Florida, Dyfed	22	Daffyd ap Gwylam buried under the yew. **N**
56	Tandridge, Surrey	36	Bees occupy a hollow in tree. **W**
57	Temple Farm* (nr Corsley), Wilts.	30	—
58	Tilmanstone, Kent	30	Badly damaged in 1987 storm. **SW**
59	Tisbury, Wilts.	31	Hollow cemented in. **N**
60	Totteridge, Herts. and Worcs.	26	**W**
61	Ulcombe, Kent	35	**W**
62	Waldershare, Kent	30	**S**
63	Wilmington, Sussex	30	—
52	Woolland, Dorset	32	**S**

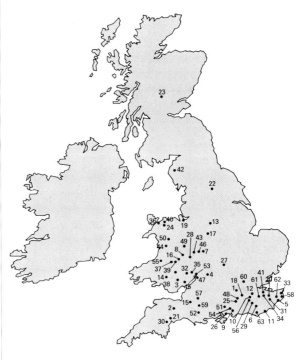

*Not situated in churchyards. Those trees marked (25+) all have a girth of over 25 feet, but have not been measured recently.

The Totteridge Yew
This ancient yew at Totteridge, near Barnet in Hertfordshire, has a girth of 26ft (8m), the same as when it was measured in 1677. Yews are thought to grow slower the older they are, which suggests that it was already very old by the time the church was built next to it.

The Fortingall Yew
In the 1700s its girth was estimated at 52ft (16m). Today only part of the ancient hulk remains.

has it that funeral processions passed through the arch made by the ancient tree. Today only a little of the shell of this ancient hulk remains, but some parts have regrown, and several newer trunks are standing in a circle with a vast hollow centre.

At Eastham, on the Wirral, another ancient yew tree stands in the churchyard near to the modern church. This is not such an impressive tree, though it is still whole, and its circumference today is only about 17ft (5.2m); yet local records of it go back to 1152, when the Manor of Eastham changed hands and the villagers entreated the new owners 'to have a charge of ye olde yew'. The tree itself appears to have changed little in 840 years.

According to the history of Fountains Abbey, as related in 1628, the monks sheltered under the great yew trees in 1132 when they were building the Abbey. These yews were known as the Seven Sisters; today just two of them (both female trees) remain.

Whereas tree-ring data had led to the reassessment — and reduction — of the ages of many great trees, including oak, such methods are inapplicable to ancient yews. All yew trees of a really great age are hollow, so ring-counting has been impossible. As a result, researchers like Allen Meredith have turned instead to documentary evidence. Like the great amateur naturalists of the past, Meredith has made the study of ancient yew trees his life's work, and has startled professional botanists with his findings.

On the basis of documentation that he has collected from all over England and Wales, Meredith has compared the known planting dates for 70 individual trees over 300 years old with their present dimensions. He has calculated that for the first 500 years the girth of a churchyard yew increases on average by 0.43in (1.1cm) per year to approximately 18ft (5½m). Yet it is clear from measurements of many very old yews that they grow very much slower than this later in their life; the ancient tree at Totteridge in north London is still 26ft (8m) in girth, just as it was in 1677. The great hollow yew at Crowhurst in Surrey apparently only grew from 30ft (9.1m) in girth in 1630 to 30ft 9in (9.4m), recorded both in 1850 and 1874.

Many ancient yews are found growing on what are known to be ancient burial sites dating from neolithic, Celtic and Saxon periods. The yew at Ashbrittle in Somerset is growing on a neolithic barrow. At Tandridge the foundations of the original Saxon church were constructed over and around the roots of an ancient yew that is still thriving today; the foundations could be seen in the crypt until this was sealed.

Meredith has also documented the positions of church buildings in relation to the ancient trees, and has proposed that this indicates the age of the sites and gives minimum ages for the trees: where the church is west or east of the yew the site is Celtic, where north or north-east of it, Saxon, and where south of the yew, neolithic.

There are records of a *samhain* (autumn) festival at Fortingall when a communal bonfire was burnt on a Bronze Age tumulus known as the Mound of the Dead (*carn nam marb*). In Ireland at least one of the five 'legendary trees' of Ireland, *Bile Tortan*, alongside which St Patrick built his first church, was a yew. Old Irish chronicles refer to the destruction

THE PRESERVATION OF ANCIENT YEWS

We may not understand their true significance to our early ancestors, but as a living link with the very ancient past these trees are clearly unique. In the last few years a campaign to protect and document ancient yews has been started by Alan Meredith and Professor David Bellamy, with the assistance of the Conservation Foundation. A general request has been made for information about ancient trees, and moves taken to ensure that at least they are protected by Tree Preservation Orders. A formal registration and national preservation scheme are envisaged and each yew is being granted its own certificate, stating its probable age.

The public response to the ancient yew campaign has been remarkable; information has been provided about hundreds of yew trees, most though not all of them in churchyards. Allen Meredith has visited many of these trees and intends to visit them all; a map of ancient yews has been compiled from his records. Perhaps the most important responses were the very many letters from people who were moved to write about the spiritual strength they had received from ancient trees, and particularly from ancient yew trees. One correspondent from Scotland wrote:

> I find yews weird trees, to say the least; whereas an oak could be called lord of the trees, the provider at the heart of our cycle, the green man, nest and home, the yew would seem to be God above trees, dark and aloof, 'other' to us, not of our cycle, or rather transcending it, the graveyard yew... distilling the negative poisons of the soil and thrusting them outwards positively above ground... It is an everpresent watcher. I think of the ancient yew of Fortingall, there when the megaliths were planted, the later Roman forts, the much later church, and it knowing all the time, being aware of something we can only feel.

After its measurements have been confirmed, each ancient yew is issued with a certificate. This one, for the Fortingall yew, confirms that the tree is probably over 5,000 years old. It could be considerably older.

The degree of neglect of some of the most important of these trees is almost unbelievable. The ancient tree at Ankerwyke, on the north bank of the Thames at Runnymede, has been forgotten for decades. Many centuries ago the Thames ran on a more southerly course, so that what is now Runnymede was on the same bank as the sacred yew, under which oaths were declared and holy ceremonies held in medieval times. This tree almost certainly marks the site where the Magna Carta was signed by King John in 1215, chosen for its ancient spiritual significance. Yet in modern times this extraordinary ancient tree was not protected, and was completely overgrown with scrub until early in 1992. Full protection and conservation of this tree and the area around it, one of the most important historic sites in England, is still awaited.

THE AGE AND GIRTH OF YEWS

Some tree-ring data has been collected from large but not yet hollow trees. One section from a yew 7ft (2.1m) in girth showed over 300 rings, and a number of samples obtained after the 1987 storm have yielded counts for trees of known girth. Combined with the rates of growth shown by the frequently measured ancient trees such as those at Crowhurst and at Eastham a tentative table of average yew growth in these islands has been produced by Allen Meredith though obviously some trees vary substantially from this curve.

Girth	Estimated Age
9ft (2.7m)	240 years
12ft (3.7m)	300 years
18ft (5.5m)	720 years
21ft (6.4m)	1,020 years
24ft 6in (7.5m)	1,360 years
27ft (8.2m)	1,800 years
30ft (9.1m)	2,400 years
33ft (10.1m)	3,000 years
35ft (10.7m)	4,400 years
35ft 6in (10.8m)	5,000 years
36ft (11.0m)	5,600 years
Over 36ft (11.0m)	Age unknown

The Fortingall yew was an estimated 52ft (16m) in the 1700s, while the Brabourne yew in Kent, which has since disappeared, was said to have a similar girth in the early 1800s.

After yews have reached a certain girth, their rate of growth slows and sometimes even stops, making it impossible to estimate their age.

The Book of Armagh
*A detail from the celebrated ancient manuscript in which there is mention of the ancient yew tree (Bile Tortan) where St Patrick built his first church.
'The circuit being completed he went out and built a church for the priest Justanus beside Bile Tortan, which is in the possession of the community of Ardbraccan, and he built another one in eastern Tortiu, in which the tribe of Tech Cirpain resides, but it is free for all time.'*

by war of sacred trees and woods: unfortunately this seems to have happened all too frequently in Irish history and though the prevalence of ancient yews at burial grounds in Ireland was recorded as long ago as AD 1184 by Geraldus Cambrensis, there are very few ancient yews known in Ireland today.

However, the widespread association of very old yews with known centres of Celtic culture is now accepted; in Wales and parts of England reasonable numbers of the trees are still standing. These ancient trees, growing at burial grounds, would have been seen by generations of Celts; they epitomized a belief in immortality, and in many places provided the spiritual focus of the whole community. But, as Meredith's researches show, this is not the whole story, for it is now clear that some of today's living trees predate the Celtic period. In other words they were already ancient sacred trees to the earlier inhabitants of these islands.

The history and pre-history of ancient yews, and their role in the spiritual lives of ancient communities, is still hardly known; few sites adjacent to ancient yews have been excavated, partly because the yews are still alive and would be damaged. Until recently, few people believed that any living yew trees could be more than perhaps 1,500 years old; but very much greater ages are now generally accepted, and it is thought perfectly possible that the Fortingall yew could be between 5,000 and 8,000 years old.

There are other living trees of a comparable age, including the bristlecone pines of California — which have the advantage of exhibiting a complete set of rings.

5

Our Rarest Trees: The Plymouth and Whitty Pear

T HE CHANGING TREE FLORA of the British Isles and Ireland since the last glacial period, which came to an end around 10,000 years ago, has been mostly a record of new arrivals. Man has greatly accelerated that process by the deliberate introduction of many species, some of which have become naturalized. At the same time some native species apparently disappeared from certain parts, such as various trees lost from the outer Hebrides, and Scots pine lost from England and Ireland — a process which may also have been accelerated by human activity. Two of the rarest native trees, both of the family *Rosaceae*, are thought to have suffered from man's activities, and are in any case of limited fertility in the present British climate.

These are the Plymouth pear (*Pyrus cordata* Desv.) and the Whitty pear (*Sorbus domestica* L.). In both cases not enough is yet known about these species for very firm conclusions to be drawn; in the case of *P. cordata* its precise taxonomic status is still being investigated; in that of *S. domestica* its credentials as a native species are unproven.

T. R. Archer Briggs
Archer Briggs, the man credited with having discovered the Plymouth pear in a hedgerow near his home.

The Plymouth Pear

In 1870 or 1871, T. R. Archer Briggs, a local naturalist, was puzzled by some wild pear plants, thought to be *Pyrus communis* L., growing in a hedge near Thornbury, on the outskirts of Plymouth in Devon. He sent them to J. Boswell Syme, the Curator of the Botanical Exchange Club, who was unable to identify the specimens; writing in his annual report for 1871 Syme noted that the inch-long leaves and the flowers were smaller than usual, and the fruit was just half an inch long and shaped more like an elongated berry. In fact he considered that it hardly deserved to be described as a pear at all. He proposed the name var. *briggsii* 'in the event of its being destitute of a name'.

The small tree, which grows to about 4½m (15ft), was later recognized as a separate species, and is now known as *Pyrus cordata*. It is a most attractive species which could grace any site with its decorative qualities; in early May it is covered with sprays of very pale cream flowers, which have some pink on the flower-buds and the outside of the petals. Unfortunately the flowers have a faint, but quite appalling smell, variously described as rotting scampi, soiled sheets or wet carpets. This is interpreted by biologists as meaning that the flowers are probably attractive to and pollinated by flies, rather than bees and wasps; my own observations were that while St Mark's flies (*Bibionidae*) are much in evidence, many other insects, including honey-, bumble- and other solitary bees, all visit the flowers.

The Plymouth Pear
This is the site where the Plymouth pear was first discovered on the outskirts of Plymouth, Devon. Its beautiful blossom is a rare sight as the flowers are only out for about five days a year.

The Plymouth pear has been incorporated into English Nature's Species Recovery Programme, which aims to establish the precise taxonomic position of the existing populations and their present status, as well as achieving their long-term self-sustaining survival in the wild; botanists at the Royal Botanic Gardens, Kew, are working with Plymouth's Nature Conservation Officer and other local experts in various studies and action programmes concerning the tree.

Fruit are being collected, and careful observations about flowering, pollinating insects and fruiting are being made on all the known trees. Associated insects are being collected, and specimens of foliage, flowers and fruit are being compared with existing specimens already in collections. Both grafting and micropropagation are being attempted, so that the long-term survival of the population both in the wild and in planted sites can eventually be guaranteed.

Recent searches in the Plymouth area have revealed a small number of other trees, including one thought to have been raised from seed in the garden of a house occupied by Briggs himself. Other specimens have been found on the west coasts of France, Spain and Portugal.

P. cordata is a very rare tree under very real threat of extinction in the UK; very few full-grown specimens exist, and much of the original site has been lost as a result of industrial development on the edge of Plymouth. While serious conservation measures such as immediate compulsory purchase are considered politically unacceptable, the rest of the site must be considered seriously at risk. The problem is that the tree seems to set very little fertile seed, and only one or two seedlings have ever been raised. Propagation from cuttings has so far also failed. There has been some success with saplings produced from suckers, though these are genetically identical to their parent trees, and so are of limited conservation value. Recently two new hedgerow sites were found near Truro in Cornwall, but on examination it became clear that they are different in form and are possibly not even the same species.

The Whitty Pear or True Service Tree

The Whitty pear (*Sorbus domestica* L.) was discovered much earlier than *Pyrus cordata*. According to the Worcestershire naturalist Norman

Hicken, the first record of this pear-like relative of the familiar rowan was in 1678, when Alderman Edmund Pitts first reported a single '*Sorbus pyriformis*' tree growing in the Wyre Forest. By the middle of the nineteenth century this tree was well known locally and a flowering branch was exhibited at the Worcestershire Naturalists' Club in 1855. In 1862 the by now ancient tree was burnt down by vandals, but grafts were already flourishing elsewhere, and two trees in the grounds of Arley Castle were claimed to have been raised from seed. A new Wyre Forest tree was planted in 1913; this too is claimed to be a direct descendant of the original tree, and is now over 10m (33 ft) tall. Other specimens can be found in botanical gardens such as Oxford, Cambridge and Kew. The tallest individual, at 23m (75 ft) is at Claremont House in Surrey.

S. domestica appears to be a Mediterranean species which probably reaches the normal limit of its natural range a little south of the British Isles. It is quite widely distributed in southern Europe, in North Africa and as far as the Middle East. So far the Wyre Forest tree is the only British specimen recorded, though some botanists believe that the tree could occur naturally on the inaccessible cliffs above the River Wye in Herefordshire and Worcestershire; if so, an interesting discovery is waiting to be made, and one that would confirm whether or not it is truly a native species.

The Whitty pear is similar to the rowan (*S. aucuparia*), but has a fissured rather than smooth bark, and attractive feathery foliage. The flowers have 5 styles (instead of 3–4 in rowan). The fruit is green turning brownish, and is less than an inch long – larger than the 'berries' of rowan, but much smaller than a typical pear. It is an attractive tree and has been planted from European stock in gardens, somewhat confusing its status as a native tree.

MICROPROPAGATION

In the last 25 years the laboratory culture of plant tissue from the smallest original samples of live vegetative matter has been perfected in many countries. Commercially this has facilitated the production of very large numbers of individual plants from a single selected parent for the retail market or for research purposes. But perhaps even more important has been the contribution made to the conservation of plants that are difficult to propagate by conventional means, including very rare plants and those that do not appear to be reproducing naturally.

The Micropropagation Unit at Kew opened in 1974, and now employs several full-time staff. It uses the *in vitro* technique both for vegetative propagation and for growing from seeds in cases where seedlings are dangerously susceptible to fungal infection. Where plant species have intimate relationships with fungal species – as, for example, with mycorrhiza – there are some drawbacks to *in vitro* culture, and this may help to explain why the technique has so far failed with some species.

Many rare plants, especially those originating in small islands, have been successfully raised in this way, although so far very few of them have been trees. Some specimens of *Pyrus cordata* have already been raised vegetatively from tiny buds, and rare trees from Socotra, St Helena, Mauritius and other places are being attempted.

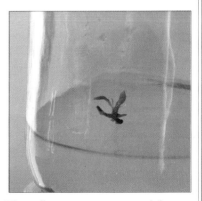

The seedlings are grown in tiny sealed jars (as here) or dishes containing nutrient-impregnated agar jelly. The specimens are effectively isolated from disease and the levels of light and temperature are carefully controlled.

6
Trees in the Web of Life

The Lobster Moth
The extraordinary appearance of its caterpillar makes it obvious how this species got its name. It is just one of a very large group of polyphagous insects that live off the foliage of a wide range of forest and fruit trees.

WHERE TREES OCCUR, they are almost always the largest organisms present, and have direct interactions with very many others. As primary producers, using photosynthesis to manufacture organic material, they make large and vital contribution to the energy cycle by providing food directly or indirectly to many sorts of organisms, from herbivorous caterpillars or grazing mammals to the fungi which live on dead wood by breaking down cellulose. The roots of large trees extend deep into the subsoil or down cracks in bedrock to extract water and minerals from these levels. This is particularly important in habitats where the upper layer of substrate is mineral-poor, such as on thin soil over bedrock, or on coastal mud flats in the tropics. When tree leaves and branches fall to the ground and decompose in such places, the minerals are either taken up directly by the decomposer organisms, or released into the soil or water below the tree.

The interactions of trees with fungi are often more complex and usually more intimate than those with other types of organism. Fungal fruiting bodies appear on many trees within a very short time after the death of a tree — so quickly that it is now clear that even when they are in an apparently healthy state, the trunk and branches of many live trees are infested with living fungi. Mycorrhizal interactions between tree roots and fungi are more familiar and extremely widespread, especially in tropical conditions. This is a symbiotic relationship; the trees gain minerals, especially nitrogen, phosphorus and potassium, while the fungi gain carbohydrates — which they are unable to manufacture themselves — and protection from fungivores and pathogens.

But what may be of mutual benefit in the natural world may not be advantageous to humans. Many organisms which under natural conditions can be in a state of balance with their tree hosts are seen by foresters and other tree growers as pests or 'enemies of trees'. The honey fungus (*Armillaria* spp.), a scourge of gardeners and foresters, is primarily a disease of introduced species — most native trees other than elm, birch, pine, apple, maple, willow and cherry being resistant. The Forestry Commission's booklet on honey fungus admits that 'it is rarely a major problem in woodland through it sometimes kills large groups of conifers in young plantations. The disease is more serious in parks, gardens, orchards and arboreta.'

To the ecologist these are all more or less artificial communities. Plantations often consist of large numbers of genetically similar individuals, such as those selected for timber quality and this is probably an important factor affecting tree susceptibility. In natural woodland trees possibly develop some resistance to the fungus, which therefore depends on finding trees under some other type of stress in which to make a successful infection. If this is the case, fungal infections could be seen as part of a natural regulatory mechanism which, by killing weaker trees, releases and therefore recycles minerals more quickly than would otherwise be the case.

The relationships between invertebrates and trees are extremely diverse, and in many parts of the world relatively little known. Even in these islands there has been no comprehensive account of them, though the interactions of trees with specific 'pests' may be very familiar. Unfortunately the approach of many arboriculturalists — like that of many farmers and horticulturalists — has tended to be largely concerned with growing better monocultures, which are now known to be particularly susceptible to attack; they are unnatural in natural systems and the system takes drastic action to correct them when they occur.

What is clear is that many plants, and especially trees, have a complex assemblage of invertebrate species associated with them in different ways. Some are specifically associated with individual tree species, such as certain moths or beetles that depend on a single food-plant, like the ash bark beetle (*Leperisinus varius*) or the elm bark beetle (*Scolytus scolytus*), while many others feed on or pollinate a limited range of species, like the bright green chrysomelid beetle (*Chrysomela alnea*).

Bracket Fungi
Although fungi are more often associated with dead trees, they can also thrive on living trees as here on this oak in Windsor Park.

Predation by Deer
In the Scottish Highlands, the greatly increased numbers of deer have effectively prevented the natural regeneration of pine or any other trees (above). Pine seedlings are quite hardy and they are able to survive some browsing by deer, although it leaves them stunted and irregular (below). When the growing shoots are repeatedly grazed, however, they inevitably die.

Vertebrates tend not to be so limited in the range of trees they are associated with: fruit-eating birds and bats (and in the tropics fish) tend to be 'cafeteria feeders' that will take what is available, though obviously preferences can be detected. Birds, for instance, use fruits in different ways; some are pulp-feeders while others depend on the actual seeds, often taking fruits as they become available, or as other food sources diminish. There is also a very large group of polyphagous invertebrates that feed on or just visit the flowers of many host species. For instance a whole group of geometrid moths (winter moths) such as the *Operophtera* species attacks the foliage of a large range of forest and fruit trees as well as shrubs.

What is the advantage to the trees of all these species living off them? For many trees there seem to be no benefits and indeed this interaction can limit the growth and even threaten the survival of trees. However for other trees the reverse is clearly true. Some depend on the availability of pollinating insects in sufficient numbers at the right time of the season to set good numbers of seed. The distribution of seeds by birds in particular, is very important. Some birds, like jays, carry large seeds and bury them, often in otherwise inaccessible places. Others eat the fruits but the seeds pass through their gut — their viability may even be enhanced as a result. Indeed the present distribution of plants in these islands, including trees, has been influenced by the activities of birds which, according to Snow and Snow, are 'the chief agents of the spread of fleshy-fruited plants' such as the species of *Sorbus*.

While animals such as deer, squirrels, rabbits, voles and mice eat fruits and seeds, and may be major agents of seed distribution, they also eat young shoots and seedlings to the detriment of trees and their survival. In the next section Donald Pigott, who has conducted experiments on seedling palatability with small animals, discusses predation of seedlings and its effect on the regeneration of trees.

Regeneration and Predation
by Donald Pigott

Many trees have the ability to regenerate vegetatively. This may be accomplished by sprouting from the base of the trunk after the tree has been cut down, or by sprouting along the roots to produce suckers, or simply by the branches touching the ground and rooting. These processes allow trees to survive in situations where regeneration from seedlings fails, but without seedlings a tree is deprived of the genetic advantages of normal seed production and of the ecological advantages of being dispersed to new sites.

When grown from seed most trees take several years before they themselves begin to flower and set seed. Beech, for example, when growing in woodland, rarely starts to produce sufficient quantities of fruit to allow seeding before it is 60–80 years old. Regeneration is the whole process from the successful establishment of seedlings through to when the new generation reaches reproductive maturity. For beech, therefore, regeneration is a slow process.

For most British trees, what is loosely described as a seed is usually a dry fruit. An acorn, for example, forms from the whole ovary, and it is not uncommon for more than one root to emerge, showing that there were two embryos inside. In the fruit of elm, maple, ash and birch the ovary wall is expanded into a wing and the seed is shed within the winged container.

It is the seed itself which contains the small plantlet, and often a nourishing storage tissue as well. The size and weight of this package varies greatly between species. An acorn when dry weighs over a gram, while the fruit of the birch weighs only a few milligrams — nearly a thousandfold difference.

The ecological significance of these differences was recognized by Sir Edward Salisbury, who drew attention to an interesting correlation. Trees which produce large quantities of small seeds or fruits, such as willows, poplars, birches and alder, are generally pioneer species, the seedlings of which will not tolerate shade and are restricted to open sites, often on bare soil such as banks of silt deposited by rivers, ground laid bare by fire or by the clearance of woodland. Trees which produce smaller quantities of large fruits tend to reproduce in more stable conditions within woodland, as in the case of beech, sessile oak, lime and maple, or in more open woodland or grassland, as in the case of common oak (see p.118).

All seeds, whether large or small, are packages of concentrated nutriment containing oils, fats, proteins and starch. These substances provide for the seedling's early growth until the new leaves are ready to take over. Inevitably they are attractive to animals, particularly as seeds

Professor Donald Pigott is director of the Cambridge University Botanic Garden and an authority on the distribution and natural history of British native trees.

The Nuthatch
Like many birds, the nuthatch depends on tree fruits to survive, as they are one of the few sources of food throughout the winter.

are often available during winter when other palatable plant tissues have largely disappeared. A complex web of adaptations and relationships have evolved between seeds and their predators.

Predation begins even before the fruits are ripe or shed. This may be by insects, which are often specific to the species of tree. For example, when acorns are examined as they fall, quite a large proportion will be found to contain a larva which converts the plant tissue to crumbly powder. This is the larva of weevil, (a *Cuculio* species), which eventually emerges through a small round hole in the acorn's coat. Sometimes damaged acorns may still germinate, but the seedlings are weak.

Other predators destroy seeds completely. Bullfinches feed on the green fruits of wych elm, neatly chopping out the seed and letting the empty wings of the fruits fall to the ground. Redpolls extract the fruits from the persistent woody cone-like catkins of alders. Grey squirrels clamber among the branches of hazels, hanging upside down like gymnasts to reach nuts on the ends of the twigs.

When fruits are shed, predation of large fruits intensifies. Pigeons feed greedily on fallen acorns and can fly away with 50–60 acorns in their full crops. Roe deer feed on fallen acorns, but probably the most important predator in woodland is again the grey squirrel. This alien species, unlike the red squirrel, spends much of its time on the ground and is apparently better adapted to digest acorns. Once an animal has satisfied its immediate hunger, it begins to remove acorns and bury them. As the adult squirrel picks up each acorn it quickly bites a small hole at the opposite end from where the acorn was attached in the cup, and removes the growing apex of the seedling. This prevents the acorn from ever germinating after burial. Young squirrels at first bury acorns whole, and may thus disperse them, but they soon learn the adult habit. Wood-mice, yellow-necked mice, bank and field voles and dormice also all feed on tree seeds, though they do less damage to the ones they hide.

So important is tree seed in the autumn diet of rodents that when the supply fails, few females survive the winter and the population collapses. Beech and sessile oak appear to have evolved a remarkable response to this dependence.

Large crops of fruits are produced at intervals of a few years, in the so-called 'mast years'. In the intervening years there is no or very little fruit. As a consequence the populations of rodents decline in the lean years; after which the quantity of fruit is suddenly so large that a high proportion escapes predation. In beech it is only mast years that lead to regeneration, and the few beech nuts and seedlings in intervening years are all destroyed. This pattern can be found in other trees, the most extreme case being many bamboos, which flower and fruit prodigiously, but only in a genetically determined periodicity of between 12 and 120 years.

It is remarkable that in no case are the seeds of common native trees either poisonous or unpalatable (except yew). Could this suggest that their arrival here after the last ice age was largely dependent on animals and birds? Even yew seeds are dispersed, and a search under a yew tree will normally produce numerous empty husks neatly opened by mice, as well as many seeds regurgitated by birds after eating the fruits.

The Juniper Carpet Moth
This well-camouflaged moth is associated with the juniper, on which its caterpillars feed.

MAST YEARS

In the mid-nineteenth century, European foresters noticed that the flower buds of many forest trees were formed in the year prior to the flowering year. From this it was suggested that the weather of the former year was probably important for flower-bud differentiation and therefore fruit formation. Various authors noted that abundant flower buds are only formed on beech during hot, dry summers, and during the period 1811 to 1922 the greater mast years in Europe followed years of summer drought. Others suggested that summer temperatures or even frost in late spring were the most important factors.

The phenomenon of mast years was studied by Professor J. D. Matthews by examining the Forestry Commission's records for beech seed availability in the years 1921 to 1950, and trying to find climatic factors to explain them. He found that during the period studied there were:

Good to very good crop (good mast year) . 10 occurrences
Moderate to poor crop .... 14 occurrences
Total crop failure .... 6 occurrences

The good mast years were irregular, and there were never two consecutive good mast years.

Matthews plotted the average air temperatures for the months of May to September in the year before good mast years. In his 30-year study period, he found that high July temperatures correlated well with good crops in the following year, and that three of the four anomalous years could be explained by late frosts in April and early May which must have destroyed flower buds. Records for the other anomalous year, 1936, were conflicting, but he concluded that the crop might have been affected by extensive late frosts in 1935. Matthews found that summer rainfall did not correlate with mast production, while amounts of sunshine in July were highly significant. From this he concluded that high temperatures, low rainfall and excess sunshine during July in the year before fruiting are essential for the production of mast in beech. But further observations showed that even in the best mast years, the quantities of fruit produced on individual trees tended to vary a great deal.

Small-seeded trees, such as birch and willow, produce large crops of seeds every year. Once they are dispersed predation is probably not significant, simply because the reward of finding a single seed is so small that no predator can effectively feed in this way.

Predation continues after germination. The young seedlings of many trees are as nutritious as the seeds themselves. The green seedlings of sycamore, ash and lime are all eaten freely by woodmice. Squirrels continue to eat the fleshy cotyledons of oak seedlings, simply biting off the young shoot. Bank voles bite through the swollen attachment of the root of oak seedlings, leaving the shoot to wither.

As seedlings grow older they remain vulnerable to voles, which, unlike mice, gnaw the bark off the stems, severing them when they are thin. They also bite off the buds. Bank voles are selective when seedlings are over a year old, and they show a marked preference for hazel, lime, ash and hornbeam, but they tend to leave oak and birch with little or no damage.

The overall effect of predation is very great. This is readily demonstrated by enclosing patches of seedlings in fine mesh cages, which allow them to survive when unprotected seedlings disappear all round. But does predation prevent regeneration? There is no simple answer. When the number of fruits is small and seedlings are sparse, then predation may destroy all that are left. When seed is plentiful however, and seedlings numerous, then many will escape. But regeneration is a very lengthy process, and it requires observation over many years to discover if the number of seedlings which do manage to escape is sufficient to ensure that there is adequate recruitment into the adult population of trees.

7
Managing Trees

What makes hazel such a special coppice wood?

'First of all it grows very fast, on good ground. When you grow it, the stools or root-stocks can be very close together so when it's time for cutting you really have a mass of poles, a lot of weight. And then it's very easy to work, it splits beautifully. You can split or cleave it with a billhook or whatever. It almost comes apart in your hand when you do it the right way. It bends beautifully like on a hurdle, it goes round a corner without losing its strength. But the only thing is once you've started coppicing hazel you must go on, you must cut it, once you leave it too long it will die, it'll get shaded out by the other trees. It really saddens me to see so much derelict hazel coppice that's been left so long it's no good any more.' — WALTER LLOYD

THE MANAGEMENT OF TREES for their many valuable products is an ancient human activity, the origins of which are unknown. Recent archaeological findings in Brazil suggest that man's activities may even have influenced the way the Amazon forest developed, when temporary clearings were regularly planted with medicinal plants, fruit trees and other game-attracting species, before being returned to nature. Certainly the 'virgin' forests of Belize in Central America are dotted with Mayan ruins a thousand years old and more; the temples of Angkor Wat in Cambodia and Great Zimbabwe in southern Africa were both 'discovered' in the modern era, deep in what were thought to be undisturbed forests. It is now suspected that several of these civilizations collapsed when their sophisticated forest management systems were destroyed by over-exploitation. This may not have happened so far in western or northern Europe, though over-exploitation has caused some environmental deterioration in both recent and historical times.

Trees have certainly been managed in these islands for a diversity of products since the earliest times. As Oliver Rackham has pointed out, we now know that much of the original wildwood, the 'natural vegetation', was cleared several millennia ago by our neolithic ancestors. Domesday records reveal that more woodland must have been cleared before the eleventh century than has been cleared since, and that even then nearly every parcel of woodland was very carefully managed for particular purposes, and its value well established. As Rackham puts it, 'for (at least) a thousand years England has had less woodland than most European countries and has taken correspondingly more care of its woods.' Timber food, foliage for animal fodder, fuel and medicinal products were all harvested on a sustainable basis, employing sophisticated management systems that make modern single-product forestry methods look crude. Many miscellaneous products, such as farm implements and household goods, were made from raw materials collected in the woods, and innumerable other items were obtained from the forests.

Coppicing

The production of many craft items, from hay-rakes to hurdles and besoms to tent-pegs, requires supplies of similar size wood. In neolithic times it was discovered that a mass of roughly equal, straight branches could be obtained from some trees if they were regularly cut at or just above ground level. This is the system known as coppicing. A very ancient practice, the origins of which are not recorded, it is a way of managing many sorts of tree on a sustainable basis. The actual length of time between cutting varies according to the tree species and the products required: ash for walking sticks 4–7 years, hazel for pottery crates or barrel hoops 7–10 years, birch for broom handles 10–15 years, and alder for clogs or oak for peeling 20–25 years.

Not only were such cycles sustainable, it was found that the process had the effect of greatly prolonging the life of the individual trees. Ancient hazel stools in England have been estimated by Rackham to be over 1,500 years old — more than ten times the normal span of uncoppiced hazel. As they say in Cumbria, 'if you want wood, you have to cut wood.' Abandoning coppiced woodlands too long between cuts soon kills many of the stools, especially when taller 'standards' such as oaks are allowed to shade out an area. The coppice thrives on being cut, but it soon succumbs to shading.

In earlier times the number of products derived from trees was enormous, and armies of men were employed coppicing woodland for industrial as well as for rural use. For instance, it is estimated that in the mid-nineteenth century the textile industry in England was using 1,500 million bobbins annually, about half of which were made from coppiced birch and alder. A single large cotton mill in Stockport is said to have used about 10 million bobbins at any one time, with a replacement rate of about 350,000 per week. Again, in the early nineteenth century a major constraint on the expanding acreage given over to hops in Kent was the availability of poles from twelve-year-old coppices. It has been calculated that in the 1830s 100,000 acres of coppice on this rotation were needed to supply the 25 million new poles required per annum. As production and population expanded there was, until the middle of the nineteenth century, an ever-increasing demand for coppice-wood, and the production of firewood, charcoal, baskets for coal and hoops for barrels all became large-scale industries.

Coppiced Woodland
This newly coppiced area is at Coldfall Wood, north London. The stools are mainly hornbeam, with some birch, and there are oak standards. Coppicing was restarted here by Haringey Council in 1990, after an interval of about 50 years.

Thereafter all the coppice industries declined, however. Many raw materials were imported, undercutting local prices, especially in the large towns and seaports; other products were superseded and replaced by mass-produced items, often made from different raw materials such as metal or, in due course, plastic. Few clogs are worn today, wire-netting has replaced hurdles, cooking is mostly done with gas or electricity instead of firewood, and few industrial processes require charcoal.

Yet all did not disappear. In the 1920s a survey carried out by Helen Fitzrandolph and Doriel Gray revealed a wide range of products still being made in small quantities by a few craftsmen in rural workshops, many of them being produced very specifically from the wood of different sorts of trees. Alder clogs were still being made, oak-bark was in demand from the tanners and to make swill-baskets, tool handles needed small ash poles, while elm was used for making chairs. All this was in addition to the uses to which large timber from standard trees was put. In some areas there was still a healthy trade, but across the country the researchers found most coppice-wood industries on their way out, which is what has happened in many parts of the country since then.

In the Lake District, where thousands of artisans once made charcoal, industrial baskets and panniers, and birch fenders for ships, nearly all of these rural industries died out. But not quite. One survivor is Walter Lloyd, a charcoal- and tent-peg-maker from Finsthwaite near Ulverston:

There's actually a terrific potential from coppice woods. Traditionally the coppice made a vast number of different products, but so many of them got taken over by plastic. Now people want to get back to real things made out of real wood from real trees. Take wooden tent-pegs; I can make them out of oak or ash coppice and sell them at 25p a time.

Making Charcoal

The wood is placed in an eight-foot-wide iron kiln and burnt with a very restricted supply of oxygen. As a result the wood is only partially burnt, reducing it to almost pure carbon. Walter Lloyd, from Finsthwaite near Ulverston, makes about 50 tons of charcoal a year from wood cut (on a sustainable basis) in the surrounding area. He uses mostly oak, ash and alder.

Marquee hirers buy a terrific number, they buy them by the thousand. The Army buy them by the hundred thousand, and one or two big camping firms order a quarter of a million at a time. Then there's the Red Cross or the refugee organizations… Well, as you can see, the demand is astronomic for things like that. Now you can make 200 to 600 tent-pegs out of oak in a day depending on your equipment and how skilled you are, but then of course you don't want to be doing just tent-pegs all day long, it would soon get boring and there's many other things to make. Take thatching spars, made out of hazel coppice; twenty million of them are being used in a year at present, there isn't enough woodland left to be coppiced, to meet these demands, because people have forgotten how to do it. Anyway I think they'd rather sit on the seat of a tractor in a nice air-conditioned cab with the wireless on than sit out in the woods with a leather apron on getting dirty, maybe wet and cold as well.

Yet, as he explained, the potential for providing rural employment in the coppice-wood industries is enormous. His main business is making charcoal, using locally cut wood and traditional iron kilns:

I load the kiln one day and fire it, then it burns for a day or a day and a half. It's got to be watched pretty carefully so it doesn't burn too quickly, so you control it by restricting the flow of air through the vents around the sides. Then I have to block all the air holes and let it cool for a day or so before I can unload it. But is it profitable? Not too bad. Trade price is about £1.75 for a 5-pound bag, and I can get about 100 bags out of a single burn in one kiln. You have to remember we're currently importing about 60,000 tons of charcoal a year; I can make maybe 50 tons in a year if I'm working hard, so you can see there's room for at least another thousand like me, and the demand from restaurants and for home barbecues is going up all the time. I don't advertise at all, I could sell ten times as much as I make at present, just by sitting here!

Walter Lloyd gets his supplies of wood for charcoal from the only traditional 'coppice wood merchant' left in south Lakeland, Bill Hogarth. Bill also says that he could sell much more than he can produce, and his list of products is surprisingly varied: he claims to make on average '46 different products from coppice woodland, and 20 of them out of hazel.'

Bill Hogarth, whose father and grandfather before him were Lakeland woodmen, buys all the small standing timber in a wood, and he's prepared to pay up to £150 per acre depending on the quality of the wood. He works on a seasonal cycle.

In the early autumn I cut hazel; most of the things I use hazel for you need the sap out — net stakes for the inshore fisheries, thatching spars, hurdles, walking sticks and so on. Birch too, now the leaves are coming off I cut birch with the sap out to make next year's besoms [birch brooms]. Then in the summer, when the sap rises, it's the oak-peeling season. I peel oak for about three months in the summer: that's a very good earner, it all goes to the specialist tanneries where they make the highest class leather, and what's left, the peeled wood, goes to make rustic furniture, or it's swill wood, for making oak-swill baskets. There's something to do here every month of the year.

Charcoal Burning

In the past, charcoal burning was far more widespread than it is today, when the great majority of charcoal is imported. During the Second World War, when this picture was taken, charcoal burners provided a vital source of fuel for many industrial processes; today oil is more often used.

The Finished Product

The charcoal produced in the Lake District is sold through garages and garden centres for home barbecues and directly to restaurants in the area.

COPPICING AND POLLARDING

The word coppice comes from the French, *couper*, meaning to cut. In England the most widespread tradition was the management of coppice woodland combined with standards. Trees were separated into two categories: those that were coppiced, such as hazel, birch, alder, hornbeam, maple, ash and, in more recent times, sweet chestnut; and those that were allowed to grow to full size as straight standards, usually oak. One problem with coppice woodland is that it does not survive much grazing by stock or deer, which therefore need to be fenced out ... so another method was widely used whereby tree production could be combined with grazing for animals on a sustainable basis. This was known as wood pasture — pastureland for grazing animals, wild or domesticated, dotted with large trees that were regularly cut for wood or foliage at a height of 2–3m (6–10ft), beyond the reach of the animals. These were known as pollards.

The trees managed in this way were, most frequently, oak and, less frequently, beech, holly, hornbeam, hawthorn and ash. This system has fallen into disuse in the last two centuries, but relics of ancient wood pasture survive, including Windsor Park (oaks and beeches), Burnham Beeches, Moccas Park (oaks) and Hatfield Forest (various species). They are impressive relics, as is apparent in Oliver Rackham's description of Staverton Park:

> ... an awesome place. Oaks of unknown age, surrealistic shapes and improbable girth moulder in the dim shade of yet mightier hollies or rise out of a sea of tall bracken. Half-fallen trees lean against other trees. There is the largest known holly in the kingdom, and the fallen trunk of almost the largest recorded birch. Big hollies and birches are rooted high in the crotches of oaks, [there is] an atmosphere of timeless decay.

Both coppicing and pollarding give trees a completely different appearance from when they have been allowed to grow naturally. Above is an old picture of pollarded hornbeams at Bayfordbury and below is an abandoned wood of coppiced hornbeam in north London.

Oak Bark Peeling
Bill Hogarth, a coppice-wood merchant, peels oak in the woods at Haybridge, Cumbria, every summer for about three months. The bark goes to high-class leather tanneries, while the peeled oak is used for rustic furniture, or as swill wood to make oak-swill baskets.

He cuts coppice woods for private landowners and the Lake District National Park Planning Board, as well as giving demonstrations of woodmanship at agricultural shows and teaching courses at the Greenwood Trust in Shropshire.

Pollarding

The word 'pollard' comes from 'poll' meaning head; the French equivalent is *têtard* and both suggest the idea of trees having their heads cut off. Rackham records the earliest signs of pollarding from around 4,800 years ago in the neolithic trackways on the Somerset Levels. Pollarding has been well documented since Anglo-Saxon times, apart from wood-pasture, many old pollards can be found in hedges, in farmland as boundary markers, or along water-courses (pollard willows or poplars). For various reasons more pollards have survived in England than anywhere else in western Europe, partly due to the survival of large estates and the preservation of 'traditional parkland'. Other countries that Rackham identifies as still having many pollards are Greece and Cyprus, where trees are often pollarded for fodder, including oaks and olives — the latter probably so as to make the harvesting of the fruits easier. A particular form of low pollarding allows goats to climb up into trees to graze the foliage.

Many pollards in places like Epping Forest, Burnham Beeches and the New Forest have not been cut for between 100 and 300 years, and for some time fears have been expressed about their health and vigour now that many have became top-heavy and been damaged by storms. Other old pollards are dying, and the total stock is diminishing. An attempt to re-pollard ancient oaks was made in 1976 at Hatfield Forest, with the aim of rejuvenating the trees. It was not successful; nine out of the ten trees died. Since then many historical ecologists and tree botanists have given this problem a good deal of attention.

Shredding

Another way of managing trees to produce fodder is shredding. The side branches are cut off at intervals to use for fodder leaving just the top tuft to grow naturally. The effect is to produce exceptionally tall and thin trees such as can be seen in some parts of Europe, like France. Apparently this technique was never popular in these islands, probably because of the windy climate.

In March 1991 pollard enthusiasts met at Burnham Beeches for a conference on 'Pollard and Veteran Tree Management', sponsored by the Corporation of London. Its main conclusions were that old pollards could be rejuvenated if enough care was taken. It is now thought that in earlier times pollarding would have been done in the summer, assuming that one of its purposes was to secure fodder for animals. It would have been done by hand, with axes, probably leaving what tree surgeons today would regard as untidy and unhealthy wounds, yet the process continued successfully for centuries. Almost certainly the whole crown of a pollard was not taken off at one time; some limbs would be left, and possibly taken off a couple of seasons later — indeed the whole process of pollarding one tree might have taken five or ten years. This approach is now being adopted at Burnham Beeches and other places, with considerable success.

It was also suggested that pollarding old trees should not be done close to the base of the branches, but that a long stub should be left — especially on beech, which produces few buds if cut close to the trunk. This too has already proved successful. Shading is also thought to be deleterious to newly pollarded trees, especially oaks, and it is now recommended that some surrounding trees may need to be cut. Many old wood pastures have been little grazed for many years, so the tendency of pollards to produce side shoots near the base is not discouraged as it would have been historically. These areas are in any case very different today to what they must have been 100 or more years ago; the relaxation of grazing pressure has resulted in the growth of often dense secondary woodland, causing additional shading on the relatively squat pollards. In places such as Windsor Park the result is a strange landscape in which these ancient trees, with their very characteristic shapes, are interspersed with unremarkable woodland and even some planted areas of alien conifers. The future management of such places is one of the most important tasks in tree conservation in these islands. If these ancient pollards and the unique habitat they create are going to survive, the secondary woodland cannot be allowed to continue growing unchecked.

Using Wood

At Glenstal Abbey near Limerick in Ireland, two monks work together to maintain the woodland and wood pasture of the 300-acre Glenstal Estate, and to produce high quality turned articles for both religious and secular purposes from 'storm-felled timber'. Little timber is actually cut unless it is in a dangerous condition, but trees are planted and they are mulched with the shavings from the lathe. Brother Ciaron is the wood-turning monk, and he is very sensitive to the particular properties of the different woods he uses:

I turn in two stages. I turn wood when it's wet; and then sometimes I leave it like that and allow the wood to dry. It's what you call seasoning — every wood has to be seasoned. Oak is quite unpleasant to turn when it's wet — it's full of tannin and your hands get covered in purple — whereas beech or ash, they're beautiful to turn wet, you get these great big creamy shavings coming off. And then the other problem about oak is that it warps very severely, so you have to leave it fairly thick because

Basket-making
Until about the turn of the century, nearly all agricultural and industrial goods were carried in baskets, many of them made of willow. These fruit baskets were being made in Somerset just before the outbreak of the Second World War.

in order to get it on centre again you have to turn away all the warped wood. On the other hand, ash hardly distorts at all, compared to oak. But it's when the wood's dried a little, when you're re-turning it, that oak is such a delight because of the grain structure — it's very tight and you get very little tearing of the fibres in the wood, it finishes beautifully.

You must remember I'm in this for the love of wood, but also for the love of money, so I always have to think of saleability. If you take walnut, that's very attractive, especially when you have the combination of the sap wood with the heart wood. Then I like sycamore, it's traditionally a wood for eating off, for plates and bowls. I find it very pleasant: you can get lovely colours when it begins to doze, that is when it starts to get a bit of fungus in it, not too much of course or it would rot. Dozed beech is very spectacular, especially where you have the combination between the natural colour and the fungus, but of course the more dozed it is the more difficult it is to get a good finish. That's why I love oak, it's always very easy to finish. I do turn yew as well and that's good — it has a beautiful red colour. The only problem is that after a week or two it fades, so you must be sure you sell your item very soon if you're turning yew, and I don't like that very much.

Wood-turning
Brother Ciaron, of Glenstal Abbey near Limerick in Ireland, has been turning wood for many years, producing high quality articles for both religious and secular purposes from storm-felled timber.

THE PROPERTIES OF DIFFERENT WOODS

The basis of many 'minor wood products' is a knowledge of how particular characteristics of different trees make them suitable for different purposes. The most obvious use of wood is, of course, burning it to provide heat, and the properties of the different woods in this regard are delightfully revealed in the old rhyme:

> *Beechwood fires are bright and clear,*
> *If the logs are kept a year;*
> *Chestnut only good they say,*
> *If for long it's laid away;*
> *Make a fire of elder tree,*
> *Death within your house shall be;*
> > *But ash new or ash old*
> > *Is fit for Queen with crown of gold.*
>
> *Birch and fir logs burn too fast,*
> *Blaze up bright and do not last;*
> *It is by the Irish said*
> *Hawthorn bakes the sweetest bread;*
> *Elmwood burns like churchyard mould —*
> *E'en the very flames are cold;*
> > *But ash green or ash brown*
> > *Is fit for Queen with golden crown.*
>
> *Poplar gives a bitter smoke,*
> *Fills your eyes and makes you choke;*
> *Apple wood will scent your room*
> *With an incense-like perfume;*
> *Oaken logs, if dry and old,*
> *Keep away the winter's cold;*
> > *But ash wet or ash dry*
> > *A king shall warm his slippers by.* ANON

An ancient ash pollard in Hatfield Forest.

Willow Growing and Osier Beds

Stripping the Willow
In the 1920s, without the benefit of modern technology, willow stripping was done by hand. As is the case today, the peeled rods were then dried in the sun before being gathered in bundles for sale.

Young willow stems (*Salix* species) have been cut for basket-making since ancient times. One- or two-year-old withies are extremely flexible and strong, especially when dried. The technique of weaving them into baskets was referred to by the ancient Egyptians, the Greeks and the Romans, while the ancient Celtic God Esus is portrayed as a woodcutter, often of willow, as in a stone bas-relief at the Musée de Cluny, Paris. In England fragments of wickerwork from wild willow dating from 100 BC have been found preserved at the ancient Glastonbury lake village site in Somerset.

Local willow-growing for basket-making has traditionally been done in low-lying areas all over these islands, but especially on the Somerset Levels, in the Ormskirk district of Lancashire, in some parts of Cambridgeshire, and in Ireland around Lough Neagh in the north and in river valleys in the west and south-east.

Walking through a willow bed in late summer or early autumn is a breathtaking experience. The beds are not so dense as to impede progress too much, but they are thick enough to envelop the walker completely in a magical, waving, rustling and ever-changing world, with beautiful light effects and occasional glimpses of wildlife. Although they are effectively monocultures, willow beds are a very attractive habitat for wildlife, especially birds such as snipe for which they provide excellent cover.

The species of willow most frequently cultivated for baskets are *S. triandra*, *S. viminalis* and *S. purpurea*, and some hybrids of these species. Ken Stott provides an easy means of distinguishing the three: *S. triandra* has a shiny-green leaf with a serrated margin, *S. viminalis* has a leaf eight times as long as it is broad, with an inrolled margin, and *S. purpurea* has a small leaf with a bloom on the underside.

But this tells only half the story, for there are very many varieties of these willow species, each with slightly different colour and weaving characteristics; willows also tend to hydridize freely, producing further shades to delight the many basket craftsmen.

It is generally accepted that the best quality baskets are made from *S. triandra* stems, the shoots of which usually grow to about 2 metres in one season. Basket willows are grown in rows a bit less than a metre apart in dense willow beds, and are cut at or near ground level every year. This

MINOR FOREST PRODUCTS

The multifarious uses of trees and woodland can still be seen in many traditional societies around the world. In woodlands similar to ours in eastern Europe and Russia, some estimates of the total production of forests including this informal sector have been made. Right are some published figures for 'minor forest products' from temperate forests in Russia in 1986, excluding small-scale timber, with estimates (for 1965) of the utilization of the yield — the estimated proportion of each product that was actually collected.

Type of Product	Production (000 tons)	Estimated utilization (%)
Hay (probably all fodder)	338.3	n/a
All fruits and berries	167.3	3.5%
Birch sap	42.7	n/a
Mushrooms	31.7	3.5%
Honey	22.9	n/a
Medicinal herbs, etc.	15.7	n/a
All nuts	10.5	25%

Willow Beds
Willow beds still dominate the landscape in small pockets of Somerset. This typical view is on King's Sedgemoor, near Burrowbridge.

'It's what you take a liking to. It's rather an arduous task. You really must love the work, you must love what you're doing to stick to it. If you didn't like it you'd find it extremely hard. But if you took a liking to it then it isn't hard at all.'
GEORGE DAVID, a traditional willow-grower from Burrowbridge, Somerset.

is, of course, a version of short-rotation coppicing. The withies that grow from the stools are traditionally cut by hand with a small sickle, and trimmed as close to the stool as possible so that in the following season the new rods do not have any old wood attached to them. Some willow-growers now use mechanical harvesters, but they still have to 'clean' the stools, which — traditional growers will tell you — is still best done by hand. The withies, willow stems, are cut every year between November and early April, traditionally after cattle have been allowed into the willow beds for a week or so to clean them by eating the weeds. Occasionally stems are left for two years to produce the 'sticks' from which stronger items such as chair legs are made. Many withy beds are 40–50 years old, and good beds will last a willow-growing family for two generations or more. Serious infestations of rust or other pests sometimes make it necessary for willow-growers to replant using short stem-cuttings, but this occurs infrequently.

In England the commercial use of willows for making containers developed in the Middle Ages, but remained relatively small-scale until the nineteenth century. In late eighteenth-century Ireland the Dublin Society gave grants to landowners to encourage commercial tree-planting of all types. The Society's records show that between 1766 and

Willows and Wetlands

At the Willows and Wetlands Visitor Centre in Stoke St Gregory, near Taunton, there is an exhibition about the willow industry and a small willow museum, in which photographs, artefacts and documents trace the history of the industry locally. It is a working willow establishment, and the whole willow process — from harvesting the withy beds through preparation to the making of baskets and willow charcoal — can be observed. Several other willow centres are open to the public, and there are many other basket-makers and shops selling willow products in different parts of the Somerset Levels.

Willow Fish Traps

These tidal fish traps are still in use today on the River Severn. They are made from 'browns' (unpeeled willow rods) as opposed to the 'whites' (peeled willow rods) that are used for high-quality baskets.

'It's not something you could learn overnight — it takes time, some people call it a skilled craft. It's not just the cutting of the willow, it's the trimming of the stump, tidying the stump up for a good growth and to make it easier for cutting the following year.'
GEORGE DAVID, a traditional willow-grower, Burrowbridge, Somerset.

1806 grants were paid for 2,800 acres of willows and poplars for basket-weaving, including 109 nurseries. A few of these 'sally gardens' still survive in Co. Dublin and surrounding areas. The great expansion of the willow industry in England was in the early nineteenth century, when Napoleon blockaded the UK and prevented willow imports from Flanders. Willow baskets were widely used for carrying light or perishable goods to markets or other points of sale, though for carrying heavier goods, such as coal or clay, oak-swill baskets were used.

Large-scale drainage of the Somerset Levels made possible a major expansion of commercial growing; this spread to various other parts of the country in response to demand, peaking around 1900. Since then there has been a steady decline, except during the First World War, when demands for containers of all kinds increased enormously. There was also a minor revival of demand during the Second World War, in this case for airborne panniers. In 1925 over 6,000 acres of willows were being grown commercially, but this had dropped to 2,000 (1,355 of these in Somerset alone) by 1953; today Stott estimates a total of only 250 acres of commercial growing, apart from willows grown by individual basket-weavers for their own use in many parts of the country. There are very few traditional growers left, though some willow beds cut by hand can still be found on the Somerset Levels.

Stott describes a variety of other uses for coppiced willow: 'The attributes of cheap propagating material, rapid establishment and rejuvenation by coppicing, combined with vigorous resilient growth that is not easily broken, have led to a wide range of uses in bioengineering, difficult environments and large-scale amenity planting.' For centuries the roots of willows have been used to bind and strengthen river-banks and prevent scouring and erosion. In Holland willow mattresses have been used in dykes to protect the polders, and for storm protection of low-lying coastal areas. Recently they have been used to stabilize the sea bed for deep-water port construction at Port Talbot, and in harbour improvements at Zeebrugge and Dunkirk. Steep mountain slopes in the Alps, such as those near ski-runs, have been secured with willow mattresses, whose full potential for holding soil and preventing landslips is only now being explored.

A new bio-engineering technique that is being developed makes use of two woven 'hurdles' of live willow, which are erected about a metre apart, the gap between being filled with earth. The willows make a living wall, which is the best device yet found for combating the noise and air pollution caused by motorway traffic; these 'willow walls' are in use in the Netherlands along the side of motorways, and experiments are being done by the Department of Transport to see if they would be appropriate in this country. Comparable in cost to concrete walls, they are graffiti-proof, will not crack, corrode or break down and require little maintenance, becoming even stronger as they age.

Other characteristics of willows make them desirable trees to cultivate. For centuries fine willow stems have been used to make high-quality artists' charcoal. Because they are flexible, their foliage is not too dense, and they can be planted much closer together than poplar, so that they are particularly suited as quick-growing wind-breaks.

BASKET WILLOWS

One-year-old willow stems, 'withies', are traditionally cut by hand using a short sickle. After cutting they are graded by length; if sold in this form with the bark still on, they are known as 'browns'. The majority of rods are peeled to make the more valuable 'whites' — these are cut in the spring and peeled directly or 'pitted', i.e. left over the winter with their ends in about 15 cm water before being peeled — or 'buffs' which are boiled for 8 hours in large tanks before being stripped. Today the rods are peeled by using a rotating drum powered by an electric motor or tractor. Peeled rods are dried in the sun before being bundled up by hand for sale, often tied with a withy 'tie'.

S. triandra rods can be used to produce good quality whites or buffs. Coarse work, such as agricultural baskets or the tidal fish-traps which are still in use on the River Severn are made from unpeeled brown rods. *S. purpurea* produces finer rods, and was once used to make whites of high quality for fancy baskets, especially around Mawdesley in Lancashire. Today *S. purpurea* is more often used in the brown form, and is much in demand from artistic basket-makers. The red- and orange-stemmed cultivars, of *S. alba* and *S. fragilis* are particularly used for river and sea defence work in the Netherlands and Belgium. There is also a tradition of using thin willow shoots to tie agricultural crops such as vines or hops; according to Stott, willow stools kept and cut for this purpose can still be seen dotting the market gardens in the Vale of Evesham. Groups of willow stools are also a common sight in damp corners of vineyards in both France and Germany. Basket-making is now increasing after many years of decline; demand for domestic use is growing and many craftsmen are experimenting with new varieties and hybrids to produce individually designed articles for an elite market.

George David is one of the few willow-growers who still cuts his 'withies' in the traditional way (above). Once the cows have been left in the willow beds for a couple of weeks to eat the weeds, cutting proceeds from November to April, weather permitting. The 'withies' are then peeled, using a rotating drum (below).

Fruit Trees and Old Orchards

Like many other domesticated plants and animals, naturally occurring varieties of fruit trees have for centuries been specially bred and selected. Local variations of soil and climate have contributed to the enormous number and diversity of these cultivars, and over the centuries other varieties and species have been brought in from outside. Several native trees produce edible fruit of sufficient interest to attract the interest of horticulturalists: apples (*Malus* spp.), pears (*Pyrus* spp.), cherries and plums (*Prunus* spp.), as well as the smaller berries of other rosaceous trees. In this chapter we will concentrate on apples and, to a lesser extent, pears.

In England, fruit trees have been cultivated since neolithic times, but numbers were supplemented when the Romans arrived, bringing with them many of their own varieties and planting orchards. The Romans also grew vines in England, and records of vineyards much further north than now provide further evidence that the climate was markedly warmer at that time.

In some other regions, such as Western Asia wild apples and pears were collected as food by prehistoric man. According to Roach, a fruit historian, carbonized apples dating from 8,500 years ago were found at Catal Huyuk in Turkey, and in excavations of prehistoric lake settlements in Switzerland remains of both crab apples and a larger, possibly cultivated variety of apple were found.

The cultivated apples of Europe are derived from *Malus pumila*, a small forest tree that occurs naturally in the Caucasus region and Turkey, though selection and cross-breeding with the crab apple

A Traditional Orchard
Although many old orchards have been destroyed in recent years, they can still be found in many parts of the country, often possessing rare varieties of fruit trees unique to the locality.

CONSERVING OUR ORCHARDS

Why conserve old orchards? The reasons given below are adapted from the list produced by Common Ground as part of their Save Our Orchards campaign.

○ They create beautiful landscapes in all seasons, from blossom-time to winter. As a result they have inspired artists and poets, as well as millions of ordinary people.

○ Fruit trees are a source of food for humans and wildlife, from birds to bees.

○ Locally grown fruit is more diverse, provides local employment and cuts down transport.

○ Orchards are an important link with local history, and have a long tradition of multiple use, from grazing sheep and pigs to recreation and picnic sites.

Common Ground suggest that in order to conserve local apples and orchards, you should find out what orchards exist in your area, who owns them and what varieties are growing there. The Royal Horticultural Society has an identification service at their Wisley garden.

○ Try to arrange for an area of old orchard to be let to the local community to care for: in some parts of Somerset it is possible to receive a grant to maintain traditional orchards.

○ Search for and encourage the retention and planting of fruit trees, such as crab-apple, medlar plum and wild pear, in local hedgerows.

○ Encourage interest in local varieties by asking about them at local shops and 'Pick Your Own' orchards or farms.

○ Grow local varieties in your garden or on nearby open spaces.

Starting a community orchard from scratch can be done with council help on vacant public land, in corners of parks, or on housing estates. Gardening societies or nurserymen will often be able to supply trees of local varieties; plant them and then look after them!

National Apple Day is 29 September.

(M. *sylvestris*) and, more recently, the Siberian crab (M. *baccata*) has also been involved. The cultivated pears of Europe are derived from *Pyrus communis* and two other species, *P. korschinskyi* and *P. heterophylla*, while in the Far East cultivated pears are derived from varieties of an Asian species, *P. serotina*.

The trees of both *Pyrus* and *Malus* are naturally very variable in form: according to Roach, the genetic make-up of the apples (and pears) cultivated today is very complex. The freedom with which hybridization between the species has occurred naturally in the past, and the thousands of years during which man has selected and bred new varieties, has further complicated their genetic composition so that seedlings arising from the fruits on any one tree give rise to many varied types, the vast majority of which will prove of little value. Many varieties, particularly the hybrids, are infertile and may not even set seed, so the propagation of valuable varieties is done vegetatively. As neither *Malus* nor *Pyrus* will propagate satisfactorily from cuttings, the technique of grafting stems onto established root-stocks was developed. The grafting technique has been exhaustively explained by R.J. Garner in his *Grafter's Handbook*.

Many varieties were named after their discoverers or owners, and great landowners such as Henry VIII employed fruiterers to search Europe for good varieties with which to establish orchards. In the Middle Ages orchards flourished and many new ones were planted; in Tudor times, according to Keith Thomas, there were so many orchards in Norwich that the place was described as 'either a city in an orchard or an orchard in a city, so equally were houses and fruit-trees planted.' Every local area, even village, had its own varieties, which were much appreciated by travellers. Unfortunately in this century the range of varieties has diminished as the storage and transport of fruit has improved. Standardized apples and pears of a few very successful varieties are now grown in vast commercial orchards, and the trends in European food legislation threaten to curtail the number even more.

Even cider manufacturers are using fewer and fewer varieties of apple — indeed they are now using a great deal of apple concentrate from other parts of the country or even abroad. In 1987 the Somerset branch of the National Farmers' Union estimated that at least 70 per cent of British cider was produced from imported fruit. It follows that local varieties of cider apples are scarcely in demand at all. Along with the decline in the use of local fruit varieties, the gradual disappearance of traditional orchards, formally such an important and well-loved element in the country landscape, has accelerated. For some years up to 1988, the Ministry of Agriculture actually gave grants for the grubbing-up of old orchards, and many have been lost to housing and industrial developments. Former orchards are preserved in name only, as Applecroft, Orchard Way, Peartree Avenue, etc., bear witness.

With the decline in traditional orchards, the National Apple Register, set up in 1990, becomes all the more important. At present over 6,000 varieties are recorded, over 2,300 of which are to be found growing in the National Fruit Collections at Brogdale near Faversham in Kent. Many varieties of other fruit trees such as pears (500 varieties), plums (350), cherries (220), as well as other soft fruits, nuts, quinces and medlars are also grown at Brogdale, which was first opened to the public in 1991. The apples include exotic-sounding varieties such as the Decio, which is claimed to be of Roman origin, and the Mela Carla, which is reputed to have been highly esteemed by King Charlemagne.

There remain many local varieties that may not be on the Register, and may be represented by single ageing trees in private orchards around the country. Several groups and organizations have started to record and collect these varieties, and in 1988 a voluntary organization, Common Ground, began a campaign called 'Save Our Orchards', which has been very successful in raising awareness and encouraging the search for forgotten varieties. They also started the increasingly successful National Apple Day, on 29 September, when 'apple events' are held in many parts of the country.

As with other efforts to collect and preserve plant varieties, it is to this naturally occurring genetic diversity that plant-breeders turn when they need improvements in such areas as disease-resistance and drought-resistance.

The Bramley Apple Perhaps the most celebrated apple variety in England is the Bramley, or 'Bramley's seedling', named after Matthew Bramley, who once owned the cottage in Southwell, Nottinghamshire, in the garden of which the original tree still grows and bears fruit. Bramleys now constitute over 90 per cent of the cooking apples produced in the UK, with some 135,000 tons being produced annually from about 28,000 acres of fruit trees. As with other varieties of fruit tree, all Bramley apples come from the grafted progeny of the original tree. The tree itself is now over 160 years old, and concern has been expressed about its condition; it is also threatened by an infection of honey fungus (*Armillaria* spp.), which is spreading from an adjacent privet hedge. A trench has been dug and filled with fungicide to

. . THE . .
Finest Apple on Earth.

BRAMLEY'S SEEDLING.

See over, also pages 6 and 7, and 4th page of Cover.

The Characteristics of the Bramley

'The apple is bright and clear; when cooked it remains firm and has a delicious taste. The crop can be gathered early and keeps very well even until May of the following year. The tree flourishes in many different soils. The blossom is not affected by frost as it is well-protected by the outer leaves. The apple is of good size and averages 6oz in weight. The tree is sturdy and does not easily become storm-damaged; it grows rapidly and is robust. The apple's core is small and the peel is thin yet firm and bruise-resistant. The tree fruits after a few years and continues to do so abundantly for decades.'

From Merryweather's
nineteenth-century sales brochure.

The Bramley Apple Tree
This is the original tree, still growing in the garden of Matthew Bramley's old cottage in Southwell, Nottinghamshire. Using modern micropropagation techniques, it has now successfully been cloned, so that the tree's genetic resources will survive after the tree itself has died.

discourage the honey fungus, but as the future of such an aged tree is uncertain, botanists from Nottingham University are working on ways of growing new individuals (clones), using modern micropropagation techniques. This has been successful: already 80 new trees have been 'weaned' from their sterile environments and are growing in soil, ready for planting out in selected orchards in the near future. Being pure trees, as opposed to those grafted on to other apple stocks, these young trees will keep the Bramley genotype intact for the future.

THE ORIGIN OF BRAMLEY'S SEEDLING APPLE

A number of versions of this story have been published: the following account is based on the research of Mrs Pat Pomeroy, 'the great great granddaughter of the lady who planted the original pip'.

The cottage in Southwell was owned by Charles and Elizabeth Brailsford from 1809 until 1837. Between 1809 and 1813 one of their daughters, Mary Ann Brailsford, planted the pips of an apple she had enjoyed, and when it grew she planted it out in the garden. She left the cottage in 1813 when she got married and, after her mother died in 1837, the family lost their connection with the cottage. Matthew Bramley, a butcher and the landlord of the White Lion in Easthorpe, bought the cottage in 1846 and lived in it until his death in 1871.

Interest in the apples from Mr Bramley's tree was first recorded in 1857, when Henry Merryweather, a local nurseryman, met a gardener with a basket of the apples. Impressed with the quality of the fruit he begged cuttings for grafting, and was given them on the condition that they were called 'Bramley's Seedling'. As a result, Merryweather's nursery planted many acres with the grafted trees, put Bramley's Seedling in their catalogue, and went on to exhibit the apples at the Royal Horticultural Society. In 1876 the apples were highly commended, and in 1893 they won a first-class certificate.

The tree has been bearing abundant fruit ever since, though some time early in this century the tree blew down in a storm, as a result of which part of the trunk is now horizontal.

Mary Ann Brailsford planted the seed which became the Bramley apple tree.

PART TWO

TREES AND THE EARTH

8

Trees as Part of the Ecosystem

Dead Wood

When trees are allowed to rot naturally they simply become a new habitat for the whole plant and animal community. Indeed, recent research has revealed that trees are just as important to the ecosystem when they are dead as they are when alive.

THE FULL COMPLEXITY of the role of trees in the ecosphere, that is, on the whole planet, is far from being fully understood. As the Brazilian ecologist and ex-Minister of the Environment José Lutzenberger has suggested, the cooling and moderating effects of the vast Amazon forest on the weather and the climate of the whole western hemisphere is critical. Without these billions of trees, which literally put a dampener on a great area of land surface, it is certain that life for the rest of us would be much more turbulent and the climatic effects much more extreme. Trees also hold vast amounts of carbon and oxygen which would otherwise be loosed into the atmosphere, moving the planet a good deal further towards unpredictable instability. One thing is absolutely certain: present trends in deforestation cannot continue. Unless we begin to appreciate and respect the contribution that trees make to the fabric of life on this planet, the shorter will be our stay here as a species.

Individually and collectively, trees have many influences on the ecosphere. In *The Triumph of the Tree*, John Stewart Collis tried to suggest the range of these effects, though new ones are still being discovered: 'Trees act as pegs, fountains, oceans, pipes and dams, their work ramifying throughout the whole economy of nature. They hold up

110

the mountains. They cushion the rain-storm. They control the floods. They maintain the springs. They break the winds. They foster the birds.'

Trees create the soil: by infiltrating roots and rootlets into cracks in the bedrock, they start the process of weathering. They draw up minerals and water from deep below the surface for other organisms to use. They hold the soil that they create; without trees, many land surfaces would be unstable, with great quantities of loose surface material washing or blowing away uncontrollably under the effects of rain and wind, leaving ultimately little but bare rock. One can see the effects of the loss of trees in many parts of the world where rates of soil erosion have accelerated alarmingly in recent times, causing disastrous alternations of flood and drought downstream. In the Himalayas, the mountains have become seriously deforested and, while there are other factors involved, it is clear that the additional burden of soil and rock debris in the tributaries of the Ganges has caused enormous problems downstream, by choking river-beds. Flooding is now endemic in the region, and low-lying areas, like the main part of Bangladesh, are often subjected to catastrophic flooding; floods now alternate with dry seasons, when there is far less water than there used to be.

Naturally Regenerating Woodland
Such a sight as this one, where tree cover is re-growing with little interference, is becoming increasingly rare. If present trends of deforestation and single-species planting continue, the balance of the ecosystem will be irrevocably upset.

TREES AND MOISTURE

John Muir, the nineteenth-century environmentalist and founder of the American Sierra Club, was one of the first modern ecologists to appreciate the role of trees in ameliorating the local environment. This is an extract from his classic account of the Yosemite Valley.

It is constantly asserted that in a vague way the Sierra was vastly wetter than it is now, and that the increasing drought will of itself extinguish the sequoia, leaving its ground to other trees supposed capable of flourishing in a drier climate. But that the sequoia can and does grow on as dry a ground as any of its rivals is manifest in a thousand places.

'Why, then,' it will be asked, 'are sequoias always found in only well watered places?' Simply because a growth of sequoias creates those streams.

The thirsty mountaineer knows well that in every sequoia grove he will find running water, but it is a mistake to suppose that the water is the cause of the grove being there; on the contrary, the grove is the cause of the water being there. Drain off the water and the trees will remain, but, cut off the trees and the streams will vanish.

Never was the cause more completely mistaken for effect than in the case of these related phenomena of sequoia woods and perennial streams.

When attention is called to the method of sequoia stream-making, it will be apprehended at once. The roots of this immense tree fill the ground, forming a thick sponge that absorbs and holds back the rain and melting snow, only allowing it to ooze and flow gently. Indeed, every fallen leaf and root-let, as well as long clasping root and prostrate trunk, may be regarded as a dam hoarding the bounty of the storm clouds and dispensing it as blessings all through the summer, instead of allowing it to go headlong in short-lived floods.

Since, then, it is a fact that thousands of sequoias are growing thriftily on what is termed dry ground, and even clinging like mountain pines to rifts in granite precipices, and since it has also been shown that the extra moisture found in connection with the denser growths is an effect of their presence, instead of a cause of their presence, then the notions as to the former extension of the species and its near approach to extinction, based upon its supposed dependence on greater moisture, are seen to be erroneous.

In Thailand, the cutting of forests in watershed areas has resulted in chronic flooding and frequent droughts; in recent years there have been catastrophic floods in the south, while fruit-growers in the east have too little water for their trees in the dry season. Yet in isolated cases, where even very small areas of forest have been carefully conserved by the local community, the streams run clear, dislodging little or no valuable topsoil, and water supplies for both domestic use and farming have been guaranteed through the driest years.

Trees themselves can hold large amounts of water in a constantly flowing system. They absorb and use the rays of the sun to evaporate water from their leaf surfaces, thus cooling the air and maintaining air and soil humidity levels sufficient for myriad other organisms to thrive.

The cooling effects are extraordinarily important; a forest has the same effect on a mass of humid air as a range of mountains, and precipitation is often caused by its cooling. Even in temperate zones, the difference in air temperature and humidity between deep forest shade and bare ground is enormous; in the tropics it is, for many organisms, an unbridgeable gap. Once forest has been cleared and the open spaces have been made too big, ground temperatures and low humidity effectively prevent the return of many species, especially trees. The seedlings of many tropical forest trees are very sensitive to drought; after all, there is little selective advantage under normal conditions. Even in temperate England, what is more refreshing than to move from the direct glare of the sun into the cool shade of woodland?

Much of Vietnam's wonderful tropical forest has been replaced by pernicious, fire-resistant grasses that smother everything, yet dry to

tinder after a few weeks without rain. They survive seasonal fires, but are almost the only plants in the country that do so. The local name, *co my* is Vietnamese for 'American grass'. The forests were destroyed by Agent Orange and by wanton fire-bombing during the Vietnam War more than 20 years ago, yet no trees have returned; the soil now gets too hot and the grassland burns every dry season, reminding many people of the war itself.

Even winter conditions are modified by trees; walk into a wood on a day of freezing snow and hard frost and you will find that under the trees the temperature is not so severe and the wind chill is less. In mist and cloud, water condenses on the leaves and trunks of trees; on the coast of Arabia and on top of the hills in the Cape Verde Islands, the trees capture water out of the atmosphere, which would otherwise pass by these rainless places.

In these islands we have less of our original forested land than in any other part of Europe and, after a few dry years, water supplies are alarmingly short. Forests that once held the water have gone. The effects of the deterioration in the ozone layer will also be greater in our relatively treeless land. We need more trees yet, as Oliver Rackham explains in Chapter 14, this does not mean that the answer is to plant trees. Trees will grow naturally in most places in these islands given half a chance, but what could be improved is the care and attention we give to those that do exist. What we do need perhaps, is a clearer understanding of the ecosystem of which trees are a part, so that their role is better appreciated. We could start with one of our own relatively simple ecosystems – that of natural woodland.

The Boi Loi Woods of Vietnam
Once tropical forest, these woods were defoliated by Agent Orange and then fire-bombed during the Vietnam War. 25 years later, few trees have returned and the area is covered with poor scrubland.

The Cape Verde Islands
Deforestation resulted in the almost total desertification of the islands, as there were no trees left to capture water from the atmosphere. The process has now been partially arrested by the watershed planting of tall cypresses and pines.

Dr George Peterken, of the Joint Nature Conservation Committee, has studied woodland and its management for many years, and it was he who proposed the classification of our woodlands that is in standard use. He is the author of *Woodland Conservation and Management*, the standard work on the subject.

A Mature Oak
This oak, in Killarney National Park, has become a habitat all of its own. It is covered in mosses, liverworts and lichens, and has ivy growing up its trunk and round its branches.

Trees as Habitats
by Dr George Peterken

Trees do more than define woodlands. They have several distinctive functions in the ecology of a woodland.

Trees create the woodland environment. Their most obvious feature is shade: daylight intensity at ground level is reduced in summer to no more than 5 per cent of its intensity above the woodland. Woods also shelter plants and animals from wind, create a humid atmosphere and reduce extremes of winter frost and summer heat to an equitable climate. They reduce total rainfall at ground level – simply because light showers evaporate from the leaves and never reach the ground – and concentrate what does reach the ground around the bases of tree trunks, down which the rainfall flows. Woods also create their own soil conditions, rich in humus formed from the decay of tree trunks, branches, leaves and other vegetation.

These conditions favour a distinctive assemblage of plants and animals. The shade excludes many of the strongly growing plants we find in fields and reduces the vigour of the rest. As a result, while the ground vegetation consists of a mixture of species, it includes some which almost require shade to survive. In deciduous woodlands, the

light is brightest beneath the trees in spring, which enables colourful displays of bluebells, primroses and anemones to develop before the leaves of the trees have fully formed. Woods also induce plants which can survive for decades as dormant seeds in the soil (the persistent seed bank) whilst growing conditions are unsuitable. Thus, for example, they spring to life when a tree dies and more light gets through, but retreat again to dormancy when the space is again occupied by a thicket of saplings. Woods are also places which cannot stand being heavily grazed: thus, they have few grasses, but many kinds of broad-leaved herbs with showy flowers.

Oddly enough, it is quite possible to have woodland conditions without trees. These can be found on cliff ledges, rock faces and cracks, beside deeply-cut streams, beneath drifts of bracken fern and even on railway embankments. These are all the places where there is some shade, high humidity or negligible grazing. On the other hand, we can find woods which are more like heathland or grassland below the trees, especially where sheep and deer have grazed for so long that the broad-leaved herbs have gone and the woodland has become open and bare.

Trees not only make the woodland conditions; they also form a substrate on which plants and animals can grow. Mosses and liverworts commonly grow around the base of the larger trees, where they use the rainwater running down the tree trunk and stay above the accumulation of leaf litter on the woodland floor. Lichens, which can stand more drought, often cover the trunk and can grow luxuriantly even on the smallest branches. In wetter climates, polypody and other ferns grow on horizontal branches, where they root in the mats of mosses. Sapling trees may start growing in the angles between the branches, and, exceptionally, root down through the rotten hollow of an older tree trunk, to form trees within a tree. The fallen logs of dead trees are worlds of their own, supporting thickets of mosses and ferns and providing a grazer-proof site where tree seedlings may successfully grow into trees.

Animals also use trees as homes. It's not just the woodpeckers that excavate holes, the starlings that take over the abandoned woodpecker holes and all the other species that nest in the angles in the branches, in the foliage of the canopy or in the thickets of saplings, but also squirrels in their dreys, the dormice in hazel bushes and the badgers in their sets, excavated beneath the roots of large trees like oaks.

Trees are more than home to many woodland species. Invertebrates use leaves as food, and some of them are so numerous that entire oak-woods are sometimes defoliated in summer. The sap that runs oozing from wounds in large trees is food for flies. Mycorrhizal fungi grow within the roots of trees and also in the litter, while other species penetrate the cores of larger older trees, forming rotten hollows which in turn act as home for other creatures. In North America and eastern Europe, for example, this is where bears have their dens. Smaller creatures burrow into the trees, especially their rotten cores, feeding off both the wood and the fungi.

Trees are climate, home and food to the woodland fauna and flora, but they are also agents in the shaping of the land. Trees which are blown over drag up their roots on one side, leaving a hollow on the

Lichen

Lichens are more drought-resistant than most mosses and liverworts and so are not restricted to the bases of tree trunks where there is more moisture. This lichen is growing on an elm trunk near Dingwall in the Scottish Highlands.

other. The fallen trunk collects leaf litter as it is blown around the wood in winter, while the hollows may fill with water from the subsoil. It has been calculated that the entire area of soil in woodland will be turned over once every 1,000 years by tree-fall alone. Where trees fall down on slopes, they drag soil and even pieces of bedrock down the slope, so aiding erosion. On the other hand, trees lying on the ground prevent serious erosion when heavy rain falls on a wood.

When branches and trunks fall into streams, they create a multitude of micro-habitats – miniature waterfalls, pools, shallows, eroding banks and shoals. They can impede the drainage of whole areas, creating damp conditions. Many woodlands in or near towns were naturally much damper and prone to waterlogging than is now the case; one of the first things that is done to promote public access appears to be the insertion

An Uprooted Hornbeam
Despite being uprooted, many trees will survive if allowed to by man, with their side branches becoming new vertical stems. Meanwhile earth displaced by the roots creates a new habitat for plants and animals. This hornbeam in Queen's Wood, London, was felled in a storm in 1989 and is thriving even though its trunk is horizontal.

of field drains in woodland, changing the natural order irrevocably – for instance, in parts of Oxleas and Shepherdleas Woods in south London, and Coldfall Wood in north London. Wherever they are allowed to lie, dead trees form a source of plant nutrients and energy which activates the whole woodland ecosystem. So, throughout both their lives and their decay, trees form the essential base upon which the ecology of the woodland depends.

The Genetic Potential of Our Trees

It may seem a long time – 10,000 years or so – since the ice age, when most of the country was a more or less barren waste, or even covered with ice, but in terms of natural environments and the speed of change in biological systems, this is a very short period indeed. It is quite clear from the history of trees in Britain that had it not been for human activities, the tree flora of these islands would be very different. Some new species, such as sycamore, would probably have invaded from

Europe even without human intervention, but others, like horse-chestnut, might not. Trees like beech and hornbeam would probably have expanded their range, while some of our familiar trees would have declined. Grazing pressures on seedlings would have been different, since grazing animals would never have reached their present high population levels, due to the controlling influence of such native, but recently extinct predators as the bear, the wolf and the lynx.

In Britain we have remarkably few species of trees and shrubs, most of which have been subject to intensive study over many generations by foresters, ecologists and naturalists. As a result, we have an immense fund of knowledge which can be used to interpret and predict the behaviour and abundance of individual species. More recently, however, we have begun to use this same information to understand the structure and dynamics of our forests and woodlands, and to analyse the ways in which environmental factors and management determine the contribution of woody vegetation to different parts of the British landscape. A key step in this endeavour has been to begin classifying trees with respect to their strategy or functional type. Efforts are now in progress to use this approach abroad, where forest conservation and management often proceed without the benefit of a long history of scientific study of the biology of native trees.

Genetic potential determines how different species make use of the changing environment in which they find themselves (or are able to advance into), and how well they compete with other species in those environments. Professor Philip Grime's team at Sheffield University is investigating the relationship between genetic potential and field success of plants. The theories he has developed to explain what he calls plant 'strategies' (see overleaf) are now accepted by scientists in many fields of biology; this concept is now being used to explain other more complex systems than ours, such as those in many species-rich tropical systems.

The Scottish Crossbill
This bird is endemic to Scotland and is closely associated with the native Scots pine. The unusual beak is used to open pine cones so that the bird can feed on the seeds.

Ecological strategies of trees
by Professor Philip Grime

In ecology, as in the rest of science, the objective is not merely to accumulate information, but rather to organize knowledge into a useful form. In the case of British trees, this leads to questions such as 'Can we classify our species into particular ecological types?' and 'Can we predict their responses to future changes in land management or global climate?'

Since the early 1970s, ecologists at Sheffield University, working for the Natural Environment Research Council, have pioneered the development of a system in which British plants (trees, shrubs, herbaceous species and lower plants) have been classified according to their essential biology in order to predict their biological behaviour. This approach has now reached the stage where a databank recording the vital attributes of common British plants can be used to predict for land managers or conservation workers the future course of vegetation development at particular sites and under specific scenarios. In order for this system to work, it has been found necessary to classify each tree according to two sets of functional characteristics. The first set refers to adult trees, whilst the second applies to tree seedlings.

Professor Philip Grime is Director of the Unit of Comparative Plant Ecology (MERC), based in the Department of Animal and Plant Sciences at the University of Sheffield. He is a plant ecologist primarily interested in vegetation dynamics, species diversity and wildlife conservation.

THE ECOLOGICAL STRATEGIES OF ADULT TREES

By recording details of the occurrence of every species of plant over a very large number of representative sites, and by conducting standard growth and germination experiments with many species as well, we have built up at Sheffield a database of information about the actual field behaviour of every (common) native species. From this data we have been able to assess the differences in strategy of plant species, and to group those with similar strategies. As a result three extremes of habitat are recognized: environmental stress, disturbance, and abundance of nutrients.

The triangular model is built up by placing these maxima at the corners of a triangle. Species can then be placed on this triangle according to their ecological strategy. The extremes are exemplified as follows:

1 *Maximum environmental stress* (poor soil and extreme climatic conditions, resulting in low plant production.)

The species characteristic of this corner of the triangle are known as the 'stress-tolerant species'. These are very slow-growing hardy trees like yew and juniper, which can survive in chronically infertile, hostile conditions.

2 *Maximum disturbance* of the environment (periodic total or part destruction of the plant as by ploughing, storm or flood damage, etc.)

The species characteristic of this corner of the triangle are known as the 'ruderal' or 'weed' species, whose strategy is to colonize disturbed ground: typically they produce vast numbers of tiny seeds (like birch and poplar) and colonize new habitats. These are specially adapted to disturbed habitats, but often get overtaken later when some of the next group arrive.

3 *Maximum nutrients and favourable conditions* such as rich soil, shelter etc., giving rise to extreme competition for nutrients between species.

The species characteristic of this corner of the triangle are known as the 'competitors', those species best able to make use of abundant nutrients and favourable conditions by, for instance, growing very big and eventually shading out other species: these are typical tall forest trees like oak and beech.

Intermediate species between the above extremes are then placed in other parts of the triangle, corresponding to their strategies. To some extent all trees are partly intermediate and do not reach the extremes that some other types of plants do. This is particularly true of severely-disturbed conditions as most woody species are long-lived and cannot persist in habitats where the vegetation is totally destroyed at frequent intervals.

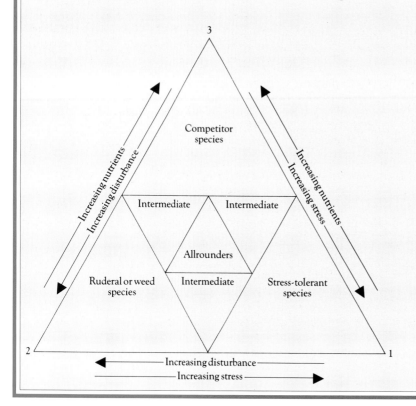

This triangle shows the three extremes of habitat to be found in the British Isles, with each corner representing the places where the conditions are most pronounced.

The bottom right-hand corner (**1**) represents conditions of **maximum environmental stress**. Trees found here are generally medium-to-small in size and very slow-growing. Examples: *juniper and yew.*

The bottom left-hand corner (**2**) represents conditions of **maximum disturbance**. Trees found here are generally medium-to-large in size and are fast-growing but not long-lived. Examples: *aspen, birch, black poplar and willows.* (None of these trees would be found growing very near the actual corner, where disturbance is at its highest.)

The top corner (**3**) represents conditions of **maximum nutrients**. Trees found here are generally the biggest trees. Examples: *ash, beech, elm, hornbeam, lime (small-leaved) and sycamore.*

A number of trees are generally found midway between 1 and 2, where there is a mixture between stress and disturbance, but still a lack of nutrients. Examples: *alder, bird cherry, crab apple, field maple, rowan, whitebeam, wild pear, wild service.*

No trees really fit into the intermediate stages between 2 and 3 and 1 and 3, although Scots pine is an allrounder and belongs in the centre of the triangle.

THE ECOLOGICAL STRATEGIES OF TREE SEEDLINGS

Strategy	Functional characteristics	Conditions under which strategy appears to enjoy a selective advantage
Vegetative expansion = **V**	New shoots which are vegetative in origin and remain attached to parent plant until well established	Productive or unproductive habitats subject to low intensities of disturbance.
Seasonal regeneration = **S**	Independent offspring (seed or vegetative propagules) produced in a single cohort	Habitats subjected to seasonally predictable disturbance by climate or biotic factors
Persistent seed or spore bank = **Bs***	Viable but dormant seeds or spores present throughout the year; some persisting more than 12 months	Habitats subjected to temporally unpredictable disturbance
Many widely dispersed seeds/spores = **W**	Offspring numerous and exceedingly buoyant in air; widely-dispersed and often of limited persistence	Habitats subjected to spatially unpredictable disturbance or relatively inaccessible (cliffs, walls, tree-trunks, mud-banks, etc.)
Persistent juveniles = **Bsd**	Offspring derived from an independent propagule, but seedling or sporeling capable of long-term persistence in a juvenile state	Unproductive habitats subjected to low intensities of disturbance

Strategy	Species which display regenerative strategy
V	Aspen, dwarf willow, holly, elm (*U. minor*), cherry
W	Ash, field maple, willows, black poplar, birch
Bs*	None in Britain
S	Hazel, ash, rowan
Bsd	Sessile oak, holly, beech, whitebeam

N.B. the same species can exhibit more than one mechanism of regeneration. For example, many willows can regenerate vegetatively (**V**) by means of suckers, but they are also widely dispersed by the production of numerous buoyant seeds (**W**). Holly, on the other hand, produces suckers in combination with persistent juveniles.

* This strategy is not present among British trees. We do have some small shrubs with very persistent seeds; the best known example is heather, which accumulates millions of persistent seeds in the soil of heathlands.

There are certain trees and shrubs – for example, oak, beech, field maple and hawthorn – in which seedling establishment is the only effective method of regeneration, and we may expect therefore that the ecology of these woody species will sometimes be restricted by the effects of environment or land management upon seed production and seedling mortality. Seed production in some trees and shrubs – such as the small-leaved lime (*Tilia cordata*) and probably wild service (*Sorbus torminalis*) – is severely reduced at northern latitudes. The causes of this phenomenon vary with species and location, but they include frost damage to flowers and the failure of fruits to reach maturity.

Within the regions in which seed production is relatively unrestricted by climate, a factor limiting the regeneration of many shrubs and trees is predation by animals and fungi. Seeds and fruits of trees are consumed by a wide range of animals and they are a primary food source for many birds, rodents and primates, as well as the larvae of insects such as micro-*Lepidoptera* and weevils. It is to be expected, therefore, that in addition to their incidental role as agents of dispersal, animals will often function as the most important factor controlling the seed output which survives and germinates. Predation also operates during the seedling phase, where fungal attack and selective feeding by small mammals and invertebrates influence seedling survival. But the most potent effects of animals on trees occur through the grazing activities of larger animals, especially sheep and deer. Where sheep are allowed to graze within woodland, it is often exceedingly difficult to find tree seedlings of any species.

9
Record Trees

'Among all the varied productions with which Nature has adorned the surface of the earth, none awakens our sympathies, or interests our imagination, so powerfully as those venerable trees which seem to have stood the lapse of ages, silent witnesses of the successive generations of man, to whose destiny they bear so touching a resemblance, alike in their budding, their prime and their decay.'

JOHN MUIR, founder of the Sierra Club, writing in 1868 of his first visit to the Yosemite Valley and the nearby redwood forests.

The Bristlecone Pine
This ancient bristlecone pine forest (opposite) is in Methuselah Grove, in the White Mountains of California. The species' longevity is directly related to the harshness of the environment in which it grows.

Clark's Nutcracker
This relative of our native jay collects bristlecone pine seeds and hides them in inaccessible cracks in rocks, so helping the pine seedlings to become established in very unhospitable terrain.

TREES ARE among the most extraordinary forms of life on the planet, and they are also extremely diverse. Record trees are usually defined as being among the largest, the tallest and most remarkably perhaps, the oldest living things. To put our native trees into a world context, they can be compared with some of the extremes of the tree world. The equable climate of these islands means that many species which, in their natural habitats, contribute to the record books can be found growing here, albeit in less spectacular form.

The Bristlecone Pines

Although the redwoods are the largest trees in the world, they are not the oldest. Some yews, including the Fortingall yew, are probably well over 5,000 years old, but as the most ancient ones are invariably hollow, it is impossible to give them a precise age. The oldest trees for which accurate ages have been measured are the ancient bristlecone pines of the White Mountains in California and the Great Basin Lake area in Nevada; 4,300 years is the greatest confirmed age of an individual living tree still standing today.

Bristlecone pine is a rather variable tree which many botanists now put in two separate species: *Pinus aristata* Ergelm. and *Pinus longaeva* D.K. Bailey.

Bristlecone pines grow at a high altitude on the west side of various semi-arid mountain ranges, from the Mexican border north to Colorado. They are an extremely hardy, slow-growing species which can survive the full force of the wind and average monthly temperatures below freezing from November through to April. Even in the summer the average temperature at the altitude in which they grow, usually 2,750–3,500m (9–11,500ft), is only 10°C (50°F), and rainfall is just 30cm (1ft) per year. These are some of the harshest conditions under which any large plants can grow. In general the trees still grow upright even in these extreme conditions, though at the highest altitudes and in some other places mats of creeping trees or Krummholz can be found. Under favourable conditions, usually above 3,000m (10,000ft), heights of 18m (60ft) or more are attained, and individuals may reach a girth of about 5m (16ft), young trees often having long straight trunks and straight limbs. But in the most exposed and drought-prone environments they apparently cease to grow any taller after reaching 4.5-9m (15-30ft) and gradually age into extraordinary contorted shapes with just a few branches of foliage. The needles are five to a bundle, deep green and aromatic, and — most unusually — they continue to function for about 40 years before they fall. The trees are sensitive to severe drought, which is recorded by unusually narrow tree-rings.

Due to the extreme age of many bristlecones and to the fact that the heartwood does not rot, they have been used for dendrochronology

Examples of Bristlecones and Redwoods planted in Britain and Ireland

Bristlecone pines have been planted in some botanic gardens in these islands: the largest specimens are at Bells Wood, Herts (12 x 28) and Leicester University Botanical Garden (12 x 25). Large specimen redwood trees can be seen in many parts of these islands, including the following record trees: *Sequoia sempervirens* at Bodnant Garden, Gwynedd (47 x 159), and at Woodstock, Co. Kilkenny (42 x 245); *Sequoiadendron giganteum* at Castle Leod, Highlands (52 x 281) and at Clunie Garden, Tayside (36 x 345).

The Mammoth Trees of Calaveras Grove

These mammoth trees, later named Sequoiadendron giganteum, *were first discovered by a hunter, A. T. Dowd, in 1852, in Calaveras County, California. Though many of the biggest trees were felled, the grove became a mecca for tourists as this woodcut shows.*

for many years, individual trees and dead trunks yielding continuous records for over 9,000 consecutive years. Such trunks have been used to calibrate radiocarbon dating results in the USA.

In many old trees, parts of the trunk and root system are already dead. Erosion exposes some roots which dry out and die; the wood immediately above them then dies as well, so that the tree may have only part of its root system fully functioning, sending water up through a single sector of healthy sapwood to a few needled limbs while the rest of the tree has become lifeless. Why do these trees grow for so long? Scientists studying plants that grow in extreme conditions have concluded that longevity is directly related to the harshness of the environment in which they live. Trees that grow very slowly often live very much longer than those that grow fast; it is a fallacy to think that very large trees are necessarily the oldest. Professor Mike Baillie, the dendrochronologist at Queen's University, Belfast, has half-seriously claimed that in some cases, size and age seem to be inversely related.

Several factors are likely to affect the longevity of bristlecones growing near the snow-line. The trees are widely scattered, so there is little competition; fewer fires reach them, their extremely slow growth results in denser, more resinous and more decay-resistant wood; and the dry and cold conditions retard the growth of decay organisms. At around 2,750m (9,000ft), the lower limit of their distribution, there is so little snow that even when temperatures are above zero, drought conditions prevail. Higher up the trees grow better as there is more snow-melt.

In spite of the extreme conditions in which they grow, bristlecones reproduce successfully by seed. Pollen is shed from mid-July to early August. The cones are dark purple, and they open to shed seeds in September or October the following year. Very aged trees still produce viable seed; one tree in the White Mountains, which is reckoned to be 4,300 years old, continues to bear cones. Seedling establishment, especially on very hostile slopes, is known to be assisted by a bird, Clark's nutcracker, which at certain times of year feeds off the small seeds of the bristlecones and often collects the seeds and buries them in the soil. As a result many bristlecones are actually small clumps of separate trees that have all germinated in nutcracker caches. A variety of other birds use the dense foliage of bristlecones for nesting. Bristlecone wood is extremely hard and is popular with artists for making woodcuts.

The Redwoods

Great trees are the largest single living organisms that exist on the earth. The largest are the two species of American redwoods: *Sequoiadendron giganteum*, the giant sequoia, and *Sequoia sempervirens*, the coast redwood. These two species do not overlap; the giant sequoia occurring between 1,200m (4,000ft) and 2,400m (8,000ft) on the western slopes of the Sierra Nevada in central California, and the coast redwood occurring along the Californian coast in a belt about 450 miles long, some distance further north than the giant sequoia. While the pencil-slim coast redwood is the world's tallest tree, the giant sequoia is much larger in terms of volume, with an immense trunk which has a very slight taper.

The redwood forests were only discovered by white Americans in the middle of the last century and they soon realized that the timber of both species was excellent. Because of the size and quantity of the trees, and the easy access, especially to the coast redwood forests, an immensely profitable logging industry rapidly built up, regardless of the native American communities dependent on the forests for their livelihood.

Logging started around 1852 and continued unabated for 60 years before the first serious conservation measures were taken. Previously the forests had been used by native Americans, such as the Sinkyone people, for hundreds and even thousands of years. They regarded the redwoods as sacred protectors of the whole forest, especially of the streams on which so much else depended. Redwood groves were the guardians of the spirits of their ancestors, whose sacred burial sites were in redwood groves; today many of these people are still trying to recover their sacred groves, and to protect them from a voracious logging industry that has never given much attention to either sustainable forest use, non-timber forest products, or the rights of the indigenous people in the area.

'So harmonious and finely balanced are even the mightiest of these monarchs in all their proportions that there is never anything overgrown or monstrous about them. One that I measured in the King's River forest was 25 feet in diameter at the ground and ten feet in diameter at 220 feet above the ground, showing the fineness of the taper of the trunk as a whole … Seeing them for the first time you are more impressed with their beauty than their size, their grandeur being in part invisible, but sooner or later it becomes manifest to the loving eye, stealing slowly on the senses…'
JOHN MUIR, Yosemite.

The Indian Fig Tree
This species of tree is thought to have the widest canopy of all: one specimen in Calcutta Botanic Gardens covers an area of nearly three acres. Recent research suggests that these great trees may in fact arise from a number of seedlings and can effectively be groups of interlocking trees, whose stems and roots have actually fused, effectively increasing the genetic diversity of the combined tree.

Such is the interest in and inspirational value of the redwoods that battles between loggers and those who wanted the redwood forests conserved, have been going on since the last century.

In 1918 the Save-the-Redwoods-League was set up by a number of prominent scientists and other public figures to raise money by public subscription to purchase redwood forest and preserve it for public enjoyment. As one of the early founders said, 'cutting the redwood for timber is like lighting your pipe with an ancient Egyptian parchment, rather than going to the trouble of getting some matches to do it.' Since then the Save-The-Redwoods-League has purchased over 135,000 acres which are not part of California's 32 Redwood State Parks. Around $2m continues to be raised every year, and more redwood groves are still being purchased. They still form only a tiny part of the original area covered with redwoods. No redwood groves have as yet been returned to their traditional owners, though a campaign to create and rehabilitate an inter-tribal wilderness in the Sinkyone area has now begun, with the active support of a native American newspaper, the *New World Times*, based in San Francisco.

The Coast Redwood

These are the tallest trees in the world and are native to a section of the Californian coast. A specimen in the Redwood National Park, which measured 112.2m (368ft) in 1990, is thought to be the tallest standing today.

RECORD TREES IN THE WORLD

The bo tree at Anuradhapura in Sri Lanka is the oldest planted tree for which there are continuous records. Originating in about 300 BC, it has been the centre of Buddhist ceremonies on the island ever since.

The Oldest Tree The bristlecone pine (*Pinus aristata* and *Pinus longaeva*) of California and Nevada. The oldest individual recorded is a *P. longaeva* at 4,800 years old. Only an ancient creosote plant (*Larrea tridentata*), at an estimated 11,700 years, is older. The oldest planted tree for which there are continuous records is the Bo tree (*Ficus religiosa*) at Anuradhapura in Sri Lanka, which originated in around 300 BC.

The Tallest Tree The coast redwood (*Sequoia sempervirens*) of California. The tallest standing today is thought to be the National Geographic Society coast redwood in the Redwood National Park, which measured 112.2m (368 ft) in October 1990. But this is not the tallest ever: a eucalyptus (*Eucalyptus regnans*) at Watts River, Victoria, Australia, was 435 ft (132.6m) tall in 1872, and is thought to have been previously over 500 ft (152m).

The Largest Tree The giant redwood (*Sequoiadendron giganteum*) of California. The largest individual recorded is the General Sherman tree in Sequoia National Park, California, which, in 1989, was 83.8m (275ft) tall and had a girth of 25m (82ft) at 1.4m (4ft 8in) above ground.

The tree with the widest canopy is the Indian fig tree (*Ficus benghalensia*) in Calcutta Botanic Garden. Over 400m (1,300ft) in circumference, it covers nearly three acres.

The Smallest Tree The dwarf willow (*Salix herbacea*), growing on the Scottish mountains, usually reaches a height of about 2.5cm (1in).

The Rarest Tree There are several species endemic to remote islands of which only a single living specimen is known: the St Helena Olive (*Nesiota elliptica*), the Caffe Marron (*Ramosmania heterophylla*) from the island of Rodrigues, and *Pennantia baylisiana* from Three Kings Island, off New Zealand.

The Northernmost Tree The Arctic willow (*Salix arctica*) which occurs on the northernmost land at lat. 83' N.

The Deepest Tree Roots A wild fig (*Ficus* spp.), at Echo Caves in South Africa has roots 120m (390ft) deep.

The Most Isolated Tree A single Norway spruce (*Picea abies*), growing on Campbell Island, Antarctica, is over 90 miles (145km) from its nearest companion on the Auckland Islands.

The dwarf willow is probably the smallest tree in the world, at around 1 inch tall. It grows on the tops of Scottish mountains.

10
The Living Fossil Tree

Professor Hsueh Chi-Ju
At the time a graduate student, Hsueh was sent to collect the first specimens of the living fossil tree in 1946. This photograph was taken in 1984, some 38 years later.

THE DISCOVERY of a 'living fossil' is one of the few events in the science of taxonomic biology likely to make the front page of major newspapers. The famous coelacanth fish, thought to have been extinct for 40 million years, made the world's headlines when it was first dredged up from the Indian Ocean; and in the mid-1940s an equally startling discovery was made in the tree world. A living tree was found in a remote part of China that was soon identified as one of the early relatives of the giant redwoods, a genus known only from the fossil record. The story, of what was soon dubbed the 'Dawn Redwood', made headlines around the war-torn world, at a time when newspapers were hardly short of events to report.

In 1941 a Japanese palaeobotanist, Professor Shigeru Miki, created an entirely new genus, *Metasequoia*, to describe some fossil trees found in Japan from the Pliocene period (1.6-5 million years ago); until then they had been confused with redwoods (*Sequoia* spp.) and bald cypresses (*Taxodium* spp.). Fossil *Metasequoia* remains have since been identified from sedimentary deposits in North America, China, Japan, Greenland and Spitzbergen.

Rumours of an unknown tree in the western part of China's Hupeh province began to circulate that same year. A Chinese forester had found an unusual tree; it was unidentifiable without its leaves, but he failed to collect a specimen. His colleagues at the National Central University were interested in his find, so he sent word to a local teacher, asking him to collect some leaves and cones and send them to him. It seems that these never arrived, but the teacher mentioned the strange tree to Professor Z. Wang of the Central Bureau of Forest Research. He collected some cones and a small branch, which he was unable to identify, and these specimens eventually reached Professor W. Cheng at the National Central University at Chungking. At first Cheng thought they were *Glyptostrobus pensilis*, the Chinese water fir, but close examination revealed strange differences; as he said later, 'the leaves and cone-scales were opposite. The specimen looked more like an American Redwood, but that was clearly ridiculous.' Intrigued, he dispatched one of his graduate students, Hsueh Chi-Ju, to collect more complete specimens, including branches bearing male cones.

The tree had been found in an obscure village in the mountains called Modaoqi. Hsueh took a steamboat two days up the Yangtze, and then had to walk 72 miles across country to Modaoqi. He soon found the tree; it was enormous, over 30m (100ft) tall and far too big to climb. It was also completely bare and without leaves. However, Hsueh managed to dislodge some small branches by throwing rocks up at them, and was delighted to find they bore both male and female cones.

Professor Cheng was astonished; the tree was clearly a new species, but what were its affinities? He sent specimens to Peking, where Dr H.

126

Hu, the Director of the Fan Memorial Institute of Biology, checked them carefully and realized what they must be, an ancient relative of the redwoods, of a type never seen before. Hsueh was dispatched again to get more samples and to find out if there were any more trees; he also measured the tree — it was 122ft (37m) high by 23ft (7m) in girth, and apparently growing vigorously.

He was also told that there was another valley 30 miles away where there was a whole grove of such trees. Hu and Cheng then sent specimens to some American scientists with whom they were corresponding: Professor E.D. Merrill, Director of the Arnold Arboretum of Harvard University in Boston and Ralph Chaney the Professor of Palaeobotany at the University of California. In the meantime Chinese scientists drafted a scientific paper describing the new species as *Metasequoia glyptostroboides* Hu & Cheng the first living example of Professor Miki's new genus, a genuine 'living fossil'.

Early in 1948 Professor Chaney decided to go to China at once to see the newly discovered tree. Accompanied by Milton Silverman, science editor of the *San Francisco Chronicle*, he took the trans-Pacific flight to China and then travelled overland across the vast country to the Szechwan border. As can be imagined, the appearance of these two Americans in the remote village of Modaoqi caused something of a stir; with the exception of a missionary or two they were the first westerners to visit the area.

In his book *Search for the Dawn Redwoods* Milton Silverman has described their arrival at the village:

Late in the afternoon the rain stopped, the clouds cleared and for the first time we walked in sunlight, climbing down the last slope into Mo-Tao-Chi. It was market day and the narrow streets were crowded. Men and women alike were dressed in padded jackets and trousers or ankle-length quilted gowns mostly dark blue or black.

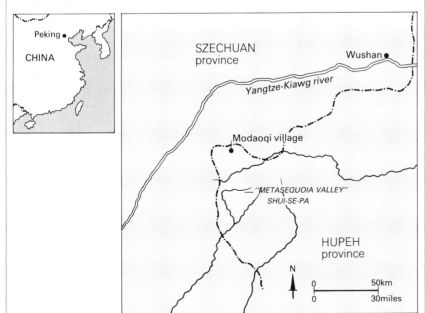

Planted *Metasequoia*

Outside its native area *Metasequoia glyptostroboides* thrives; it is now widely planted in China, especially along roadsides. Research by John Kuser into the health of the trees in botanical gardens, arboreta and other institutional grounds in the US revealed that the trees were thriving in most of the places where they had been planted. In 1981 the tallest American tree in Williamsburg, Virginia, measured 31m (102ft) and was still growing at a rate of about 60cm (2ft) per year — suggesting that by 1991 it must have been at least 36m (120ft) tall.

In 1981 many other trees had reached heights of around 23m (75ft) in America and in various parts of Europe, including Britain. In Britain M. *glyptostroboides* has been planted in many botanical gardens and Forestry Commission estates. The largest specimens today are at Leonardslee, Sussex (30 x 58) and Central Park, Bournemouth (26 x 99)

The Home of the *Metasequoia*
The first Metasequoia was discovered in the remote village of Modaoqi in the western part of Hupeh province. A whole forest of the trees was later found less than 30 miles (50km) away in the Valley of the Tiger near Shui-Se-Pa. It has since become known as 'Metasequoia Valley'.

At the edge of the town was a towering tree, perhaps a hundred feet high and about ten feet in diameter at the base. It was practically bare of needles, and its long, graceful branches were outlined sharply against the sky.

'This is the big Metasequoia,' announced Mr Hwa, our guide. But Chaney was stunned, he had forgotten what Cheng had told him about the tree. 'My God, it's the only redwood tree in the world that's deciduous, and it's dropped all its needles!'

At the great spreading base of the tree was a small shrine, where villagers came to pray and make offerings; it was a sacred tree. 'There must be a god in the tree,' a sixty-year-old villager told us through an interpreter, 'it's the biggest, strongest, straightest tree for many days travel, bigger than any other we have ever seen.'

After asking local villagers they then travelled several days further west to an even more remote valley, where they found a whole forest of *Metasequoia* trees in a place called the Valley of the Tiger, near Shui-Se-Pa. Counting over a thousand trees, they collected cones, branches and even some live seedlings.

Later that year, a larger team of American and Chinese scientists visited the area. The American group was headed by Dr Gressitt of the California Academy of Sciences, who collected a large number of specimens and seeds. In America and elsewhere it had been found that

'Metasequoia Valley'

By 1980, when this photograph was taken, much of the Metasequoia forest near Shui-Se-Pa had lost out to paddy fields. But, as can be seen, many individual trees still remain, though there is little or no natural regeneration.

the seed viability was good; many institutions succeeded in raising seedlings and started planting out the trees. The distribution of seeds happened just in time; within months of Gressitt's expedition, the Red Army defeated the Kuomintang, a Communist government headed by Mao Tse Tung was installed, and all travel to the area was forbidden.

Nothing further was heard of the dawn redwoods in China for nearly 30 years; the area was closed to foreigners and scientific exchanges stopped. There was serious deforestation in that part of China and evidence from elsewhere suggested that this would have got worse: had the dawn redwoods survived?

They certainly had survived in botanic gardens throughout the world so that when the first scientific exchanges between China and the outside world took place in the late 1970s, many of the planted trees were already fine specimens. This was true for *Metasequoia*, as well as for various other rare Chinese trees such as dove trees and paperbark maples, which had been collected in the 1930s and earlier. When an official Chinese delegation visited the Arnold Arboretum in 1979 they were delighted to find these Chinese trees growing well in New England; some of the Chinese scientists had not visited those parts of China themselves and had never seen the trees before.

In 1980 an expedition of American and Chinese botanists was allowed to visit and study the *Metasequoias*. At Modaoqi they found the original tree still standing — though the small shrine had been removed during the Cultural Revolution — and hundreds of other *Metasequoias* had been planted along the roads near the village. There were still many trees at Shui-Se-Pa, but the area had lost nearly all its natural forest — all but the steepest slopes being turned into agricultural land.

Since 1974 the Bureau of Forestry of the Lichuan Xian area, which includes both the *Metasequoia* sites, has stationed foresters in the area; one of their jobs has been to keep a census of the trees up to date every four years. By 1980, 5,420 trees with a diameter at breast height of over 20cm (8in) had been measured, of which nearly 1,800 were large, mature seed-producing trees, several of them over 50m (164ft) tall.

Since the 1940s a number of trees and groups of trees have also been found at various other places in the region, within about 40 miles of Modaoqi. In its natural habitat *Metasequoia* is now protected by the Chinese government, and not even small trees may be cut. However intense fuel-wood cutting and cultivation in the area had already resulted in an absence of seedlings in 1980. A number of other plants had been recorded as associated with *Metasequoia* at Shui-Se-Pa, but by 1980 most of these had disappeared. It is not known what the present situation is. As a result of their visit the American botanists estimated that 'the protected status of *Metasequoia* will probably ensure their survival for the immediate future', but they were concerned that 'the lack of protection for the surrounding habitat will result in little if any natural reproduction.' The thickets near many of the trees that had been reported in the 1940s had by now gone, yet these were the very places where seedlings had been growing; it was feared that in their enthusiasm to monitor the adult trees the local foresters may have contributed to the destruction of suitable germination sites.

The Living Fossil Tree
This is the original Metasequoia *from which Hsueh collected his samples in 1946. The photograph was taken in 1980.*

11

Socotra's Strange Trees

The Sack-of-Potatoes Tree
Known locally as 'Desert Rose' on account of the attractive pink flowers it produces in winter, this tree (above) can sometimes suggest the human form, with the navel-like depressions in its trunk.

The Cucumber Tree
The only cucumber that grows into a tree (opposite), it can also shed all its leaves and withdraw into this white carapace-like trunk during periods of extreme drought.

Why Socotra's Trees are Unique

As Darwin first noted, small oceanic islands can produce numerous species of closely related organisms — birds in particular — that are found nowhere else. Plants exhibit the same phenomenon, and the island of Socotra — like Mauritius, further to the south in the Indian Ocean — is one such treasure-house. Socotra has been separated from the mainland long enough for many unusual tree species to have evolved in the absence of large grazing mammals but with the stresses caused by regular sustained drought.

FOR CENTURIES, herbalists and astrologers knew of a mysterious substance with powerful healing and even magical properties known as dragon's blood. It came in hard rounded lumps that looked as if they could indeed be the dried droplets of blood from a large animal — even a dragon. Ancient writers such as Pliny also described a strange mountainous island where dragons were thought to live, far away in the eastern ocean. Rumour of a dragon's island called Socotra was also linked with the tales of Sinbad the Sailor, who was shipwrecked on an island where the monstrous bird known as the roc lived. Nor was the mysterious and alarming aura that surrounded Socotra entirely dispelled when the first modern scientific expedition, led by the Scottish botanist I. B. Balfour, visited the island in the 1880s; there was no sign of dragons, but in their place were a whole range of plants unlike any that had ever been seen before. Above the coastal plain they found that much of the island was wooded, yet of all the trees they found, practically none resembled any previously known species.

Since Balfour's time there have been several further biological expeditions to Socotra. In terms of sheer numbers of species, the tropical rain forests of both the Old World and the New World are perhaps more interesting: a wider range of indigenous tree species can be found in a hectare of Amazonia than occur in Socotra or the whole of Britain and Ireland for that matter. But the trees of Socotra are about as different from our native trees as they could be. Indeed, the only family of trees we share is the *Buxaceae*, or box trees. Not only are most of Socotra's trees found growing naturally nowhere else on earth, but the regular periods of severe drought have resulted in some very odd-looking specimens. Swollen-trunked and bottle-shaped trees predominate, giving a surreal look to the entire landscape.

Socotra has been isolated from Africa and Arabia since Tertiary times (1.6-5 million years ago), and indeed the higher mountains are thought never to have been submerged since the Pre-Cambrian period. During this long isolation many unique plants have evolved. Indeed what excites botanists and tree enthusiasts so much, is that of around 800 plant species now recorded from the island, over a third are endemic, including 25 trees.

Socotra's Trees

Dragon's blood does not after all come from dragons, real or imaginary, but is the dried resin of one of these endemic trees. Distantly related to palms, the dragon's blood tree (*Dracaena cinnabari*) looks at a distance like a giant mushroom. It tends to grow on exposed surfaces, especially cliff tops, which gives its appearance an even more dramatic air. The main trunk grows straight for about 3 to 4 metres before dividing into a host of equal branches; these then form an inverted cone, with a circular

Socotra's Climate

The climate of Socotra is sub-tropical but dry, with a prolonged and fierce dry season during several months of the year when hot north-east trade winds blast the island, causing serious droughts. Rain usually falls in December and January, and less frequently in May and June, but the amounts are irregular. Total rainfall is more than for other low-lying parts of the Arabian region, averaging between 150mm (6in) on the north coast and around 500mm (20in) in the Hagghier Mountains.

The Island of Socotra

Socotra lies just off the Horn of Africa, about 150 miles (210km) east of the north Somalian coast. The island is about 80 miles (130km) from end to end (west to east) and, at its widest, is no more than 25 miles (40km) across.

area of spiky foliage on the top. A single tree is a strange enough sight; a hillside covered with dragon's blood trees is one of the wonders of the tree world.

Even stranger than the dragon's blood tree is another of Socotra's endemic trees, the cucumber tree (*Dendrosicyos socotranum*). This has a bloated whitish trunk which grows to a height of about 4m (13ft) and is topped with an untidy crown of short stubby branches. The leaves seem to emerge from the ends of the branches like dark green toothpaste squeezed from a monstrous white tube. In the regular drought conditions the leaves turn brown and drop off, leaving the smooth woody parts to brave the dry summer winds. *D. socotranum* is the only member of the cucumber family, *Cucurbitaceae*, that grows into a tree, and is perhaps typical of the strange organisms that can evolve, given time, in isolated places. The seedlings are probably eaten by goats, but the cucumber tree may have evolved without the presence of large grazing herbivores, though the island does have a small desert gazelle. Today the only seedlings of the cucumber tree that survive the attentions of the goats appear to be those which establish themselves under heavy cover, such as the dead leaves around date palms or among dense and low bushes in semi-desert areas. At times of extreme drought, the local people sometimes cut down cucumber trees and feed the pith and soft heartwood to the goats.

In the winter months, after the rains, *D. socotranum* flowers and fruits; the flowers are small and yellow with narrow greenish-yellow petals, while the fruits are diminutive cucumbers which turn red on ripening. On Socotra the cucumber tree grows on the coastal plain and up on to the lower slopes of the mountains — some limestone and some granitic. In spite of its often rather droopy appearance, as if its trunk was an insufficiently inflated rubber toy, the cucumber tree appears to be highly successful at resisting drought as it can be found thriving even in the desert of the Nogud Plain, on the south side of the island, and on the most exposed cliffs on the north coast, which face the full force of the north-east trade winds.

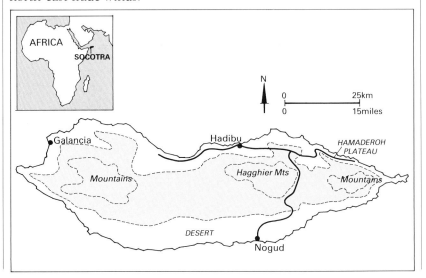

Growing among both the cucumber trees near the coast and the dragon's blood trees further up the mountain slopes, is an even more extraordinary tree, a sort of slug of the tree world known as the sack-of-potatoes tree (*Adenium socotranum*). This poisonous lump, with its ridiculous apology for foliage apparently added on as an afterthought, could be mistaken for a sculptor's reject, a failed attempt at the portrayal of bulk without content. Disturbingly, some individual trees seem to suggest the human form — an impression that is reinforced by the frequent small depressions in the smooth bark, which look like navels in a pale unhealthy human skin. Apparently contradicting its strange appearance, the tree produces a mass of attractive pink flowers in the winter, as a result of which it is also known in the local language as the 'desert rose'. A poison, a cardiac glycoside, is extracted from the soft *Adenium* wood and used to poison fish, much as some related *Adenium* species are used in Africa. Socotrans throw chips of *Adenium* wood into pools when the fish are abundant, making them lethargic and therefore easy to catch.

The seeds are probably distributed by birds, and *Adenium* trees often germinate in the most unpromising places — on cliffs and even in crevices on single limestone boulders. The seedlings start off quite normally, but when they reach about 30cm (12in), they begin to assume the appearance of a traditional Chianti bottle, and for the rest of their lives they grow outwards at least as much as upwards. This is obviously an even more successful drought-resisting strategy than that of the cucumber tree; *Adenium* groves cover hundreds of hillsides throughout the island, looking like giant bottles that have been set up on a fantastic fairground stall.

Ever since Balfour's first visit, scientists have been fascinated by two less obviously strange but much rarer endemic trees — *Dirachma socotrana*, a botanical curiosity that has petals and sepals in rings of eight, and *Punica protopunica*, the only known wild relative of the pomegranate. Both have been given Red Data Book status by the International Union for the Conservation of Nature, as they are only known to exist at one or two isolated sites, with small numbers of trees growing at each.

Dirachma socotrana is a small wiry tree that grows in crevices on the limestone hills. Its attractive foliage looks similar to that of oak with much smaller leaves; it is not a particularly striking tree, but it has been the subject of two separate botanical controversies. The small white flowers are most unusual in having seven or eight petals; the fruits are like those of a geranium. Balfour placed it taxonomically in the *Geraniaceae*, but since then botanists have argued whether it should be in a family of its own, the *Dirachmaceae*, or regarded as an anomalous member of the *Geraniaceae*. The second controversy involves its wood, and its 'endangered' status. It was thought that the tree only occurred at a single site, and when Dr Q. Kronk, a Cambridge botanist who visited the island in 1985 on behalf of the World Wildlife Fund, failed to find any examples, alarm bells sounded. Concern was expressed about its possible extinction as the result of its alleged cutting by local people for its sweet-smelling wood.

Wild Pomegranates
Socotra is the home of the only known wild relative of the pomegranate. The specimens found there vary greatly in shape, size and colour, suggesting a large genetic diversity which could be useful for plant breeders in the future.

DRAGON'S BLOOD

The people of Socotra have, for centuries, collected the lumps of resin that ooze out from between the branches on certain mature trees. To obtain the best quality of dragon's blood, specific trees are climbed at certain times of year, and the resin drops carefully collected. The commoner variety is made from freshly-trimmed sections of the bark, which are stripped off with a large knife, pounded with a stone, and then cooked in a pan over a wood fire; the bark quickly turns a dark red and becomes a thick oily mass, which is cooled on a stone in hamburger-size cakes. Dragon's blood contains various compounds including cinnabar (mercuric chloride), and its known medicinal effects are as a strong astringent, and as an involuntary muscle relaxant. It is used on Socotra both internally and externally for treating a wide range of ailments, and throughout Arabia is much in demand, as it is thought to have magical as well as curative properties. Dragon's blood is also used as a dark red glaze on local pottery, from water-vessels to censers for burning aromatic resins.

A relative of the dragon tree of the Canary Islands, dragon's blood trees are endemic to Socotra. They can be found covering whole hillsides on the island, creating one of the strangest landscapes in the world.

Recently Dr Tony Miller of Edinburgh Botanic Gardens and Dr Luigi Guarino of the International Board for Plant Genetic Resources have visited the island with Yemeni scientists from the El-Kod Research Station in Aden to assess and map the flora of the whole island, particularly looking at the endangered endemic species. With the help of local people and the ethnographer Dr Miranda Morris, they established that fears for the immediate future of *D. socotrana* were fortunately unfounded. The aromatic wood in question, known locally as 'drachmam', is now known to come from another endemic but much commoner tree, *Cephalocroton socotrana*, and in any case is never cut; only the dead wood is collected. The odourless wood of *Dirachma socotrana* is known locally as 'tifit', and has little importance.

The importance of trees to human survival on Socotra in the face of regular severe droughts is very well understood by the whole community. There is no formal government in the country areas, where the land and grazing rights are held by family clans, sisters as well as brothers inheriting land, livestock and goods such as date palms. The people keep goats, sheep, camels, donkeys and the local Socotran breed of dwarf cattle. Date palms are cultivated in the river valleys, and, apart from rice, which has been imported in the last ten years or so, Socotrans depend mostly on dates, milk, meat, and wild fruits. They live in small hamlets of stone-built huts that belong to members of a single clan.

As a result of interviewing local people all over Socotra, Dr Morris has established that nearly all the trees, as well as many other plants, are used for fuel, food, animal fodder, building materials, medicines, dyes, glue, fibres, tanning materials, insecticides, cosmetics, tinder, and other products — including a sticky lime with which to trap birds, manufactured from the latex of a species of fig. Several endemic trees are used as fodder for animals, and a number of gums and resins are collected.

All the trees in each area are carefully conserved by the members of the clan, who know very well that in times of drought they will need them to provide fodder for their animals, without which their supplies of milk would be endangered.

As a result, and presumably arising from bitter experience, there are very strict rules about which trees should be used for what purpose and when. Indeed there is effectively a total ban on the felling of useful live trees at all times except in emergency. The only live woody plants that are felled are the ubiquitous *Croton socotranum* shrubs and one or two other unimportant trees. At a very early age children learn that only dead wood should be collected for firewood.

This situation was demonstrated in a dramatic way when an old man took me to see a tree of the *Zizyphus* species that he had just felled in order to build a new hut to replace one that had been washed away in the recent floods. Three herdsmen discovered him trimming it into shape, and wanted to arrest him for cutting a growing tree and arraign him before the whole clan. Only after detailed explanations were they persuaded that the cutting was justified. Social pressure for the conservation of trees is extremely strong, and there is local concern in some areas about the paucity of certain sorts of tree seedling, and the possibility of over-grazing by goats. This is tempered by the knowledge that the numbers of livestock have been very much higher within living memory, without apparently damaging the island's vegetation too severely.

Two species of Socotran trees are used for collecting resin for frankincense (*Boswellia socotrana*) and myrrh (*Commiphora planifrons*), but these are not the only uses of these trees. The entire ecosystem has clearly provided a wide range of products to the local people on a sustainable basis for several millennia, and though some of the vegetation seems overgrazed, there is little sign of the soil erosion found in many other semi-arid parts of the world that are exposed to intense grazing pressure. Several Socotran trees are lopped for fodder during the dry season on a regular basis, including the frankincense tree.

The present status of the endemic flora of Socotra is a matter of debate, but at present stocking levels it is thought that the system is in balance and is not being degraded. None the less, recent scientific surveys by Dr Miller's team have concluded that very careful monitoring of the fragile yet genetically unique flora is essential, if irretrievable damage is not to result from some of the planned developments — such as widespread tube-well construction, leading to the expansion of both grazing flocks and arable cultivation.

The People of Socotra

The population of the island is entirely Moslem, of mixed African and Arabic descent, and probably numbers around 40-50,000 at present. Arabic is spoken on the coast, but the main language, Socotran, is a non-Arabic language and is related to the languages spoken in parts of Dhofar in Arabia. At one time, possibly up to the seventeenth century, the island was Christian, and archaeologists have uncovered the remains of at least one early church. The Portuguese occupied Socotra between 1507 and 1511, after which it was ruled by the Mahri Sultan from what is now the eastern part of southern Yemen. In the late nineteenth century the Sultan accepted British 'protection' for the entire sultanate. After independence in 1967 the sultanate was abolished and the island became part of the independent state of South Yemen. This was united with North Yemen in 1991 to form the Republic of Yemen, with its capital in Sana'a.

12

The Folklore of Trees

The Money Tree

The 'money tree' at Clanenagh, Co. Laois, stands outside a graveyard a few miles from Portlaoise on the main Dublin to Limerick road. An old sycamore pollard, it is associated with the Holy Well of St Fintan, though this is some distance away. Tradition has it that St Fintan dropped some water on the tree and that the ever-damp hollow in the trunk is taken to be a trickle of holy water. Pilgrims used to tie clothing on the tree for luck, but in recent years a tradition has developed of hammering coins into the bark. There are now thousands of such coins in the tree, which also seems to have suffered somewhat from having innumerable small pieces cut from its trunk as lucky mementoes.

'*The roots of the tree are in the underworld, within the earth; the trunk of the tree is in the middle-earth where we live and walk; and the branches of the tree reach up towards the heavens, towards the sun. People recognize that trees are sacred, it's where they connect with the spirit of the earth, the spirit of life.*'

HAZEL BIRCH of Tree Spirit

SACRED TREES are found in every country, and for some people their first response to a tree is a spiritual one. Even in the materialistic western world, nobody laughs about trees, though the idea of 'communing with Nature' may be considered eccentric or amusing. In many cultures trees are held to be sacred, even feared. Individual trees are at the very centre of certain civilizations; to many American Indians and other indigenous peoples all over the world, many trees are sacred, and their ancestral groves are the holiest places on earth.

Buddha gained enlightenment while sitting under a Bo or Bhodi tree (*Ficus religiosa*), from the family *Moraceae*; detailed records at Anuradhapura in Sri Lanka show that the Bo tree which is still standing there has been at the focal point of the spiritual life of the island for over 2,300 years. Oak and yew trees were at the spiritual centre of Celtic, Saxon and other early civilizations in Britain and Ireland. The fact that Jesus was crucified on a wooden cross created an inextricable link between trees and Christian witness, though the fact that trees were revered before Christianity has inevitably connected them in the minds of some Christians with paganism. Indeed early Christian missionaries were generally hostile to sacred trees: in the eleventh century the Church made it an offence to build a sanctuary around a tree. In Ireland there is a widespread belief, of pre-Christian origin, that the 'little people' live in or near fairy trees: they must at all costs be respected, otherwise harm will come to those involved.

The folklore of trees in Britain is still little documented, except as incidental items about country customs or passing references in accounts of cultural history. Three or four thousand years ago these islands were more or less covered with trees, as was most of northern and central Europe until much more recently. Trees and forests must then have had a much greater impact on people's consciousness; as Frazer points out in *The Golden Bough*, 'nothing could be more natural than the worship of trees' throughout Europe at a time when the solitude, gloom and silence of the vast forests made a deep impression even on Roman Emperors. He suggests that researches into the etymology of the Teutonic word 'temple' make it probable that the oldest sanctuaries among the Germans at least, were natural woods and sacred groves. Yet, although trees were at the centre of the spiritual and cultural life of the Celts, this concept may be difficult for most contemporary researchers to accept: in most published works on Celtic culture and history little mention is made of trees or their spiritual significance. Those who are leading investigations into the cultural and spiritual aspects of trees are not generally historians at all. Two of the leading figures are Roy Vickery, a professional scientist and the curator of Flowering Plants at the Natural History Museum, London, and Dr Patricia Lysaght of University College, Dublin, a lawyer and an expert on the Irish language.

Tree lore is much better recorded in Ireland and in northern Europe — both areas in which ancient traditions involving trees are still found or at least remembered — than in mainland Britain. There are very few records of ancient folk traditions centred on trees in England, Scotland and Wales; in spite of the survival of many ancient yew trees, few of the beliefs and traditions surrounding them can still be traced. Indeed the existence of important ancient yews, such as that at Ankerwycke, formerly part of Runnymede, was forgotten until Allen Meredith's recent researches (see p.82-84).

Keith Thomas mentions a few fragmentary beliefs which suggest that folklore of the kind that is well-documented in Ireland may also have been widespread in England at least, and probably also in Wales and Scotland: that rowan could protect against witchcraft — in Cheshire it was thought bad luck to cut one down — and that ash trees over holy wells, such as St Bertram's Well in Staffordshire, were not to be damaged. He also quotes 'Histories from the Forest of Dean' in which miners would only take an oath on the Bible if they were holding a holly stick at the same time. But today such memories are scarce.

Sacred Trees of Ireland

In Ireland the term sacred tree is taken to mean a tree that is 'treated with a certain reverence which normally protects them from wilful damage or cutting'. This still applies to many ancient trees in Ireland, whether or not they have other holy or supernatural connections. Dr A.T. Lucas, former director of the National Museum of Ireland, refers to celebrated trees such as the 'Big Bell Tree' in Co. Tipperary, the Red Cross Tree and the 'Monument Tree' of Co. Meath and a tree known as 'Gurthavella' in Co. Kilkenny. A famous ash tree, now disappeared, the *crann o hullo* at Killura in Co. Cork, was claimed to be endowed with a very special property: anyone in possession of even the smallest

Who or what are 'the fairies'?

The belief in a hidden race of people, close to humans but normally invisible to us, is a very ancient and widespread one. According to an eighth-century hymn, the Irish worshipped the gods of the *sidh* (the modern 'fairy faith') until St Patrick converted them. Christianity provided a new frame of reverence in which to place them: they became the fallen angels, not good enough for heaven but, on the other hand, not bad enough for hell.

Since the Great Famine of the mid-nineteenth century, popular religious belief, including fairy lore and other aspects of traditional culture, has generally declined, but because of the secretive nature of fairylore it is hard to quantify this or trace the details. Although fairy legends are still told in Ireland, few of them are set in the very recent past. Fairylore has largely lost its hold on the people, and its remaining vestiges are connected with sacred sites on the landscape, such as fairy glens and lone trees.

The Great Ash of Leix
One of the most famous 'named trees' of medieval Ireland, it finally died and was removed in the early nineteenth century.

RAG TREES

At some holy wells, the trees are known as 'prayer trees' or 'rag trees'. Fragments of cloth or garments are tied to the branches as offerings, a custom that can be found in many countries. At Paphos in Cyprus, for example, a terebinth tree (*Pistacia terebinthus*) that grows from the ancient underground chapel dedicated to Ayia Solomon, a local early Christian martyr, is continually festooned with offerings from people hoping for cures for particular ailments. Since most of the garments tied to the branches appear to be handkerchiefs it seems very likely that the main affliction for which help is sought is heartbreak!

There are few such trees in England, though the arbor tree at Aston-on-Clun, Shropshire, is always decorated and has a tradition that cut pieces of its branches will bring fertility, especially for newly-married couples in the area. The early stages of popular consecration can be observed near Enfield on the A10 Cambridge road out of London, at the site of a fatal road accident some years ago. A horse chestnut tree, one of a long roadside line, is regularly garlanded and festooned with flowers, originally just by the mother of the dead youth. Other people have started adding small offerings, but presumably now 'for luck', like a wishing well. And at Barnes Common, in south London, the sycamore tree which caused the death in a car crash of the pop musician Marc Bolan in 1973 is still regularly bedecked with flowers, fan-letters and a variety of other memorabilia, fifteen years after his death.

Marc Bolan died when his car hit this sycamore (above) on Barnes Common, London. The terebinth tree (below) at Paphos, Cyprus.

fragment of it would never die from drowning, with the result that in the nineteenth century, large numbers of would-be emigrants from all parts of Ireland provided themselves with chips or twigs of this particular tree. Many trees at holy wells are still thought to offer such protection, and pieces are still cut from them and kept by pilgrims and local people.

Another widespread characteristic of sacred trees is that of affording sanctuary. In ancient Greek mythology, Orestes, fleeing from the Furies, found sanctuary under Apollo's laurel, and there are many similar tales right up to the present time. Since yew trees pre-date Christian churches here it may even be that the tradition of the church offering sanctuary was in part an inherited tradition that became 'Christianized'.

Specific categories of Irish sacred trees identified by Lucas include trees sited at the places where ancient chieftains or kings of Ireland were inaugurated, trees associated with saints (and therefore with churches), trees associated with funerals, trees at holy wells, and 'lone bushes' or fairy trees.

The spiritual and earthly power of rulers or chieftains in ancient Ireland is thought to have been closely related to sacred trees and their survival as an appropriate adjunct to a chiefly or kingly residence. They were almost certainly more than this, centres of ritual or holy places at the centre of tribal territories. In times of war they would therefore be prime targets, their destruction symbolizing the total submission of the tribe. There are many accounts in early Irish manuscripts of such trees or even groves of trees being destroyed by conquering armies or rival chieftains.

Holy wells can be traced back to the earliest written records in Ireland; there may be as many as 3,000 holy wells in Ireland, many of which have individual trees associated with them. Lucas made a random survey of 210 such wells scattered across the country, and found that by far the commonest associated trees were 'whitethorn' (hawthorn)

St Patrick's Well
The holy water from this well near Enfield, Co. West Meath, is claimed to cure eye disease. The water emerges from between the roots of an ancient ash tree.

MARIE FITZPATRICK'S FAIRY TREE

Near the shore at Ballyshannon is another and larger ivy-covered fairy tree, on land belonging to Mrs Marie Fitzpatrick.

Mrs Fitzpatrick's tree is a hawthorn; there are many local tales about misfortunes occurring to people who did not 'respect' it. A farmer lost his cattle after using branches from the tree to keep them from breaking out of a field; another man who burned some of the branches was dead within the year, and at his wake the neighbours were shocked to see that he had become 'like a fairy man, all wizened'. Marie Fitzpatrick also relates a story she was told by an aunt who died in 1989: apparently her children found some green pods under the tree, and 'when she opened them there were what looked like little men inside. She made the children put them back under the tree immediately.'

Wish-bone shaped,
One arm upright, on guard, bearded in green,
the other horizontal,
Giving suck to its tiny offspring,
I stand beneath its out-stretched arm,
Lean against the trunk,
Ponder on the half-remembered lore.
An aura of mystery entraps
A haunting thought;
Am I deceived in seeing it a tree?
Or,
Have people just made it
A monument to magic of the past?
In the unsure silence all around,
I am whispering innocence,
That strokes the gnarled bark,
That suffered many seasons,
Living near a Donegal shore.

Jimmy Burke's Fairy Tree

Jimmy Burke (below) is the owner of the land in the Blue Stack Mountains in Co. Donegal where this fairy tree (above right) stands. Misfortune is said to visit all those who attempt to damage or destroy this small but aged rowan.

(103), and ash (75) which together made up 85 per cent of the total, others being oak (7), willow (6), elder (5), holly (4), rowan (3), alder (3), elm (2), yew (1), and fir (1). He goes on to say that the frequency of ash — an important timber tree in a much deforested country — is in itself 'a testimony to the sacred character of the trees growing there, for nothing else could have saved them from use as fuel or timber in a country as starved of wood as was the greater part of Ireland during the eighteenth and nineteenth centuries, when the dearth of timber was such that the winning of semi-fossil bog-timber developed into a major rural industry.'

Although ancient yew trees are very scarce in Ireland today — two examples from Co. Wicklow are the only ones over 6m (20ft) in girth — there are many references to yew trees in ancient chronicles and in 'fairy tales', oral history of the kind collected by Séan ó Eochaidh in his authoritative *Fairy Legends from Donegal*. According to a typical tale,

> *Oilean an Iuir (Island of Yew) has always been an enchanted island and the tree which grows in it is enchanted also. It used to be said that the best curach ribs (for boat-building) in Tir Chonaill could be made from the tree, but no-one ever had the courage to cut a bit from it... A fisherman from Gola began to gather some of the wood, and immediately the water in the lake began to rise until waves were going clean over the island. A man herding across the lake shouted to him to throw down the wood or he would be drowned. No sooner had he done so than the lake calmed down until it was as smooth as the page of a book. Since then no-one has ever gone back to gather curach ribs there.*

There are myriad tales about fairy trees causing misfortune to those that damage or destroy them. It was widely claimed that the De Lorean car factory in Belfast failed because a fairy tree had been removed to make way for it, and in many places roads have been re-routed and planned buildings re-located to take account of fairy trees.

At Shanveen in the Blue Stack Mountains, Co. Donegal, a local man, the late Jimmy Burke, had at least two fairy trees growing on his land. One of these, a small rowan, grows on an isolated pile of rocks, in the middle of a bog: according to Jimmy Burke, 'If you damaged the tree you could wake up in the morning and find your hair gone; I do go in the field where it is but I would never touch it or have anything to do with it. If you interfered with the tree, or tried to cut it, you can be sure something would come upon you.'

This particular fairy tree bears an ancient scar on its trunk. According to Jimmy this dates from an attempt by three youths to cut it down and destroy it 50 years ago: 'They were trying to break it, but they weren't able to, though they did split it and trampled on it. But the next day the tree was up again and it's been growing away ever since.'

Joseph of Arimathea
According to legend, the original Glastonbury thorn grew from Joseph's staff when he pushed it into the ground on Wearyall Hill in AD 63.

Sacred Trees of Britain

In England perhaps the most celebrated sacred tree is the Glastonbury Thorn. According to legend, the original tree originated from Joseph of Arimathea's staff, after he had thrust it into the ground on Wearyall Hill on his arrival in Britain in AD 63. Some writers have suggested that the fact of its growing was seen as a miracle, and because of the Holy Thorn Joseph settled in Glastonbury. The fact that the tree bloomed at or near Christmas (12 days later than now, in the old Gregorian calendar) was taken as further evidence that it was a holy tree. It is said that the ancient stump of the original tree remained visible on Wearyall Hill until the mid-eighteenth century, though this seems most unlikely. Many trees since then have been grown from cuttings of the original and its descendants. The oldest Holy Thorn in Glastonbury, which was planted outside St John's Church around 1900, finally died in 1991, but

The Old Holy Thorn
This holy thorn, in front of St John's Church, Glastonbury, died in 1991. Its mantle has now been assumed by a younger thorn growing nearby.

THE SIGNIFICANCE OF TREES IN ANCIENT SCOTLAND

by Ian Brodie

The forest and its trees had a profound significance for the Celtic peoples — and nowhere more so than in Scotland. Indeed, the name 'Caledonia', which was used throughout history by many writers from Ptolemy and the Romans onwards is probably derived from the Celtic words *coille* and *dun*, which translate as 'forest fortress'.

To the ancient inhabitants of Scotland — whether pre-Celts, Brythonic Celts or the later Goedelic Celts — the forest was of immense importance and significance as a place that provided sanctuary in times of conflict, food in the form of meat, plants and fungi, fuel with which to heat and light their houses, and timber for building both houses and fortifications.

Amongst Celts, the main tree species were known by different names and, each letter in the Gaelic alphabet is the name of a tree. Children were taught their alphabet by listing the trees rather than by the letters, which was useful as an aid to memory and also helped the children to learn about the forest around them. For example, A=*Ahhall*, Apple tree; B=*Beith*, Birch tree; C=*Calltuinn*, Hazel tree; D=*Dair*, Oak tree; etc.

It was not just individual trees that were sacred; the very forest itself was believed to be the spiritual home for several gods and goddesses, including Deirdre, who was known to the Greeks as Diana. There were also areas of forest around sacred wells where cloths were hung on the branches of trees as offerings, a practice that is still continued in parts of rural Scotland today.

Different tribes used certain forest trees as totems, a practice which has continued down to the present day. The clans had 'plant badges' as part of their cultural identification. For example, the clan Brodie was associated with juniper, Cameron with oak, Colquhoun with hazel, Fraser with yew and Grant with pine.

Around 6-7,000 years ago up to 80 per cent of Scotland was covered in forest, but much of this has now disappeared or been destroyed. It is however, still very easy to find out what types of tree grew in areas now completely devoid of trees by looking at the place names, which still include the Gaelic names of particular trees. These fall into two categories, the first of which has the word more or less unaltered in spelling, whilst the second is partially hidden because the word may have been anglicized. Examples of the first would include Carn Beith (the birch cairn) and Loch Ghiuthsachan (the loch of the pines), whereas examples of the second include Callander/Coille an Darrach (the oak forest) and Calton Hill/Calltuinn (the hill of the hazels). To many Scots these names are a constant reminder of what their homeland has lost.

The forest was of vital significance to the Celts, providing sanctuary, food and fuel. However the days when Scotland used to be covered in vast swathes of woodland are long gone and now little naturally regenerating forest remains.

younger trees grow nearby and in the grounds of the ruined Abbey, and in many other places including Wells, Bath and Appleton Thorn in Cheshire.

At Appleton, there has been a succession of trees derived from an original cutting brought to Cheshire about 1178 by Adam de Dutton, a Crusader knight who made a pilgrimage to Glastonbury to give thanks for his safe return from the Holy Land. In medieval times there was an annual festival of 'bawning' or decorating the throne in June; this old custom was resurrected in 1973, and now takes place on the third Saturday in June every year. Further afield, a tree said to have been brought from Glastonbury grows in the New York Botanic Garden, where it blooms in spring and in late autumn, but not at Christmas.

The legend of a tree growing from dry staffs, usually in the hands of saints is found fairly frequently in Britain. For instance, a fig tree which grows from the south wall of the church at St Newlyn East in Cornwall, is said to have sprouted from the staff of St Newlina, an obscure virgin martyr. Again there is a tradition that anyone harming the tree will suffer, and, in 1978, the then vicar recorded that 'from time to time the tree has to be pruned, but by a remarkable series of coincidences some of those who have done so have met with misfortune or death'.

May Festivals

The summer festival of May Day, or *Bealtaine* in Scotland and Ireland, can be traced back to Celtic traditions of dividing the year into two halves, May Day signalling the start of the warmer summer half. The other seasonal festivals are of similarly ancient origin; *Lughnasa* (Lammas), the harvest festival in early August, *Samhain*, which marks the beginning of winter in October, and the ancient festival of the winter solstice that has now become Christmas.

Several 'verdure traditions', symbolizing the vitality and fertility of summer are still found in Ireland: May flowers, May bough, May bush, and the maypole. The maypole tradition is the only one also found in England, although the May bush tradition appears only in the eastern parts of Ireland and is thought to have come from England.

THE MAYPOLE

The maypole tradition as a spring festival is widespread in Europe. Maypoles are erected and act as the central point for celebrations on May Day in various places in England though they are mostly recent revivals of popular ancient customs. Historically the May King and May Queen were chosen from among the local young people, who then went to a nearby forest to cut and bring in a maypole. The type of tree varied in different places, but it would sometimes be birch or, in Germany, fir. This would be erected, often after the bark had been peeled, and decorated with ribbons, flowers or green foliage. The local people would then assemble and dance round the maypole to 'awaken the spirits of spring and ward off evil spirits'. Such activities can still be found in many parts of Europe. In England May festivals are held in several places among them St Mary's in the Scilly Isles, Torrington in Devon, Cerne Abbas in Dorset and St Martha's Hill in Guildford but it is not clear whether any of these are long-standing traditions rather than recent revivals. The Floral or Furry Dance at Helston in Cornwall has a similar significance, and is held on 8 May. Maypole traditions were also found in Ireland, but only in parts of Ulster and the south-east, where English influence was strongest. There seems to be no indigenous tradition of maypoles or May bushes in Ireland.

The May flowers are fresh seasonal blooms such as primroses, cowslips, marsh marigolds etc. that are scattered on doorsteps and window-sills, house and cow-byre roofs, and around wells.

The May bough consists of the small branch of a newly leafed tree (hazel, elder, rowan or ash, but not hawthorn) that is usually brought into the house unadorned, and placed over the door, on window-sills or over the fire. May (hawthorn) blooms are not brought into the house; this is widely thought to be unlucky even in England. In Co. Cork branches of sycamore, known as 'summer tree', are used as May bough.

The May bush is usually a small whitethorn (hawthorn) bush in full leaf that is cut on May Eve and decorated with yellow May flowers and blue flowers, such as bluebells, to signify the Virgin Mary. The shells of eggs that were laid on Good Friday may also be added. The May bush is then set up, usually in front of the house, to be ready for May morning, when it will – according to Patricia Lysaght – 'reaffirm boundaries at the boundary-less time between the seasons, and protect the milk and the dairy products at that particular time'. The May bush then stays on show for a week or two, or until all the flowers have withered.

These various May traditions do not overlap; they occur in different parts of Ireland, May bough being found exclusively in the south-west (Munster) and the others found widely elsewhere.

The May festival is particularly associated with milk and dairy products, which were the staple items of diet in Ireland before the introduction of the potato. The productivity of the cows being of prime importance, many folk traditions concerned the health and well-being of cows (trees being symbolic or actual fodder), while failures of milk yield were commonly ascribed to magic, the fairies or other supernatural forces. Part of the tradition of *Bealtaine* also involves boundary marking with sprigs of rowan or quicken tree, again aimed at protecting stock from 'magic'.

Christmas Trees

Another festival which has a tree at its centre is Christmas, although the contemporary form of Christmas tree is not an ancient tradition here. It was introduced from Germany by the Royal Family in the nineteenth century, and one of the most celebrated examples was a Christmas tree put up at a children's party given by a member of Queen Caroline's court in 1821. The custom was confirmed in 1841, when Queen Victoria and Prince Albert had their first Christmas tree at Windsor Castle, while the tradition of erecting a Christmas tree in Trafalgar Square dates from 1947. The tree is donated by the people of Oslo in gratitude for British support during the Second World War.

The use of evergreen boughs to decorate houses around the midwinter solstice is of very ancient origin; the Romans used laurel and bay, but in these islands holly is generally used. The early Church forbade the custom, condemning it as 'savouring of paganism', but according to the Celt historian, Hole, it was 'too deeply rooted for such prohibitions to have much effect.' The significance of evergreen is that it symbolizes the return of the sun, and thereby the leaves on all the other trees, and the fertility of the coming season.

Christmas Tree at Windsor Castle
A drawing by J. L. Williams of Queen Victoria, Prince Albert and their children around the Christmas tree in 1848. It was the Royal Family who first introduced the custom of Christmas trees to Britain.

144

13

The Inspiration of Trees

IN BRITAIN, as in the rest of Europe, it took many millennia for trees in their wild state to be appreciated as objects of beauty, worthy of protection and conservation. They were too much a symbol of untamed nature, of the wildwood from which every acre of farmland had been wrested arduously by axe and by fire.

The idea of the carefully planned landscape, a neat and tidy version of reality which at the same time symbolized man's domination over nature, was largely a creation of the eighteenth and nineteenth centuries. 'Before that,' as Professor Keith Thomas has written, 'forests had been synonymous with wildness and danger as the word 'savage' (from the Latin *silva*, a wood) reminds us. Early man, it has plausibly been suggested, preferred open country to woodland because it was safer.'

A mid-nineteenth-century dictionary suggested, as appropriate epithets for a forest: 'dreadful', 'gloomy', 'wild', 'uncouth', and the 'haunt of wild animals'. It followed that the haunt of civilized men was not in the forest or even close to trees, and that the progress of mankind was from the forest to the field. A Victorian Prime Minister, Gladstone, boasted that his main form of relaxation was 'chopping down trees'; he arranged well-publicized tree-felling exhibitions to demonstrate that 'to cut down trees is to strike a blow for progress'.

Parts of the west of Ireland are today almost treeless, and have been so for generations; people coming from these areas to the more wooded country round Dublin are shocked at how backward the district seems, and some claim to feel uncomfortable near so many trees. This idea that progress or even social refinement means leaving trees behind may be a contributory factor to the absence of trees in many suburbs and newer residential parts of cities, especially in the Third World. In Thailand, trees in Bangkok and Chiangmai have been decimated as part of the 'modernization' of these cities; one of the few sanctuaries left in Bangkok is around the university, where staff and students have successfully campaigned to protect venerable trees.

Paradoxically, there has also been a trend towards planting trees, for timber, for shade and for aesthetic reasons, not only in Europe but in many other parts of the world, where it is accepted and understood that spiritual benefit can be gained from the proximity of trees. In Buddhist countries like Thailand, the tradition of the forest monastery, where monks and lay people alike can purify the soul from the agitations of modern life, has long been revered. As early as the seventeenth century some voices in England could be heard speaking out in favour of trees, and not simply in terms of their commercial value. Keith Thomas quotes

The tree which moves some to tears of joy is in the Eyes of others only a Green thing that stands in the way. Some see Nature all Ridicule and Deformity.....and some scarce see Nature at all. But to the Eyes of the Man of Imagination, Nature is Imagination itself.

WILLIAM BLAKE, 1799

one Walter Blith, who admitted that the hedgerow tree was not just useful, but also 'a thing of delight', and recommended planting oak, ash and elm not just for profit but to be 'most delightful and honourable unto men of ingenious spirits'. And in 1697, Leonard Meager confirmed that trees could afford 'pleasant and delightful prospects to the eye'. In 1650, 200 mature timber trees at Nonesuch House were spared being felled, as they were 'essential to the magnificence of the structure' and materially contributed to 'the pleasantness of the seat'.

Over the centuries trees have acted as a source of inspiration to many writers, poets and artists, and have often been portrayed as the key to the different seasons of the year. One such writer was Henry Thoreau, who lived in a hut in the woods of Concord, Maine, USA, from July 1845 to September 1847. He kept a detailed list of natural events which he later published under the title of *Walden*. The following extracts from his writing concern the pine tree and the seasons.

BETTER DEAD OR ALIVE *by Henry Thoreau*

Few come to the woods to see how the pine lives and grows and spires, lifting its evergreen arms to the light, to see its perfect success. Most are content to behold it in the shape of many broad boards brought to market, and deem that its true success. The pine is no more lumber than man is, and to be made into boards and houses is no more its true and highest use than the truest use of man is to be cut down and made into manure. A pine cut down, a dead pine, is no more a pine than a dead human carcass is a man. Is it the lumberman who is the friend and lover of the pine, stands nearest to it, and understands its nature best? Is it the tanner or turpentine distiller who posterity will fable was changed into a pine at last? No, no, it is the poet who makes the truest use of the pine, who does not fondle it with an axe, or tickle it with a saw, or stroke it with a plane. It is the poet who loves it as his own shadow in the air, and lets it stand. It is as immortal as I am, and will go to as high a heaven, there to tower above me still. Can he who has only discovered the value of whale-bone and whale-oil be said to have discovered the true uses of the whale? Can he who slays the elephant for his ivory be said to have seen the elephant? No, these are petty and accidental uses. Just as if a stronger race were to kill us in order to make buttons and flageolets of our bones, and then prate of the usefulness of man. Every creature is better alive than dead, both men and moose and pine-trees, as life is more beautiful than death.

Henry Thoreau was one of the first writers to extol the inspirational effects of trees and woods. He observed every nuance of the seasons by living in the woods of New England and keeping a detailed diary of his impressions.

THE SEASONS *by Henry Thoreau*

March

I perceive Spring in the softened air…Looking through this transparent vapor, all surfaces, not osiers and open water alone, look more vivid. The hardness of winter is relaxed. There is fine effluence surrounding the wood, as if the sap had begun to stir and you could detect it a mile off. Such is the difference between an object seen through a warm, moist and soft air and a cold, dry, hard one. Such is the genialness of nature that the trees appear to have put out feelers by which the senses apprehend them more tenderly. I do not know that the woods are ever more beautiful, or affect me more.

Early June

Within a little more than a fortnight the woods, from bare twigs, have become a sea of verdure, and young shoots have contended with one another in the race. The leaves are unfurled all over the country…

Shade is produced, and the birds are concealed and their economies go forward uninterruptedly, and a covert is afforded to animals generally. But thousands of worms and insects are preying on the leaves while they are young and tender. Myriads of little parasols are suddenly spread all the country over, to shield the earth and the roots of the trees from the parching heat, and they begin to flutter and rustle in the breeze.

The large buds, suddenly pushing out late in the spring from dry sticks which had seemed to be dead, developed themselves as by magic into graceful green and tender boughs, an inch in diameter; and sometimes as I sat at my window, so heedlessly did they grow and tax their weak joints, I heard a fresh and tender bough suddenly fall like a fan to the ground, when there was not a breath of air stirring, broken off by its own weight.

October

Standing on the railroad I look across the pond to Pine Hill, where the outside trees and the shrubs scattered generally through the wood glow through the green, yellow, and scarlet, like fires just kindled at the base of the trees, – a general conflagration just fairly under way, soon to envelop every tree. The hillside forest is all aglow along its edge and in all its cracks and fissures, and soon the flames will leap upwards to the tops of the tallest trees.

A great part of the pine-needles have just fallen. See the carpet of pale-brown needles under this pine. How light it lies upon the grass, and that great rock, and the wall, resting thick on its top and its shelves, and on the bushes and underwood, hanging lightly! They are not yet flat and reddish, but a more delicate pale brown, and

The colours of autumn.

lie up light as joggle-sticks, just dropped. The ground is nearly concealed by them. How beautifully they die, making cheerfully their annual contribution to the soil! They fall to rise again; as if they knew that it was not one annual deposit alone that made this rich mold in which pine trees grow. They live in the soil whose fertility and bulk they increase, and in the forests that spring from it.

November

The landscape looked singularly clean and pure and dry, the air, like a pure glass, being laid over the picture, the trees so tidy, and stripped of their leaves; as if they had been swept; ice on the water and winter in the air, but yet not a particle of snow on the ground. The woods, divested in great part of their leaves, are being ventilated.

It is the season of perfect works, of hard, tough, ripe twigs, not of tender buds and leaves. The leaves have made their wood, and a myriad new withies stand up all around pointing to the sky, able to survive the cold. It is only the perennial that you see, the iron age of the year.

TREES AND POETRY

The Irish poet Brendan Kennelly feels a particular affinity with trees, and has written a number of different poems which draw on them for inspiration.

WILLOW

To understand
A little of how a shaken love
May be sustained

Consider
The giant stillness
Of a willow

After a storm.
This morning it is more than peaceful
But last night that great form

Was tossed and hit
By what seemed to me
A kind of cosmic hate,

An infernal desire
To harass and confuse,
Mangle and bewilder

So that now I cannot grasp
The death of nightmare,
How it has passed away

Or changed to this
Stillness,
This clean peace

That seems unshakeable.
A branch beyond my reach says
'It is well'

For me to feel
The transfiguring breath
Of evil

Because yesterday
The roots by which I live
Lodged in apathetic clay,

But for that fury,
How should I be rid of the slow death?
How should I know

That what a storm can do
Is to terrify my roots
And make me new?

Dick Warner interviews Brendan Kennelly

DW: Have trees always been an inspiration to you?

BK: The place I grew up in, North Kerry, had trees growing more or less everywhere – you could hide amongst them and play all sorts of games. There were two lines of trees on the way to church, and on the road to school there were trees as well. I have a special feeling for the ash because I remember one teacher who wasn't a very good teacher, who was a very unhappy man I think. He used to pick the stick with which he used to slap the boys from the ash tree, and since then I've had a fairly ambiguous relationship with ash trees. And I think that's the key word –'relationship' – because trees are living things, and in the course of a year they proceed from almost a state of birth-like nakedness to being completely covered over and then shedding themselves again. So they're moody, and this aspect – this change of life and mood and feeling – this seems to be very true of the way poets work themselves, in relation to their own feelings and their own lives.

DW: And these symbols, do you find they keep cropping up in your poetry?

BK: Yes – ash and other trees as well. I think one of the most heart-rending sights in the world is to see a tree fallen, particularly after a storm. It's all the more ironically tragic because of the state of peace that often follows a storm. One of the poems where I tried to express this was when I was going through a fairly tough period in my own life, a kind of stormy existence. And I saw a willow tree, fallen after a storm, and it struck me as rather like myself, that I had to pick myself up and learn from the tree. Even though the tree couldn't get up I did try to. So the tree taught me to renew myself.

DW: Moving away from your own poetry, does it strike you that trees have been important symbols to a wide variety of poets?

BK: Absolutely. The greatest poet of Ireland, W. B. Yeats, was obsessed with trees, and he said somewhere 'study that tree and you'll know more about yourself'. If you're looking for an objective correlative for your own emotional life, a tree is a perfect living object with its own changing moods, to help you grasp and express the changing moods of your own inner life. This runs right through literature, and in our time, when trees are being polluted, they are used by English and American poets, and poets throughout the world, as symbolizing the way we have poisoned our own civilization; they're true to the inner life of our civilization.

PART THREE

THE FUTURE OF TREES

14

Planting Trees

ANY DISCUSSION on tree planting should perhaps be qualified by the knowledge that 99 per cent of all tree seedlings that grow into mature trees do so naturally, without human help. Thus, in the context of tree conservation, protecting trees will always be more important than planting them. Planting trees is nevertheless a very significant act to many peoples in many cultures and in this chapter several authors write about the subject from different viewpoints. Oliver Rackham looks at tree planting from an historical perspective. Rob Soutar and Dr George Peterken are most concerned about the conservation and recovery of our native flora and associated fauna, while Alan Mitchell has strong views about the merits of many introduced trees.

The contributors to this chapter are Dr Oliver Rackham on planting amenity trees, Rob Soutar and Dr George Peterken on native trees and shrubs for nature conservation and Alan Mitchell on the rationale for planting exotic trees.

Planting Amenity Trees
by Oliver Rackham

As a historical ecologist, I have noticed that the late twentieth century lacks a proper theory or philosophy of tree planting. More trees must have been planted in the last 20 years than in any 20 years previously (I exclude commercial forestry, or what is thought to be commercial forestry). Yet we of the 1990s do not have the clear ideas about what amenity trees are for, or where to put them, or what species to choose, that the seventeenth-century French or the Victorian English had.

Trees are popularly and vaguely thought of as a 'good thing'. People think they can play god and have power to control the destinies of all other fellow-creatures. This leads to the myth of the tree as artefact. A

Dr Oliver Rackham, who tutors in the Botany Department at Cambridge and is a research fellow at Corpus Christi College, is an acknowledged authority on the countryside, particularly trees, woodland and wood pasture. Among his books are *Trees and Woodland in the British Landscape, Ancient Woodland: Its History, Vegetation and Uses in England* and *History of the British Countryside.*

tree is a sort of post with leaves on, manufactured in a garden centre, put in a hole in the ground, and ending when it is cut down or blown down; planting a tree is much the same as planting any other sort of post. This myth is believed in the face of any number of examples to the contrary. Trees, therefore, are sprinkled around the landscape in a random and meaningless way. Many refuse the destiny foisted on them, and die. Those that survive too often clash with conservation values. Conservation of existing trees is neglected.

Principles of tree planting for the 1990s ought to be based on the analysis of past experience. We should ask what values we expect from trees and how effectively do planted trees provide these values?

Planted Trees of the Past and Present The idea of amenity trees goes back to the Ancient Greeks, if not to the Garden of Eden. In Ancient Greece (as in Greece today), some sacred groves were natural woods, some were plantations. The Grove of Herakles at Nemea was a formal plantation of cypress, an exotic tree.

In the Middle Ages, besides woodland and wood pasture, there were hedgerow trees, trees around manor houses, in gardens and orchards. Some of these non-woodland trees were natural, others planted. For example, in fourteenth-century Norfolk we find young ash trees pulled up in the local woods to plant round the manor house. One could also purchase nursery plants of elm, hazel, willow and poplar. All of these were probably vegetatively reproduced; in the Middle Ages people would have been puzzled by the modern custom of trading in species that anyone can grow from seed for nothing.

We do not find records of trees planted in woods. Even sowing acorns in a field was an exceptional act, to be set down among the memorable deeds of a great abbot or squire.

Exotic trees appear from the sixteenth century onwards. One of the earliest was sycamore, which made its debut in Cornish churchyards. Experiments were made with trees from the eastern North American colonies: false-acacia is the only one which has caught on. New trees were invented by gardeners or introduced from foreign gardens: for example, London plane, Lombardy poplar (once thought to be a timber tree) and a succession of cultivar poplars. There has been a sequence of fashions in newly introduced exotic trees; horse chestnut, Dutch elm, Wellingtonia (redwood), Wheatley elm, *Metasequoia* from China, monkey puzzle from Chile and, latterly, Leyland cypress.

Place of Tree Planting in the Landscape Planted trees have had an important place in the landscape, increasing down the centuries. One is tempted to treat them as all-important and to forget about wild trees. This is right for certain very formal tree-scapes, for example around Newmarket, but reality is more complex. England is not just a succession of Newmarkets. Even today it is quite easy to find a landscape – in Suffolk, or Sussex, or Herefordshire – in which there are no trees that have definitely been planted.

Hedgerow trees are partly planted and partly wild. We now think more of planted trees, but this is because planting is an action which may be put on record, whereas the birth of a wild tree is never recorded. Hedgerow trees are known to have been at their most prolific in the early eighteenth century, and again in the early twentieth. Both periods came after agricultural recessions, when not much planting was done. Hedgerow trees can, therefore, be an index of neglect: they arise unnoticed, at times when there is no money to spend on preventing them from growing.

Wild trees can be significant, even in towns. The part of Cambridge where I live is dominated by ash trees, which grew up in people's gardens when the area was a little run-down and untidy. Elsewhere, most kinds of industrial wasteland – quarries, gravel pits, coal tips, furnaces, gunpowder factories – turn into woodland without anyone doing anything at all.

Wild trees are very important in eighteenth- and nineteenth-century landscape parks. Creating a park involved preserving trees already there, to give it an air of respectable antiquity from the start. Many had been hedgerow trees in the seventeenth century. Humphrey Repton, the greatest of landscape designers, expressly wrote about the importance of preserving ancient trees.

Amenity trees may arise in unpredictable ways. Often they began as something entirely different. For example, the rows of gnarled Scots pines – now part of the character of the Breckland – were originally not intended to be trees at all. They were planted for hedges in the early nineteenth century. To keep a pine down into the form of a hedge requires a great deal of cutting, which can only be done in times of prosperity. After a few decades the attempt was abandoned: the pines grew up into trees, but still retained gnarled bases from their hedge-cut youth. As amenity trees they have four advantages: they are long-lived, very wind-firm, no good as timber and have a distinctive gnarled base, which saves them from being boringly straight like other Scots pines. It has a meaning and marks them as belonging to a particular part of the country. The gnarled base may also be of value as a habitat. Although exotic, these are very successful amenity trees, but they owe their value to a chance sequence of events which would be almost impossible to reproduce.

Planting for the Future: Where and Whether to Plant Trees Tree planters all too often assume that: every landscape ought to be a tree'd one; trees are necessarily better than what has gone before; and trees will not come unless planted.

In some landscapes, trees could technically be grown, but are entirely out of place. For well over a century, conservationists have opposed planting on moorland and have usually lost. In the early days, when nearly half of Great Britain was treeless moorland, this probably did not matter much. But times have changed, and what remains of the wild moorland becomes valuable for itself – especially the moors of the far north, which are wholly natural tundra that has never been wooded. The time is not far off – it may already have come – when it can be said of moorland planting that enough is enough.

In the farmed or industrial landscape, trees appear on almost any land that is abandoned. At first the public thinks of them as scrub, which is bad (except for birds), but in about 20 years they turn by magic into woodland, which is good. Seventy years ago, this process of succession was a hot theme of ecology; research was being done, and books written – and students examined – on how it happens. But unreason has triumphed: this knowledge has been forgotten by the political ecologists of today and books on trees rarely mention it. The proposal has been canvassed for creating a new forest by planting trees in south Essex. This is doubtless an admirable idea, yet the promoters seem unaware that thousands of acres of woodland sprang up on derelict land in south-east Essex in the 1930s and 1940s. These woods now constitute two country parks, yet, because they cost nothing, their origin has been forgotten.

Attempts to increase tree numbers are the chief threat to heathland, chalk grassland and fen. These rich and delightful kinds of vegetation are now only a fraction of their former extent. When invaded by trees they turn into undistinguished kinds of woodland. In conservation terms, they are much more important as they are than new woodland.

Choice of Species All too often, the advice one gets from local authorities and wildlife trusts is an exhortation to plant native trees, a poorly-argued case for doing so, an inaccurate list of what are native species and, maybe, a claim as to what trees grow on what type of soil.

Such advice may be misleading. Just how strong are the virtues of native trees? Do planted native trees supply those virtues as well as wild ones? Not necessarily; a virtue of oak, for example, is that it provides nest sites for barn owls. This, however, is only true of old pollard oaks and no newly planted oak is the slightest use to a barn owl.

Soil does not strongly determine where trees grow. Most native trees grow on many different soils; some, like oak, grow almost anywhere. Advice about soil can have disastrous effects. For example, the idea somehow got about in the eighteenth century that beech is the ideal tree for dry chalklands. No amount of drought or storm can persuade planters that this is a mistake. Worse still, advice about native trees is too vague. It leaves the advisee with a list of a dozen species and no suggestion of how to get a short-list.

Planting and Conservation Tree planting is supposed to help the cause of conservation in various ways. The most general objective is to take carbon dioxide out of the atmosphere. Undeniably, having more trees will work in the right direction – but to a minute degree. For its practical effect, telling people to plant trees is like telling them to drink more water to keep down rising sea-levels. Anyone really concerned about CO_2 should work at preventing the destruction of peat bogs.

Much recent planting seems to have the object of making every rare native tree into a common tree. Two examples are service and small-leaved lime. Is this what conservation is about?

Service and lime are trees with a definite meaning: they grow in particular kinds of ancient wood. They are rare trees – but not very rare – and much of their appeal depends on there not being many of them around. Amenity is not served by making them commonplace, nor is conservation. They are not threatened. All through history they have been rare, and have not much diminished; they have taken care of themselves without being planted. They are very difficult to kill: the Forestry Commission spent 20 years trying – with all the power of science – to get rid of lime from its woods and failed. Even if Parliament were to make it a felony to have lime or service on one's land, they would still not be in much danger of extinction. Every planted lime or service – except formal avenues, which cannot be confused with wild trees – alters the values that lime and service stand for.

Native trees are wildlife, and we should allow them to be wildlife. To plant native trees in order to conserve the tree is like a captive-breeding programme for a rare antelope, with the object of returning the animals to the wild. This is purposeful only if it meets certain criteria. The animal or plant should not only be rare, but its survival in the wild precarious. There should be some reason why conservation of the habitat is not enough to perpetuate it. I can think of only two trees that meet these conditions: black poplar and wild pear.

There is a case for planting, not to conserve trees as wildlife themselves, but specifically as a habitat for other kinds of wildlife. Here too, one should ask what exactly is intended. Wildlife is not something homogeneous which can be provided for as a whole, but consists rather of thousands of species, each with its own requirements. Which species are faring badly because of shortage of a particular kind of tree? Will planting more trees make them fare better?

Among the infinity of tree-inhabiting wildlife, there are three main categories which are faring badly because of lack of suitable trees: those which need ancient trees, coppiced trees and dead trees. None of these will be helped by planting more trees. To promote these creatures we need to take care of ancient trees and trees that are going to become ancient; to resume coppicing; and not to tidy away dead trees. (The hope that planting trees in 1990 ensures that there will be ancient trees in 2490 is an illusion. Only a very small fraction of trees are allowed to become ancient. Sweden lacks ancient trees today, not because fifteenth-century Swedes failed to plant them, but because nineteenth-century Swedes cut down all old trees.)

Far be it for me to say that planting trees is irrelevant to wildlife conservation. There is a connection, but it is not a strong one, and is easily overstated.

Amenity Versus Timber Trees Economics have been promoted in the last 70 years as if they were the supreme value in tree planting. This is a dangerous illusion because of the mismatch between money, a short-term value, and the length of time which trees take to grow. When the time comes to cut down the trees, the purpose for which they were planted may have disappeared (for example, the poplars planted for match-making in the 1950s). If the trees do have a value, few owners will take the trouble (even if they have kept the records) to work out how much they cost to grow. In practice, only very rarely will anyone care enough to find out whether the enterprise has made a profit.

The first requirement of an amenity tree is that our successors should not mistake it for a timber tree and cut it down. The timber value appears earlier in the tree's life than the amenity value; if felled for timber it has lost most of its value as amenity. Nevertheless, there have been uneasy attempts to combine the two values. This works best with cherry – a short-lived tree whose timber value comes relatively late in its life, and which grows again from suckers.

Cherry is a very valuable tree because it is rare and precious furniture wood. Few of us would object to all the cherry planting that there has been recently, but as a means of making an income from timber, it is self-defeating. Nobody can say whether cherry will still be a fashionable furniture wood in 80 years, but if it is, it will no longer be rare, and therefore will no longer be precious.

The Common Market, in its folly, has imposed legislation requiring commercial plants of certain trees, including oak and beech, to come from certified sources. The sources are chosen because they are thought to provide good timber trees – not for amenity qualities. Even on its own terms, this too may be self-defeating. What constitutes a good timber tree is subject to fashion, like other human values; the oaks that the Victorians selected as good timber trees are not what we would select today. The wheel of fashion will not remain forever stuck at 1990. Good timber trees, according to the standards of the 1980s, are bad amenity trees: all genetically the same, straight, smooth and fast-growing. Whether this Euro-oak will still be thought a good timber tree in the 2080s remains to be seen, but it is not what English oak is about. Its crookedness, epicormic twigs and corkscrew shapes give oak its meaning and its value as habitat.

Learning From the Great Storms The great storm of October 1987 brought out the worst in people's ignorance of trees. It was thought of as a tragedy and a once-only event. Its consequences could be put right by planting trees according to practices ruling before the storm. There was never a thought that the storm could reveal how modern planting practice might be improved. In 1990, it was demonstrated that the 1987 storm was not a once-only event, but there was still no thought of learning from what had happened.

The storms were more destructive to planted than wild trees. Three possible reasons come to mind. Trees have been brought from all over the world and set down more or less at random; not surprisingly, some of them have been put in places where they do not root well. Planted trees tend to be overcrowded, as witness the fact that trees on the edge of a plantation fared better than those in the interior. There is also the suspicion that transplanting may permanently alter a tree's roots.

The majority of storm-damaged trees remained alive. Most trees were killed by clearing-up operations, not by the storm. An uprooted tree, left alone, probably had a greater chance of survival than the tree transplanted to replace it.

The storms should have exploded the belief that it is old, decrepit trees that are 'dangerous' and liable to windblow. The majority of broken and uprooted trees were young. Some kinds were much more susceptible than others, for example, beech on chalk. Monterey pine, from California, grows extremely fast in the unfamiliar climate of south-west England, but produces very little root, and at 60 years – and three feet thick – it crashes down. Any big young Monterey pine, or beech on dry chalk, is a 'dangerous tree', in a way that ancient oaks are not. That is not to say that we should cut down all beeches and Monterey pines, but when we plant them in future, we should put them in places where it will not matter when they fall down.

After the Storm
The Great Storm of 1987 resulted in many scenes of devastation such as this one. It was particularly severe on planted trees, which suffered from overcrowding and from being planted in places where they did not root well.

TREE-SHELTERS

'God, they're an eyesore!'

'Dreadful plastic things!'

'Makes the whole place look like the Martians have landed.'

'If I could meet the nutter who invented them, I'd sort him out.'

'The single most important contribution to arboriculture this century.'

Tree-shelters certainly arouse strong feelings, but to give young tree-seedlings a good start in life they are unequalled. Yet this idea of 'providing each seedling with its own individual greenhouse' as inventor Graham Tuley puts it, is only about five years old. Since the correction of various teething problems such as the best diameter and the most suitable material to use, the success of the idea has been phenomenal. In 1992 total production was around 10 million and is increasingly rapidly.

The Origin of Tree-shelters As a Forestry Commission researcher, Graham Tuley was investigating the establishment of trees in very small sites, too small to be eligible for woodland grants. His idea was, that with their individual greenhouses (maintaining both temperature and more important, humidity), the seedlings would be able 'to develop their roots in the real world before the shoots were stressed'. By the time the shoot emerged, the roots would be well established.

Graham Tuley with some examples of his invention

Field trials showed that he was right. Seedlings grew well and other benefits of the shelters soon became obvious. One of the most important stresses that the seedlings avoided was that caused by being eaten. Instead of being 'a cafeteria for rabbits', a plantation of young trees could be completely protected from grazing in their 'Tuley Tubes'. They were also protected from severe weather, and field workers could easily find them, even in places where the surrounding vegetation was dense. Where herbicides were in use to kill weeds, these could be applied right up to the seedling without splashing it.

After the first few years of experimentation, it is these additional benefits that have actually proved the most important; the planting of young broad-leaved seedlings is now far more efficient than before, because so few individual trees are lost in the first year or two, restricting the need for replanting. For the shelters to be successful, they must be carefully staked and must not have a gap at the surface of the soil. The strong shelters now produced – for example, by *Tubex Ltd* – can be driven a few centimetres into the soil preventing access by voles. They do not, however, reduce the need for good weed-control, and the manufacturers recommend their use with a dark plastic mulch-mat, or ordinary mulching with organic material, such as pulverized bark or a square of old carpet.

Not all tree seedlings thrive in tree-shelters, but most native trees do – with the possible exception of beech.

The material used now is photodegradable and is designed to last a few years and then disintegrate on site: this may look unsightly for a time, but does allow for normal tree growth. Shelters are now made in several colours: green, pale buff and brown, and these can be used singly or in combination, depending on the predominant colour of the surrounding vegetation.

Tree-shelters cost about 55 pence each at present, depending on size etc., but the unit price is decreasing. The Forestry Commission has produced a comprehensive guide to Tree-shelters and their use (Potter 1991), which is available from them.

Native Trees and Shrubs for Nature Conservation
by Rob Soutar and Dr George Peterken

Rob Soutar has worked for Scottish National Heritage and the Joint Nature Conservation Committee as a woodland ecologist with a special interest in native tree species distribution. He has since joined the Forest Enterprise.
Dr George Peterken works for the Joint Nature Conservation Committee and is the author of *Woodland Conservation and Management*, the standard work on the subject.

Native tree and shrub species are not only valuable components of the natural heritage of Britain — they also provide much of the native wildlife with its natural habitats. Some native tree and shrub species are commonly associated with a prodigious diversity and biomass of wildlife, whilst other less bountiful species provide habitat for specialized flora and fauna. Native oaks, for example, support more insects than any other British tree, while native buckthorns only support the larvae of the Brimstone butterfly. Whatever the abundance or rarity of their associated wildlife, tree and shrub species are usually of their highest value to nature conservation when they grow in places where they would occur naturally in the absence of human disturbance or assistance throughout the ages.

Indigenous tree and shrub species are not necessarily native everywhere in the U.K. Beech, for example, is native to southern England and south-east Wales, yet not to northern Britain (it is common as a planted tree and as self-sown individuals springing from seed produced by planted trees). Conversely, Scots pine was once native to England and Wales but was naturally replaced by broad-leaved species, and is now regarded as native only to the Scottish Highlands. Regeneration of pine in lowland Britain is always associated with planted trees.

From the nature conservation point of view, the ideal way to create new woodlands is to encourage natural regeneration from trees and shrubs which themselves spring from a continuous line of self-sown ancestors. Land close to a good seed source may well become rapidly and adequately stocked, and there will be some sites where self-sown trees are already established. However, most new woodlands are created by planting because natural regeneration is regarded as impractical or too costly. For this reason, nature conservation advice cannot be restricted to the natural regeneration ideal and must encompass planting.

The map shows 13 zones in which different species are recommended for use in afforestation and amenity planting programmes. The boundaries reflect the broad pattern of natural distribution, but are not precise. They most closely follow the presumed natural distribution of Scots pine, small-leaved lime, bird cherry, hornbeam and beech.

The natural geographical limits of native species are complex and seldom known with precision. In the compilation of lists of species suitable for each zone, many details of distribution have been necessarily ignored in order to concentrate on the broad pattern. Most species match tolerably well with their particular combination of zones; the most conspicuous misfit among the larger trees is probably black poplar. Some guidance on the site requirements of each species is also given. Our aim is to encourage the successful establishment of British species in regions and on soils where they are indigenous, so that the character and composition of local and regional treescapes, and their associated wildlife, are maintained. The map and table are not suitable for use in the management of ancient and semi-natural woodland, where more detailed information is needed.

When creating new woodlands, it is best to plant the same native species that occur in nearby ancient and semi-natural woodland. It will be usually most appropriate to encourage common and already widespread species rather than rarer ones. The needs of the latter are often poorly understood. If used, they may well be planted on sites or soils where they would not naturally occur or thrive; such a result could be expensive and of little value to nature conservation.

Planting of native trees and shrubs can damage nature conservation interests, even if they are planted in the appropriate zones. This applies particularly to species with local forms, and to those whose distributions are of scientific interest. The problem with planting, even in the correct zone, is that scientific information, including local genetic variability, may be lost or confused. For this reason, it is recommended that certain species in selected zones should only be planted if stock of local origin is used and if a record is made of the planting. Seed should be collected from semi-natural stands, no further away than, say, 10 miles from where the stock is to be planted.

NATIVE SPECIES TO ENCOURAGE IN THE NUMBERED ZONES

LARGER TREES	A	B	C	D	E	F	G	H	I	J	K	L	M	a	b	c	d	e	f
alder, black		●	●	●	●	●	●	●	●	●	●	●	●	●				●	
apple, crab					L	●	●	●		●	●	●	●	●	●			●	
ash			●	●	●	●	●	●	●	●	●	●	●	●	●			●	●
aspen	●	●	●	●	●										●		●	●	●
aspen						●	●	●	●	●	●	●			●			●	●
beech								●	●	●					●		●	●	●
birch, downy	●	●	●	●	●	●	●	●	●	●	●	●	●	●	●	●	●	●	●
birch, silver		●	●	●	●	●	●	●	●	●	●	●	●	●	●	●	●	●	●
cherry, bird			●	●	●	●		L						●				●	
cherry, gean			●	●	●	●	●	●	●	●	●	●			●			●	
elm, wych			●	●	●	●	●	●	●	●	●				●		●	●	
hornbeam								●	●						●	●		●	
lime, small-leaved						L									●			●	
lime, small-leaved							L	L	L	L	L	L		●	●	●		●	
lime, large-leaved							L	L		L					●			●	
maple, field						L	●	●	●	●	●	●	●	●	●			●	
oak, common				●	●	●	●	●	●	●	●	●	●	●		●	●	●	●
oak, sessile				●	●	●	●	L	L	L	L	L	●		●		●	●	
pine, Scots				●	●										●	●		●	
poplar, black							L	L	L	L	L	L		●		●			
rowan	●	●	●	●	●	●	●	●	●	●	●	●	●		●			●	
service-tree							L	L	L	L	L	L	L		●	●		●	
whitebeam			L			L					L				●			●	●
whitebeam								L							●		●	●	●
willow, crack						●	●	●	●	●	●	●	●	●				●	●
willow, goat		●	●	●	●	●	●	●	●	●	●	●	●	●	●			●	●
willow, white					●	●	●	●	●	●	●	●	●	●				●	●
yew						L				L	L			●				●	

SMALLER TREES	A	B	C	D	E	F	G	H	I	J	K	L	M	a	b	c	d	e	f
box										L	L				●			●	
hawthorn, common			●	●	●	●	●	●	●	●	●	●	●	●	●	●	●	●	●
hawthorn, Midland							L	L	L	L					●			●	
hazel	●	●	●	●	●	●	●	●	●	●	●	●	●	●	●			●	●
holly		●	●	●	●	●	●	●	●	●	●	●	●		●		●	●	
juniper	L	L	L	L	L	L	L			L	L				●		●	●	●
willow, almond							●	●	●	●	●			●				●	
willow, bay					●	●	●							●				●	
willow, eared	●	●	●	●	●	●	●	●	●	●	●	●	●	●			●	●	●
willow, grey	●	●	●	●	●	●	●	●	●	●	●	●	●	●			●	●	●
willow, osier						●	●	●	●	●	●	●	●	●				●	
willow, purple					●	●	●	●	●	●	●	●	●	●				●	●

L = only stock of local origin should be used. SOILS: a = wet sites b = light, dry soils c = heavy soils d = acid e = neutral or alkaline f = exposed sites

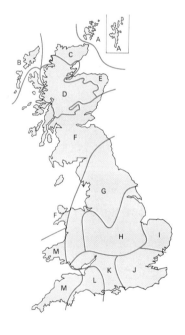

The Rationale for Planting Exotic Trees
by Alan Mitchell

Alan Mitchell, an ex-forester, is Director of TROBI (Tree Register of the British Isles) and author of *A Field Guide to the Trees of Britain and Northern Europe*.

I like a tree to get on with it – it has to be vigorous, because it's got to get big or it goes on the bonfire – or else it has to be very pretty – otherwise I wouldn't bother to find room for it in the first place. I like good foliage and interesting flowers – a tree has got to have character.

A half-serious rejoinder to the question 'Why would you plant exotic trees?' is 'Because there is no point in planting natives – they plant themselves.' The gales of the last four years have shown how efficiently native trees replace themselves. Country-wide, all native species – except the wild service tree and the black poplar – seed themselves adequately and none is in need of the 'conservation' which is now mindlessly attached to everything growing. Jays plant hundreds of millions of oak trees every mast-year – most of them, it seems in my garden-beds – yet I am begged every so often to go and save an oak seedling from eradication, 'since they are now so rare'. A hundred thousand seedlings of Scots pines are removed from Frensham Common each year in the National Trust and Surrey Trust 'Pine-Pulls' designed to save the heathland for snakes and natterjack toads. Except locally, sometimes, native trees are in little need of being planted.

There are, however, even more cogent reasons for planting exotics than this negative one. One is that few exotic trees plant themselves, so if we value their 'conservation' here, we must plant them. One obvious exception is the sycamore. Less obvious and very local are the natural seedlings of western hemlock, western red cedar, Lawson cypress, Norway maple, and sweet chestnut, with far fewer Monterey, maritime and eastern white pines, red oak, silver fir and a few others. If we want the noble spires of giant sequoias and grand firs to tower out of the monotonous domed tops of so much of our woodland, the delights of walking in larch woods, and of monumental cedars of Lebanon to grace our lawns and parks, we must plant them.

Another reason is that replacing woods by natural seeding, or by planting the same native species, is a very conservative approach which can add nothing to the variety of species and, usually, very little to the quality. We have only about 35 native trees, a minority of which can grow to great size, and only four of those are strictly native to all regions, the others being confined to England or to Scotland. Furthermore, with only 35 species, we are exceedingly unlikely to have among them the best ones we could have for growth, amenity or any special requirements, on all kinds of soils and sites. For example, no native tree can thrive like the sycamore, giving shelter in extreme maritime exposure on limestone soils at over 300m (1,000ft) and none can withstand that exposure on sands at low levels like the bishop pine from California.

Nor is any attractive native tree particularly well suited to city life. Our trees are nearly all forest-edge species, needing woodland soils and clear air, a cool temperature and high humidity. For paved root-runs, heat reflected from buildings and drying winds of polluted air, we need gingko, robinia, planes, honey-locusts and others selected from all over the world.

Our native trees are singularly devoid of attractive flowers. If they are big trees, they bear catkins or insignificant flowers; only small ones like the rowan have noticeable flowers – with the exception of the great display of the wild cherry. The horse chestnuts, catalpas, spectacular cherries and apples – invaluable in street parks and gardens – are all exotics. Another drawback to natives is that they bring all their pests and diseases with them from the woods. Who wants a garden or street tree with leaves tattered and blighted, if a range of shiny-leafed, healthy, insect-free exotics is available?

A garden is a planting designed to be distinct from its background, not to merge into it, and to be decorative. In a wooded countryside it can do this only by being formed of different (and superior) tree species. In effect, this is saying that it must be planted largely with exotics. The world's great gardens are all collections of trees exotic to the country of the garden. Westonbirt, Sheffield Park, Powerscourt, Leonardslee, Longwood, Winterthur … they all owe everything to exotics, and so do millions of very much smaller gardens.

A panoramic landscape in Britain is a monotony of rolling, formless tree crowns, and is visually uninteresting without a lake or mountain. In lowlands, where these are absent, it depends on church spires or a good clutch of cooling towers for the eye to rest on, to distance the elements and to which to return. In most areas, however, this essential ingredient can be found in the planting of giant sequoia or a Lombardy poplar or two and clumps of big Douglas firs and mixed conifers in an estate or even a garden.

Our birds need exotics in gardens and forests. Almost no native tree other than yew has a leaf to hide a nest in March and April, when they are most needed. The Lawson cypress from California, universal in gardens and churchyards, and now the Leyland cypress, are the sites for most of the garden bird nests in town and country; the western hemlock and Douglas fir in forests built up the high populations we now enjoy of goldcrests and redpolls, while the sitka spruces, in the forests of Dumfriesshire, restocked the locally extinct sparrow-hawk in its recovery to former numbers everywhere. A recently added bonus of exotic trees is the now thriving colonies of breeding golden orioles in Suffolk. They nest exclusively in the hybrid Robusta poplar and, until a decade or two ago, a single nest was a great rarity.

The vagaries of geology, in the forms of northward continental drift and ice ages, have deprived Britain of all but an outlying fragment of an impoverished North European flora. It may be nice to preserve some areas for that flora alone, but as a general policy of planting for many purposes, it is perverse to restrict ourselves to these few trees. The wealth of the world's flora is available to us.

A great number of splendid trees grow better here than they do in their native areas – a general rule in exotic plants – and our basic 35 species can be augmented to 2,500 at least. Is it not common sense to exploit fully our remarkably benign climate and grow the plants which have and still are being introduced from other countries by man to make our gardens the envy of the world and so enrich our towns, cities, villages and countryside?

15

Tree Organizations and Tree Campaigns

TREES STIR UP strong emotions in people all over the world, Britain and Ireland being no exception. So much concern has been expressed about the wanton destruction of trees – usually in the name of 'progress', that campaigns to save trees at a local level are familiar in many parts of the country. The sense of outrage provoked by plans to destroy a substantial part of a unique piece of ancient woodland (Oxleas Woods) in south-east London to make way for a new trunk road, has resulted in demonstrations and rallies for the last four years (see Alarm UK). In Ireland similar concerns have been raised over a road scheme which threatens oak woods at Glen of the Downs, Co. Wicklow. Indeed, campaigners in these islands have gained confidence from news of other campaigns and demonstrations about trees and forests, often against even more implacable authorities, from Thailand to Tasmania and Brazil to British Columbia.

Both here and abroad, support for tree and woodland organizations is growing – as is their influence. General conservation organizations – such as the Worldwide Fund for Nature – are increasingly including trees and other plants in their campaigns to conserve nature. The significance of trees as 'keystone' elements (those on which a large number of other organisms depend) in so many ecosystems, is becoming more clearly understood: trees have become an unmistakable symbol for the whole of the natural world.

Here, as in most countries, there are statutory bodies concerned with trees, but most of them are primarily forestry organizations. In this book there has been little or no mention of forestry as such for there are already many excellent publications on that predominantly commercial subject. Some of the activities, publications and services offered by forestry bodies are also very relevant to an interest in individual trees – and native ones in particular. However, it is perhaps due in part to the inadequacies and even tunnel-vision of some foresters that many of the groups mentioned here have been set up. Indeed, it would appear that the one thing most tree groups have in common, apart from their love of trees, is their often fierce criticism of such statutory bodies and of the lack of vision and unsustainability of many of their policies.

Not all tree groups are 'militant' campaigners; there are also gentler groups like Tree Spirit, more intellectual groups like the Reading Tree Club and primarily statistical groups like the Tree Register of the British Isles. The government-sponsored Tree Council is also included, because it does support a number of tree initiatives quite apart from strictly forestry matters, though, as an organization, it is perceived by many as

'Is there no nook of English ground secure
From rash assault?
WILLIAM WORDSWORTH

Crann sa Chathair
Bob Geldof, here pictured with the founder of Crann, Jan Alexander, was just one of the thousands of Irish people involved in Crann sa Chathair (Crann in the City), a tree-planting campaign organized to celebrate the Dublin millenium in 1988. 1,000 trees were planted in each of ten specially selected areas of the city, making a grand total of 10,000 trees.

being dominated by commercial forestry interests. There are tree groups in these islands to cater for just about every particular interest to do with trees; their management, appreciation and uses. The folklore field is sadly sparsely inhabited – although there is a small group called the Sacred Trees Trust – and I know of no society concerned specifically with that wonderful genus *Sorbus*, but not much else is missing!

The list below concentrates on groups specifically interested in trees (apart from Alarm UK), as opposed to those for whom trees are just one aspect of their work, like the Botanical Society of the British Isles, Plantlife and the Woodland Trust.

Alarm UK, 13 Stockwell Road, London SW9 9AU

Alarm UK This national organization actively opposes damaging road-building schemes. It has over 120 member organizations, most of whom are currently campaigning against schemes in their own areas. Some of the proposed road schemes would demolish homes and businesses; many more would destroy precious city parklands and concrete over yet more acres of our valued British countryside.

Among other things Alarm UK is currently involved in the prolonged battle to save the 8,000-year-old Oxleas Wood in south-east London, with its many avenues of historic trees, from being decimated by the proposed four-lane highway – the East London River Crossing.

The Bees and Trees Trust, 36 Rock Lane, Ludlow, Shropshire, SY8 1ST
Founder: Paul Hand

The Bees and Trees Trust The Trust sees its work partly as direct conservation and partly as providing education and raising general consciousness about the importance of trees. Its aims are to foster the interaction of bees and trees – especially fruit trees – and to promote and conserve traditional local varieties of fruit and native strains of bees. One of the main activities is teaching urban children rural skills, such as skep-making and grafting, and increasing their awareness of the natural interaction of pollinating insects and trees.

With these aims in mind, existing traditional orchards are being sought and then either purchased to be conserved by the Trust or, in some cases, have already been donated to the Trust. These orchards are being 'renovated', with new trees planted in gaps and the trees identified. The bee population in all local orchards is being increased. Bumblebees are being encouraged by providing them with nesting materials, while honeybees are being brought into the orchards in traditional skeps. Local schoolchildren are involved in various conservation activities such as finding and naming local fruit varieties and then learning to graft them on to established trees.

Already a small local orchard has been started next to a housing estate on the outskirts of Ludlow. It consists of native fruit trees and rare cultivars, together with various bee-attracting flowers and shrubs, which have mostly been planted by local children. With the help of many local community organizations and the British Trust for Conservation Volunteers, a whole network of such orchards is planned.

All aspects of traditional beekeeping are encouraged by the Trust and demonstrations are given at agricultural shows and local fêtes. Already a number of little-known varieties of apple (not previously registered at the National Fruit Collection) have been located and identified.

The Conservation Foundation The Foundation exists to promote the relationship between commercial sponsors and conservation and it has acted as midwife to many important projects concerned with trees.

Among its many activities, the Foundation co-ordinated the Yew Tree Campaign, initiated by Allen Meredith and Dr David Bellamy, which, since 1988, has been involved in collecting details of ancient yew trees. After confirmed measurements have been made, signed certificates recording the estimated age of the tree are issued. To celebrate the 777th anniversary of the signing of the Magna Carta in 1215, the signatories of the Yew Tree Certificate gathered under the ancient yew tree at Ankerwycke to sign a new environmental Magna Carta.

Another project is Elms Across Europe, sponsored by Pitney Bowes Ltd. It has resulted in a disease-resistant hybrid elm, developed in the USA and known as Sapporo Autumn Gold, being widely planted in urban tree-planting schemes.

The Conservation Foundation, 1 Kensington Gore, London SW7 2AR

Crann – Re-leafing Ireland Crann was founded in 1986 to promote the planting of broad-leaved trees throughout Ireland. With only about 1.2 per cent of Ireland's land area under broad-leaved tree cover, Crann's emphasis has been on developmental opportunities associated with broad-leaved trees rather than preservation. All aspects of Crann's work focuses on promoting the growing of broad-leaved trees and on making information on how to do it available to as wide an audience as possible.

With increasing pressure on farming communities in Ireland to diversify land use out of intensive agriculture, and with the new farm premium grants being added to the increased afforestation grants through the Department of Energy Forest Service, tree farming is now an option for farmers to consider. One of Crann's main aims is to create a multi-purpose, mixed forestry resource in south Leitrim, the area where Crann is based. It wants to co-ordinate planting programmes on a small scale, with each participating farmer planting species suited to the different soil types and individual situations.

Crann branches have now also been set up in several other areas and have concentrated on different activities depending on local circumstances; such as educational activities with youngsters and community tree-planting schemes. Two training courses, of 48 weeks each, have been run with the help of FAS (the government training agency) and Crann has produced three slide packs and a video for use in schools and by the general public, as well as two posters – the beginning of an intended series on tree identification and propagation.

Crann has also organized many workshops and seminars on tree-related themes for groups as varied as school teachers, farmers and community groups. These have resulted in thousands of trees being planted and managed throughout Ireland.

Among the campaigns Crann has organized was *Crann sa Chathair* (Crann in the City), a Crann/Allied Irish Bank co-operation for the Dublin millennium in 1988. 10,000 trees were planted – 1,000 in ten different areas – with advice and guidance from Crann. This project attracted extensive media coverage and hundreds of city dwellers learned how to improve their environment through planting trees.

Crann, Aughavas, via Cavan, Co. Leitrim, Ireland Founder: Ms Jan Alexander

Another was the Oak Glen project, initiated by Crann in September 1990, in association with Coillte (the Irish Forestry Board) and the general public. A 65-acre site in County Wicklow, owned by Coillte, has been planted with Ireland's National Tree, sessile oak, though unfortunately – through lack of availability – it has not been possible to use native seed. As the costs of planting oak on this scale are prohibitive – the deer fence alone cost 19,000 punts – the public were invited to sponsor a tree at £10.00 each in order to make this project possible. For this amount, the sponsor received a specially designed certificate in their name or in the name of a loved one. Seven trees are actually planted per sponsored tree, but six will be felled over a period of 100 years.

The Green Wood Trust, Rose Cottage, Dale Road, Coalbrookdale, Telford, Shropshire, TF8 7DS

The Green Wood Trust The Trust exists to promote woodmanship; to encourage the effective management of woodlands and the development of products using home-produced timber. Woodland management should combine the best of modern and traditional techniques, especially through coppicing, which provides a continuing supply of green timber as well as encouraging a diversity of wildlife.

Good design and aesthetic awareness are essential for the development of new products. From a manufacturing base, the Trust also provides a venue for art and sculpture and training for young craftsmen and designers.

Traditional woodland crafts have virtually disappeared in the British Isles. By recording and reviving these techniques of working unseasoned timber, the Trust is developing its potential in new ways, some for production and others primarily for recreation. A comprehensive range of traditional craft courses are held during the summer months, ranging from coracle-making to timber-frame building. Courses in 1992 included two to three day courses on: traditional charcoal burning, chair bodging, making oak-swill baskets, apple-grafting, making straw bee skeps, gates and hurdles, using a pole lathe, making coracles, willow baskets and coppice management. (A similar selection of woodmanship courses are now available each year at Hay Bridge Nature Reserve, Bouth, Ulverston, Cumbria [Tel: 0229 861412], the contact being Anne Frahn.)

An indigenous tree nursery completes the Trust's cycle of activity. This has been established at the Coalbrookdale Station site, using seed taken from local woodland so as to preserve the local gene pool.

Reading Tree Club, 38 New Road, Reading RG1 5JD
Secretary: Catharine Olver

Reading Tree Club The Club members enjoy and study trees together. The Club evolved in 1980 from a Reading University extra-mural class and the original core interest was tree-watching: the observation and recognition of local trees.

As the group has developed, there have been opportunities for meetings and outings on an increasingly wide range of tree topics. Tree professionals of all kinds have been generous in accepting the challenge of an invitation from a group that would rather be stretched than talked down to; and the presence in the membership of botanists, carpenters, arboriculturists and landscape architects ensures lively meetings. The sharing of interests and information infects everyone with enthusiasm for trees and timber.

The Club is a forum for tree issues. Estate foresters talk about windblow and financial uncertainty; development foresters about fuelwood, community woodland and agro-forestry. Speakers from the Forestry Commission, the Timber Research and Development Association, the Tree Council, the Local Authority and the Department of the Environment all explain the roles of their organizations. Experts have come to discuss tropical forests, research about rattans and the satellite monitoring of vegetation change.

Tree biology events explore tree physiology, taxonomy, ecology – first there was a sniff-in for aromatic trees, then a feel-in for hairy ones. Outstanding single genus studies have been an oak evening (with Alan Mitchell and 60 oak branches from the Hillier Arboretum) and a *Sorbus* day at Winkworth Arboretum, (with Hugh McAlister, when lunch ended with tastings of eau-de-vie from two French *Sorbus* species and *Sorbus domestica*-flavoured brandy). The club has held evenings of tropical fruit, essential oils, tree-derived honeys and a sequence of apple evenings, followed by a pear expedition to Brogdale. Christmas treats have included frankincense and myrrh, and a tasting of nuts and the preserved tree fruits of the Mediterranean.

On tree-watching trips, the combined experience of the members means that all are learning together, with both beginners and experienced tree-watchers going on trips to famous sites such as Kingley Vale (yews), the Avon Gorge (whitebeams), Pamber Heath (wild service trees) and Hatfield Forest (ancient pollards).

Expeditions through the year culminate in the annual weekend. From the 1983 Isle of Wight adventure through to the 1991 journey to Castle Howard and Thorp Perrow, the group has built up a body of shared tree memories, with highspots like the St Lucy cherry at Joyce Green Hospital, Dartford, and the *Tilia maximowicziana* at Hergest Croft, Herefordshire. The club welcomes all levels of learners and pricing is designed to exclude as few as possible. Plans for longer trips to Ireland and Cornwall are being discussed with Oxford and Claremont Tree Clubs. Then the Channel Islands? Normandy? the Netherlands?

Learning through enjoying trees transforms every journey, up the Amazon or up the road to the shops. And an informed public is the best tree preservative!

Scottish Native Woods Campaign Today, native woodland covers only one per cent of Scotland's land area, and over 90 per cent of what is left lies within the Highlands. This is a unique relic of the original Caledonian Forest, the richest and most diverse wildlife home in Scotland, with an 8,000-year pedigree.

Highland woods are amongst the most natural in Britain and their survival, along with that of our other remaining native woodlands, cannot depend solely upon nature reserves, which are not designed for widespread conservation. A much broader approach was needed, working in the wider countryside and highlighting the many benefits of such woodland. Working with the landowners is central, key to persuading them that managing native woodlands sustainably is improving their economic value. The Scottish Native Woods Campaign pioneered

Scottish Native Woods Campaign,
3 Kenmore Street, Aberfeldy,
Perthshire, PH15 2AW
Director: Alan Drever

REFORESTING SCOTLAND

The aims of this campaign are, firstly, to tell the story of Scottish deforestation and the destruction of the Great Wood of Caledon; secondly, to promote ecological restoration and rural development through the establishment of sustainable land-use, based on a network of mixed forests; thirdly, to establish the link between the bare hills of Scotland and worldwide deforestation.

The campaign is co-ordinated by Bernard Planterose, editor of one of the most lively magazines there is on the subject of trees, *Tree Planters Guide to the Galaxy*. A recent edition included the following items: an editorial asking whether the new Scottish Natural Heritage will take on the goals of ecological restoration and sustainable land-use; 'Paradise Logged' – an account of the destruction of the Canadian Temperate Rainforest; the Isle Martin story – ten years of tree-planting on a small west-coast island; an account of seed storage concentrating on stratification techniques; a report on the state of the Siberian taiga and its future; an account of an organic tree nursery; a news round-up.

Reforesting Scotland, 51 Lorne Road, Edinburgh EH6 8QJ

important research into improving native hardwood markets and is following this up by demonstrating the suitability of these hardwoods for a variety of particularly high-value products such as flooring and furniture. Birch is particularly important as over half our native woodlands are dominated by this tree.

SNWC makes a point of involving the wider community and one special initiative is the primary-school-based, native tree nursery project: Growing Up With Trees. Children literally grow up with their native trees, from seed collection through to planting out several years later, looking after them along the way in their own nursery. The project is geared to small rural schools. One nursery, three metres square, can produce around 100 trees for planting out every year – a project of much more value than the common one-off tree-planting activity. In one-teacher schools, children grow up with trees for up to seven years, such as at Georgetown, beside Loch Rannoch in Perthshire – one of over 80 schools involved in the project. Its long-term nature offers special opportunities of links with the classroom.

Through children, the wider community are encouraged to become involved – particularly parents, some of whom even manage the project. Some landowners are also co-operating by providing small areas of land for children to establish areas of new native woodland.

The Tree Council, 35 Belgrave Square, London SW1X 8QN
Information and Publicity Officer: Fiona Anderson

The Tree Council Britain is one of the least wooded countries in Europe, with only ten per cent tree cover compared with, for example, 27 per cent in France, and 31 per cent in Spain. Much of lowland Britain was originally covered in broad-leaved woodland, but now two-thirds of our woodland is coniferous and mainly evergreen. During the last 50 years, 45 per cent of our ancient, semi-natural woodland has been cleared or converted to plantation. In the storms of 1987 and 1990 19 million trees were blown down. Dutch elm disease has killed 21 million trees. Unless there is a continuing programme of promoting natural regeneration, managing woods and planting trees as future replacements for existing stock, the landscapes we now cherish will inevitably deteriorate.

The Tree Council was founded in 1974 with major support from the Department of the Environment and, in 1978, it became an independ-fent registered charity.

Its main aim is to improve the environment in town and country by promoting the planting and conservation of trees and woods throughout Great Britain. For members, the council has 46 national organizations concerned with trees, which are involved in such diverse areas as arboriculture, conservation, forestry, landowning, the landscape, farming, education, planning and amenity. Government departments and their agencies sit on the Council in a consultative capacity.

The Tree Council acts as a forum for its members, to identify national tree problems and to provide initiatives for co-operation. Its wide membership equips it to foster collaboration between individuals, voluntary groups, public and private landowners, corporate interests and local authorities. As an independent, representative and non-profit-making organization, the Tree Council is able to put forward a balanced and national view to central and local government, industry and other organizations and individuals.

Each November, the Tree Council organizes National Tree Week, the UK's largest annual tree-planting campaign and a nationwide festival of trees. Its purpose is to raise public awareness of the importance of trees and to encourage tree planting and good management. Thousands of voluntary organizations – schools, local authorities and tree wardens, amongst many others – organize planting, management and other tree events throughout the UK. A record 750,000 trees were planted during National Tree Week in 1991.

THE TREE WARDEN SCHEME

This national initiative is co-ordinated and promoted by the Tree Council. Tree wardens are volunteers who gather information about their local trees, give advice on tree matters, protect threatened trees and encourage local practical tree projects. In rural areas of England, wardens are appointed by their parish council; in Wales, Scotland, Northern Ireland and in towns, they are appointed by other community organizations.

By the summer of 1992, there were schemes running in 29 counties and three major urban areas in England and Wales, with over 3,000 wardens having been appointed; the first schemes in Scotland are now being launched. Tree wardens need not be tree experts – only enthusiasts – as the Tree Council provides each warden with a detailed information pack and organizes, with county councils and the British Trust for Conservation Volunteers, a series of optional one-day training courses in all the participating counties.

Trees are not immortal and our trees and woods face many threats – development, urban sprawl, intensive agriculture, neglect. We need to take action now if future generations are to enjoy the beauty and variety of our landscapes. To be most effective, this action should be taken by people on the spot, by people who have most to gain from the protection and enhancement of their immediate environment.

Among the activities they become involved in are: gathering information and doing surveys of their local trees, so as to discover where practical help and advice are needed to develop ideas for projects and become aware of trees under threat; giving advice – a key element in the tree warden's role. Wardens will not necessarily have all the answers, but they will soon learn where to find them. Local people can often see what needs to be done to protect trees before council officials, and tree wardens help to ensure compliance with tree preservation orders and planning consents by informing their local council of trees threatened by, for example, development and building work; they organize, or encourage others to organize, practical tree projects. Tree wardens have for instance, persuaded farmers to plant hedgerow trees and manage woods, created nature reserves, initiated successful prosecutions against developers, organized tree competitions and woodland walks with schools, created town tree trails, written historical analyses of parish woods, surveyed tree bat roosts, planted trees on derelict ground and in school playing fields, set up tree nurseries, created 'green corridors' between villages, organized tree art and even poetry competitions.

If you would like to become a tree warden, contact the Tree Council to see if there is a scheme running in your area.

The Tree Council also holds quarterly forums where member organizations debate tree topics of current concern. It arranges national conferences and seminars to bring together a wide variety of groups and views on tree matters.

The Tree Council answers enquiries from the public and, when appropriate, directs enquirers to the technical help which member organizations can provide. It obtains wide publicity for National Tree Week and other Tree Council initiatives in the national, regional and local media. It publishes a magazine, *Tree News*, which is distributed to members, government departments and, on request, to other interested organizations and individuals. A range of other publications is also available.

The Tree Council runs its own tree-planting grant scheme and particularly welcomes applications from local groups and schools. Grants, which are inevitably small, are available for planting trees where local people can enjoy them.

Member organizations pay annual subscriptions and the Department of the Environment makes a grant towards administrative costs, but the Tree Council depends principally on donations, legacies and sponsorship to maintain and expand its activities. The Council is jointly controlled by its members and is administered by a staff of four from its London office.

Trees For Life, Findhorn Foundation, Forres, Grampian IV36 0TZ
Director: Alan Watson
Winner: 1991 Ford British Conservation Project of the Year Award.

Trees For Life The aim of the Trees for Life project is to return a large area – about 600 square miles – in the Highlands to its naturally forested condition and, eventually, to reintroduce some of the missing species of wildlife which have disappeared with the forest. The project seeks to be a working model of ecological restoration and a pilot project for the larger-scale restoration efforts which will be needed in many parts of the world. It works in close co-operation with government bodies (including the Forestry Commission), private landowners and various other interested parties.

There are three main aspects to the project: first, fencing off areas on the periphery of the surviving forest remnants to facilitate the natural regeneration of the forest; second, planting completely deforested areas with young trees grown from seed collected from the nearest surviving native trees (in 1992, 16,300 seedlings were planted); third, the removal of non-native species of trees which have been underplanted in some of the remnants of the old forest.

The project also includes an extensive volunteer programme, whereby people can participate in week-long work camps to help restore the forest, and public presentations and other educational work.

Tree Register of the British Isles (TROBI), 2 Church Cottages, Westmeston, Hassocks, West Sussex BN6 8RJ
Founder and Director: Alan Mitchell

The Tree Register of the British Isles The Register lists location, height and girth of specimen trees of over 1,900 species of tree, both natural and planted, but especially those in gardens and arboreta. There are over 95,000 individual records and several thousand new ones are added annually.

The trees are measured at intervals so that the records give a unique set of growth data which can be sorted according to latitude, climate and region. TROBI gives as its main aim the identification and recording of exceptional trees, together with any special features of them or of the sites where they are growing. Champion trees (the largest recorded specimens) can also be an important gene bank, valuable for propagation purposes, and are listed every few years.

In these islands, only about 20 native species qualify (on grounds of size) for the Register – the overwhelming majority of the records being for introduced species. The concept of a tree register is potentially of vital significance in other countries, especially those where the tree flora is overwhelmingly of native species. The importance for conservation and for raising awareness about trees and the tree heritage cannot be over-estimated. Up to now, such a register only exists, in a rather different form, in New Zealand and the US, but many other countries would benefit from the establishment of such a scheme.

Tree Spirit The birth of Tree Spirit goes back to 1984, when Martin Blount organized a local petition calling for the Forestry Commission to pursue a more ecologically sound management of the local forest – Wyre Forest. This attracted a fair amount of local media coverage and strong support from many people. From this response, the seeds of Tree Spirit were sown.

Tree Spirit, Hawkbatch Farm, Arley, near Bewdley, Hereford and Worcester DY12 3AH
Secretary: Martin Blount

In an inaugural meeting it was decided that tree-planting projects should go hand in hand with making people aware of the many aspects of trees – their growth, wildlife, timber uses, medicinal uses, folklore, etc. The aim was to create more respect for our tree friends and maybe a healthier, more holistic attitude towards the earth and all its inhabitants as well.

The first undertakings were a number of small tree-planting projects for local landowners and parish councils, and starting the production of a magazine, which covers the many facets of trees – from growing an acorn to meditating with a favourite tree. Indeed, individual responses to trees is actively encouraged by the group.

The annual moot or meeting of Tree Spirit members and friends has provided a good opportunity to discuss future projects, to meet like-minded folk and to enjoy the beauty of the natural world. The Tree Spirit meetings are held not in some cosy, heated convention room, but out of doors amongst the trees, the wildlife – where the earth, the air, the sun and the water can truly be felt and appreciated.

HAZEL BIRCH (NÉE ALISON SMITH) OF TREE SPIRIT

'Trees, for me basically are friends. When I have been going through bad times in my life, I find I have drawn very close to the spirit of the trees, I find that I can connect with them. At other times I'd find just being with them clarifies things in myself. If you approach a tree with a spirit of love, of openness, perhaps you will feel the aura of peace they give off. At times they come through to me with clear messages... It was a tree that told me I was pregnant, believe me or not!'

Q: *What's actually happening when a group of you gather round and bless a tree as you plant it?*

'When a group of people come together and they're chanelling their focus, all their energy, their love and their intent into planting a tree, then it will grow and flourish and it represents all trees throughout the world, and you hope at the same time that people's awareness of trees will grow as the tree grows.'

A PERSONAL CAMPAIGN: THE JOYS OF TREE PLANTING

by Dick Warner

There seems to be a pretty universal urge to collect things. Or maybe it isn't that universal – maybe women are more sensible about postage stamps, vintage cars and 60s rock albums. Anyway, I collect trees.

I've got about five or six hundred and my ambition is to own a thousand before I end up in the great forest in the sky. This means that parts of the two acres I live on are already rather thickly wooded. But it's amazing how many trees can fit into an acre. I have just about every common species from northern Europe, plus a few exotics from other continents. But there are always some gaps to be filled. I have to get another baby yew to replace the one that died last winter.

Growing a tree produces so much return for so little effort. Okay, I devote the odd day in winter or early spring to planting, but this is pleasant exercise for the middle-aged, if you take it at the right pace. In summer, I wander around pulling weeds away from the smaller saplings and repairing the odd wind-blown stake or frayed tie. A little pruning, if one or more exuberant items in the collection are getting out of hand and obstructing a path – and that's about all. It really is the lazy man's form of gardening – or it would be if I didn't keep a few escapist sheep as well.

As collections go, mine has cost remarkably little over the dozen or so years I've been building it up. The most I have ever paid for a tree was £12 for a large Japanese larch I fancied in a garden centre. But many of my trees are grown from seed – a fascinating and rewarding activity in itself. Others are seedlings dug up from the wild. The experts frown on this as a way of collecting trees; but then many of the same experts are in the business of selling tree seedlings and therefore not totally unbiased. It's worked very well for me. I've had great satisfaction from proudly bearing home a four-foot horse chestnut, or even an attractive maple seeding. Almost all of them have grown on very well, even when I've been caught without a spade or trowel and had to extricate them with my bare hands from the leaf mould of a wood.

Of course you have to establish two things before you take a tree seedling from the wild: first of all, that it doesn't belong to anyone – or, if it does, that they have given permission; secondly, that it won't survive and flourish in the place it germinated. Trees on roadside verges I regard as fair game and many seedlings growing under a full forest canopy are doomed to death from light starvation.

No, getting trees is not a problem. Getting the land to plant them on can be. I'm lucky with my two acres, which had some fine ash trees already when I bought it, as well as some lesser species like hawthorn, blackthorn, elder and crab apple, which gave the collection a head start.

But you don't necessarily have to own land in order to start planting. Much council land and commonage – or land surrounding schools and factories – is eminently suitable and the people in charge seldom refuse the offer of planting a grove or two.

There are many satisfactions to be gained from watching trees grow. I sometimes point out to the unconverted the products I get from my trees – my house is heated by wood and the coppiceable species on the land are just getting to the stage where I can crop a few logs. The garden is shaded, protected from the wind. There are nuts and berries and the thorny branch used to block a gap where the sheep are escaping. But really these are incidental. More important is the fact that I have added some enduring beauty to the landscape and the benefits that the trees and their products give to other creatures. Ireland was once a forest country and now has less trees per acre than anywhere in Europe, south of Iceland. The birds and the animals, the insects and the ferns and fungi that depend on the forest are now amongst our more endangered species. My wood is helping them a little.

But the really compelling justification for planting and caring for trees is the pleasure it brings. I walk around with my hands in my pockets and, in February, I see the first buds burst on the elder. In April, it is the glory of the blackthorn blossom that does me good, in May the wild cherry. In summer there is the sturdy new growth of a young ash to admire and in autumn, the colour of the two American maples at the north end of the garden. Winter is made a little greener and warmer by a Scots pine and a couple of hollies I can see from the kitchen window – if, that is, I can keep the sheep away from them.

Perhaps in my old age I shall become eccentric and wander around talking to my family of trees. Threatening them with steel discipline if they don't perform, encouraging them when they're growing well. But what harm will I be doing anyone? Excuse me. I'm just going to pop outside and check if the bees have found the pussy-willow and at the same time see whether the larches are in flower yet.

16

The Future of Trees

This afternoon, being on Fair Haven Hill, I heard the sound of a saw, and soon after from the Cliff saw two men sawing down a noble pine beneath, about forty rods off ... the last of a dozen or more which were left when the forest was cut and for fifteen years have waved in solitary majesty over the sprout-land. I saw them like beavers or insects gnawing at the trunk of this noble tree, the diminutive manikins with their cross-cut saw which could scarcely span it ... I watch closely to see when it begins to move. Now the sawers stop, and with an axe open it a little on the side towards which it leans, that it may break the faster, and now their saw goes again. Now surely it is going; it is inclined one quarter of the quadrant, and, breathless, I expect its crashing fall. But no, I was mistaken; it has not moved an inch; it stands at the same angle as at first. It is fifteen minutes yet to its fall.

Still its branches wave in the wind, as if it were destined to stand for a century, and the wind soughs through its needles as of yore; it is still a forest tree, the most majestic tree that waves over Musketaquid.

The silvery sheen of sunlight is reflected from its needles; it still affords an inaccessible crotch for the squirrel's nest; not a lichen has forsaken its mast-like stem, its raking mast, – the hill is the hulk.

Now, now's the moment! The manikins at its base are fleeing from their crime. They have dropped the guilty saw and axe. How slowly and majestically it starts! As if it were only swayed by a summer breeze, and would return without a sigh to its location in the air.

And now it fans the hillside with its fall, and lies down to its bed in the valley, from which it is never to rise, as softly as a feather, folding its green mantle about it like a warrior, as if, tired of standing, it embraces the earth with silent joy, returning its elements to the dust again. But hark! ... You only saw, but did not hear. There now comes up a deafening crash to these rocks, advertising you that even trees do not die without a groan ... It is lumber ... When the fish hawk in the spring revisits the banks of the Muskatequid, he will circle in vain to find his accustomed perch, and the hen-hawk will mourn for the pines lofty enough to protect his brood ... I hear no knell tolled, I see no procession of mourners in the streets, or the woodland aisles. The squirrel has leaped to another tree; the hawk has circled farther off, and has now settled upon a new eyrie, but the woodman is preparing to lay his axe to the root of that also.

H. D. THOREAU, Walden, 1854

Henry David Thoreau claimed that he was born 'in the nick of time' when he could learn as a boy to love the New England countryside 'in which wild nature had not yet completely been tamed.' After building his own cabin in the woods next to Walden Pond, he conducted what was then seen as a revolutionary experiment, by moving in and living in the woods in an effort to get closer to nature. He is one of the few writers who have made it a priority to remain in harmony with nature. His first instinct when walking in the woods was one of intense, unfettered wonderment. As a guide to the experience of nature he is perhaps unequalled.

W E LIVE IN THE AGE of the chainsaw and the age of the bulldozer. Everywhere, trees in their natural state are being destroyed on a grand scale, virgin forests cut down for short-term profit without regard for the environmmental cost. Countries like Brazil are apparently engaged in a grotesque race to catch up with the levels of deforestation found in the 'developed' nations. As was the case in

Europe in the seventeenth and eighteenth centuries, trees have become a commodity throughout much of the world, not valued for what Robert Louis Stevenson described as 'that emanation that so wonderfully changes and renews a weary spirit', but viewed as so many board feet of sawn timber. Trees which fail to produce good timber become 'weed species', to be cut out or reduced to so many tons of wood chips. Natural woodland or forest is considered 'untidy', undeveloped, and in urgent need of 'improvement' by man. According to the historian Keith Thomas, any wild country in England, whether mountainous or forested, was regarded by seventeenth-century travellers as dangerous and ugly; and today the rain forests of the tropics are perceived in similarly hostile terms – as a challenge to modern technology.

Around the globe, the timber industry is hard at work trying to justify its activities. The Japanese, for example, claim that since only five per cent of the damage to tropical forests is done by commercial logging, there is no need to give it up. According to a Japanese spokesman for JANT in Papua New Guinea, his company's clearing of virgin rain forest and conversion of the trees into wood-chips for cardboard is a great achievement. 'We have 200 kinds of species (sic) all mixed up in this forest, so I think it will be better for us to cut all over the area first and then plant it, selecting just some useful species.' Useful, that is, to cardboard manufacturers.

Keith Thomas has traced changing public attitudes to the natural world over the last few centuries and, in his book *Man and the Changing World*, he quotes various chroniclers of the countryside who were among the first to articulate ideas that are all too prevalent today. In 1769, Mrs Elizabeth Carter was regretting that so much of the English countryside was still 'disgraced by ... tracts of uncultivated land'; while at around the same time, the agriculturalist Arthur Young was anxious to bring 'the wastelands of the kingdom into useful culture'. Both reflect a particular view of nature which is common even today, and not just in the developing countries. The wholesale destruction of primary forest is not restricted to Malaysia or Brazil. Neither the USA nor Canada apparently has the political will to prevent the catastrophic looting in Oregon and British Columbia of some of the greatest temperate rain forests in the world. Even in England, where our ancient forests have been reduced to fragments, they are still being destroyed to make way for motorways. Seeking to deflect criticism of his Department's appalling record, the British Minister of Transport recently came up with one of the most ridiculous statements ever to be issued from that source of public vandalism, namely that 'roads are good for the environment ... we planted more trees than the Forestry Commission last year.'

It is quite true that millions of trees are being planted and credit is claimed on behalf of large multinational companies, forestry agencies and even governments; yet they have little hope of ever reaching maturity and practically none of standing for their natural lives. Tree plantations of stunning uniformity are still referred to as 'forests' – rather like calling a grass tennis court, savannah – and some of them, like those planted in the Flow Country of Sutherland in order to gain tax benefits, are obviously in unsuitable places.

Once again, such attitudes were anticipated by those seventeenth-century writers who extolled the virtues of man's ordering of the countryside. In 1676, Ralph Austen eulogized his fruit trees as follows: 'it is a great pleasure and delight to walk among you, so many beautiful ... trees; seeing ye grow so handsomely and uniform; ye grow in order, in straight lines every way a man will look.' Had he lived this century, he would surely have written in similar vein about conifers. Tourists are enticed into our modern tree plantations by dishonest signs advertising 'Forest Walks'. Better by far to follow the example of Alan Watson, the photographer and driving force behind Trees For Life, who prefers walking among the ancient pines of Glen Affric. 'I feel my spirit uplifted here. Every tree here is an individual, no two are the same. They are as different from each other as people.'

In some places, natural forests like the Great Caledonian Pine Forest have even been 'improved' by the addition of healthier stock – sitka spruce from Germany or birch from Bulgaria, perhaps – inserted between ancient Scots pines that are supposedly moribund. It is to the credit of campaigners that such policies are gradually being eradicated and even corrected by the removal of these aliens, at least in some areas considered to be of major conservation value.

The phrase 'dead wood' has unfortunate negative connotations in contemporary English, implying that it is something that should be removed, cut out lest it hold back the thrusting energy of youth or prevent maximum growth. Old and dead trees are tidied up and cleared away instead of being allowed to rot, whether standing or fallen, with the result that the rich array of insects, birds and other creatures that depend on such habitats find it increasingly hard to survive. To many foresters 'sustainable logging' means taking away dead trees. Yet studies in places where dead trees are allowed to rot naturally have revealed that for the whole plant and animal community trees are just as important when they are dead as they are when alive. Yet how many people, from park-keepers to farmers, from gardeners to foresters, make it their policy to leave old or damaged trees and resist the urge to tidy them up?

In the Great Storm of October 1987, millions of trees were blown down across southern England and bordering areas of continental Europe. After the initial shock, there was an extraordinary upwelling of popular emotion about this loss, much of it arising from an uncomprehending horror of the damage done. It was accompanied by a great urge to clear up and remove all the fallen branches and tree-trunks, so that new trees could be planted. Ecologists – well aware of the periodic catastrophes that affect nearly all biological systems – advised caution. Many had noticed that younger, planted trees had suffered disproportionately. In some of the great parks like Windsor, none of the really ancient trees had been destroyed – hollow trees survived the storm best of all. Yet elsewhere whole plantations were devastated.

Either way, many trees have a remarkable regenerative capacity, being able to survive after losing limbs or even being blown down. And when woodland is allowed to heal itself, the result is in many ways more diverse, ecologically richer and altogether more natural. In the London area, the storm rectified overnight the single most unnatural feature of local woods: the complete absence of dead and decaying tree trunks. Since then, woodpeckers, spiders, beetles, small mammals, tree seedlings and very many other organisms have found a richer habitat and are thriving in increased numbers due to the change.

The word 'regeneration' occurs rarely in writings about forestry, yet in these islands, as many gardeners are aware, little need be done to produce woodland aside from encouraging some of the thousands of tree seedlings that appear every year. (In tropical conditions, recovery of destroyed forest is more difficult; soil and air temperatures shoot up when forest is cleared and, if the clearings become too large, seedlings cannot get established.) Many smaller trees will regrow from cut stems and pioneer species will produce a canopy very quickly; with a little encouragement forest will regenerate, though it may take centuries for the natural forest to return. In Scotland, for example, where projects such as Trees For Life are in hand to recover the Caledonian Pine Forest, it will take a hundred years or more to restore mature pine forest in what are at present deforested areas.

We need to distinguish between tree-farms, amenity trees and natural habitats. Much tree-planting here and abroad is really tree-farming, with carefully selected and often introduced species of strictly limited genetic diversity being planted in monocultures or oligocultures. These are often fast-growing species planted for maximum timber production, with a relatively short rotation planned. Consideration is rarely given to the ecological cost in terms of soil and water conservation, though, in some countries like Costa Rica, such plantations have succeeded in meeting local fuel needs and reducing local deforestation.

Eucalyptus species are very popular around the world, because the seeds are tiny – millions to the kilo –, their viability is high and, even more importantly perhaps, the chipboard and pulp industries find the wood useful. In temperate conditions, pines and poplars are the equivalent species. Growing such trees is big business and, in some places, an appropriate use of land. But such trees, mass-produced for a particular purpose, lack the variety needed to make an equivalent contribution to the ecosystem as trees growing naturally. Using them on a large scale to replace real forest is nothing short of vandalism. The fact that this is often encouraged and even instigated by international agencies such as FAO and the World Bank, in which the developed nations have the major voice, makes us at least partly responsible.

But there are signs of change. Alternative voices are beginning to be heard. The restoration and rehabilitation of ancient forests is being discussed and trees are being revalued. Ancient traditions of management such as coppicing and pollarding are being revived, woodmanship and the special knowledge of forest peoples are being favourably re-evaluated, even by the World Bank and the Ministry of Overseas Development. Tree groups and campaigns are growing fast; demonstrators are massing to oppose large projects which set out to destroy forests. Internationally, trees are now the focus of attention for many groups, some of whom have to operate in very hostile climates. In Kenya, Professor Wangari Mathai, the leader of the Green Belt Movement and winner of the Africa Prize for leadership in the sustainable end to hunger, has been brutally beaten by the police for campaigning about the environment. So reviled is her attitude that President Arap Moi has said publicly that she 'must have insects in her brain'. In Thailand and Malaysia, campaigners against the building of dams and logging primary forest have been assaulted and imprisoned, yet they are continuing their struggle and are gaining ground as acceptance of the vital contribution that trees make to the environment grows around the world.

The need to protect large animals from over-exploitation and even extinction has become generally established, but the notion of conserving plants as valuable or endangered species in themselves, rather than simply as part of the habitats needed by large animals, is a much newer idea to many people.

In remote forests, in places such as the Amazon region and the eastern Himalayas, new trees are still being found and described for the first time. Despite this, the diversity of the tree world is threatened, and not just by forest clearance in the rain forest. Some of the world's rarest and most endangered trees are found on small islands such as Socotra, St Helena, Mauritius and Rodrigues. The numbers of some species growing in the wild are already so small that any decrease could threaten their survival. The strange trees on Socotra exist only as populations of a few hundred and there are some trees, such as the St Helena Olive and the Cafe Marron of Rodrigues, where there is only one known specimen left alive. Yet the islanders have until recently been unaware of their significance and on many islands the introduction of goats and other herbivores has effectively prevented the natural regeneration of native trees. Only now are measures being taken to counteract this.

Wendy Strahm, plant conservation officer for the World Wildlife Fund in Mauritius, has produced a Red Data Book for the plants of Rodrigues, drawing attention to the endangered trees and other plants of that extraordinary island. She has also begun active recovery programmes in Rodrigues and Mauritius, involving protection and propagation in safe places, such as offshore islands, as well as securing important sites as nature reserves and educating the public about its responsibilities. She is now working on a Red Data Book for Mauritius, whose endangered plants include many fine timber trees and palms.

By contrast, a recent world scheme for conserving rare conifers reflects the more likely fate of many forest habitats. Instead of putting the emphasis on preserving the natural habitat of the trees, the scheme relies on 'ex-situ' planting – bringing specimens to grow in gardens and arboreta throughout these islands, the climate of which is equable enough to enable almost every endangered species to grow.

So trees are becoming the subject of active conservation, not just because their products are useful, but because endangered species are seen as worth conserving in themselves. But for trees to have a real future on this increasingly overcrowded planet, it is essential that we recover our respect for them. Although, particularly in the country, there are still traditions in which trees are revered and respected, they are, in England, much less prevalent than in the past. Only in Ireland and in country areas of continental Europe do trees still assume a general spiritual significance.

However, the evidence from certain other societies around the world suggests that all is not lost; that there are peoples who still have a respectful attitude towards trees. To cut a live tree on the Island of Socotra today is to incur the wrath of the whole community. Children are taught from a very early age only to collect dead wood for firewood. Live trees may only be cut in an emergency and social pressure ensures compliance. Likewise the Kuna of Panama and the Yanomami of Brazil and Venezuela have an equally respectful attitude to trees, based on a deep understanding of their myriad properties and products. Many of these peoples have lived in the forests for extremely long periods of time and moves are now afoot to capitalize on the knowledge they possess, especially in the areas of new drugs and other products. But what may yet be of greater import, is these peoples' experience in using trees, while at the same time preserving the forest for future generations. Recent archaeological finds in the Amazon valley have revealed 5,000-year-old cities with irrigation schemes, suggesting that the forest is not as 'natural' as previously assumed. Indeed it now appears likely that the reviled 'slash-and-burn' agriculture, widely blamed for forest destruction (60 per cent, as opposed to commercial logging's 10 per cent [according to FAO]), in fact made a major, or even predominant contribution to creating the forests that we see today.

On the Miritiparana River in Colombia, the Yucuna people have pursued this method for hundreds of years. Areas to be felled are carefully selected and then cultivated for two seasons. After felling they are left for several years while fast-growing secondary forest fills the gap. This is ideal firewood which is then cut for this purpose before another two seasons' crops are grown. The plots are then left for many generations – long enough for the big timber trees to grow, but not before an array of fruit trees and other game-attracting trees and medicinal plants have been sown. Like other forest peoples, the Yucuna often trek long distances to collect particular fruits or nuts at a special time of year, or to find particular game animals in the right season. These are not random wanderings. Having lived in the same forest for so long, the Yucuna know exactly where the things they need are to be found; after all, it was their own ancestors who planted the trees. It is no wonder, perhaps, that the spirits of the ancestors are so important to the welfare of the community. Ancestor worship may not be the style of English woodmen, but it is with real pride that Bill Hogarth points out that certain woods were last cut by his father, or even his grandfather, on particular dates. Because of their longevity, real work with trees requires several generations of people. We would do well to remember that and learn to respect those ancient trees that have seen many human generations. In Papua New Guinea there is a saying that 'Our forests are a gift from our ancestors which must be passed on to our children', while in the words of Chief Seattle, of what is now Oregon, 'The earth does not belong to man, but man to the earth.' We would do well to remember that too.

TREE INFORMATION

A Diary of Tree Events

5 January **Burning the Ashen Faggot** This ancient Somerset folk tradition takes place at the King William IV public house, Curry Rivel, Somerset.

6 January **Wassailing the Apple Trees** Apple trees are encouraged to bear a good crop by 'shooting them' at Carhampton, Somerset.

6 January **Apple Howling** organized by the Chanctonbury Ring Morris Men, Henfield, Sussex.

14 January **Chinese New Year** Associated with peach trees and peach blossom.

February/March **Ash Wednesday** Children in Hampshire and Sussex carry ash twigs to school; those who don't can expect to have their feet stamped on!

March **Irish Tree Week** Week of tree-planting in Ireland co-ordinated by the Tree Council of Ireland.

March/April **Palm Sunday** Flowering sallow branches used as 'palm', yew fronds in Ireland and box at French Protestant Church of Notre Dame in Soho Square, central London.

30 April/1 May **May Festival** Ancient Celtic Bealtaine festival held in Ireland. May boughs and may bushes set up. Maypoles are the centre of celebrations in some places in England.

7 or 8 May **Flora Day or Furry Day** Young people bring branches, mainly sycamore, into the town of Helston, Cornwall, and perform the Hal-an-Tow play and songs. The famous furry dance or floral dance occurs there on the same day.

29 May approx. **Oak Apple Day or Arbor Day (formerly Restoration Day)** An English festival commemorating the restoration of the monarchy on 29 May 1660. It was started by Charles II, who had earlier evaded the Roundheads by hiding in an oak tree. At St Neot, Cornwall, an oak branch is placed on top of the tower of the parish church. Worcester City Hall gates are decorated with oak branches, while at Aston on Clun, children process to the arbor tree and there are Morris dancers and a village carnival.

29 May **Grovely Day** At Great Wishford, Wiltshire, the villagers go into Grovely Wood and collect oak boughs. At 10 a.m. they proceed to Salisbury Cathedral and perform a dance in the nave; the celebrations are to commemorate the granting of grazing and wood-gathering rights to the villagers.

29 May **Founders Day** At the Royal Hospital, Chelsea, London, the statue of King Charles II is covered in oak branches; pensioners and guests wear oak sprigs in their buttonholes.

June **Bawning the Thorn** A festival of decorating the Holy Thorn at Appleton Thorn in Cheshire takes place on the third Saturday of the month. The 'thorn' is a cutting from the Glastonbury Thorn.

August **St Cedd** At Polstead, Suffolk, a service in commemoration of St Cedd is held beside the remains of the gospel oak on the first Sunday of the month.

21 September **Apple Day** A recent innovation by the Common Ground group and others to arouse public interest in the need to conserve local varieties of apple.

October **Samhaine** Celtic festival at the start of the winter season.

October **World Conker Championships** These championships have been held on the second Sunday of the month at Ashton, Northamptonshire, since 1965.

November/December **National Tree Week** The U.K. Tree Council co-ordinates a week of national tree-planting. It includes a newly created Tree-Dressing Day around 1 December.

December **Christmas Tree in Trafalgar Square** The tree has been an annual gift of the citizens of Oslo to the citizens of London since 1947, in gratitude for support during the Second World War.

18 December **Clipping the Thorn** Outside St John's Church, Glastonbury, Somerset, the Holy Thorn is clipped by the oldest child of St John's Infant School; the ceremony is attended by the vicar, the mayor and aldermen.

24 December **Burning the Ashen Faggot** This ceremony takes place at the Luttrell Arms, Dunster, Somerset.

24 December **Christmas** Christmas trees (normally fir or spruce) are erected and decorated both inside and outside houses and in public places to celebrate Christmas. The custom is said to have been introduced into this country by Queen Victoria's consort, Prince Albert. The trees are traditionally taken down on Twelfth Night (6 January).

25 December **Christmas Day** Celebration of the ancient festival of the winter solstice. Traditionally, yule logs are burnt.

Characteristics of Native Trees

Latin names in classification order with Family headings, common name, method of pollination, method of reproduction
[M = Monoecious, D = Dioecious, H = Hermaphrodite] *Trees which are largely infertile.

GYMNOSPERMAE (all British species are evergreen)
PINACEAE
Pinus sylvestris L.	Scots pine	wind	M

CUPRESSACEAE
Juniperus communis L.	juniper	probably wind	D
Taxus baccata L.	yew	wind	D

ANGIOSPERMAE (All British species are deciduous with the exceptions of arbutus, box and holly.)
TILIACEAE
Tilia platyphyllos Scop.	large-leaved lime	bees etc.	H
Tilia cordata Miller	small-leaved lime	bees etc.	H
(*Tilia x europea* L.	common lime	bees etc.	H*)

ACERACEAE
Acer campestre L.	field maple	various small insects	M

AQUIFOLIACEAE
Ilex aquifolium L.	holly	bees	D

BUXACEAE
Buxus sempervirens L.	box	bees/flies	M

ROSACEAE
Prunus padus L.	bird cherry	various insects	H
Prunus avium (L.) L.	gean, wild cherry	various insects	H
Crataegus laevigata (Poiret) DC.	midland hawthorn	flies etc.	H
Crataegus monogyna Jacq.	hawthorn	flies etc.	H
Sorbus aucuparia L.	rowan, mountain ash	various insects	H
Sorbus aria (L.) Crantz	common whitebeam	flies etc.	H
Sorbus domestica L.	true service	various insects	H
Sorbus torminalis (L.) Crantz	wild service tree	various insects	H
other *Sorbus* spp. (approx 16 species, many endemic)	various insects		H

ROSACEAE (cont.)
Pyrus cordata Desv.	Plymouth pear	flies, bees	H
Pyrus pyraster (L.) Burgstr.	wild pear	insects	H
Malus sylvestris Miller	crab apple	bees etc.	H

ULMACEAE
Ulmus glabra Hudson	wych elm	wind	H
Ulmus minor Miller (incl. *U. procera* Salisb. and *U. carpinifolia* G. Suckow.)	elm (incl. English elm)	wind	H

BETULACEAE
Betula pendula Roth.	silver birch	wind	M*
Betula pubescens Ehrh.	downy birch	wind	M*
Alnus glutinosa (L.) Gaertner	alder	wind	M*

CORYLACEAE
Carpinus betulus L.	hornbeam	wind	M
Corylus avellana L.	hazel, cobnut	wind	M

FAGACEAE
Fagus sylvatica L.	beech	wind	M
Quercus robur L.	common/pedunculate oak	wind	M
Quercus petraea (Mattuschka) Libel.	durmast/sessile oak	wind	M

SALICACEAE
Populus tremula L.	aspen	wind	D
Populus nigra L.	black poplar	wind	D
Salix pentandra L.	bay willow	insects	D
Salix fragilis L.	crack willow	insects	D
Salix alba L.	white willow	insects	D
Salix triandra L.	almond willow	insects	D
Salix purpurea L.	purple willow	insects	D
Salix viminalis L.	osier	insects	D
Salix caprea L.	goat willow	insects	D
Salix aurita L.	eared willow	insects	D
Salix cinerea L.	grey willow	insects	D
Salix herbacea L.	dwarf willow	insects	D

ERICACEAE
Arbutus unedo (L.)	arbutus/strawberry tree	wind	H

OLEACEAE
Fraxinus excelsior L.	ash	wind	H

Values for life history traits of major tree species
KEY:

DMAX	Maximum diameter at 1.3m (d.b.h.)
HMAX	Maximum height
AMAX	Maximum age in years
GMAX	Growth constant (the higher the number, the faster the growth rate)
WDEN	Wood density kgm^{-3}
WRES	Wood decay resistance (1 = low, 5 = high)

SSIZE	Weight of 1,000 seeds
SCROP	Frequency of good seed crop in years
SMINP	Age to first seed productions
SGDEL	Seed germinability group, (1 – germinate immediately, 2 – germination delayed, 3 – germination after longer delay)

SPECIES	DMAX (cm)	HMAX (cm)	AMAX	GMAX	WDEN (kgm^{-3})	WRES	SSIZE (g)	SCROP (Year)	SMINP (Year)	SGDEL
Ruderals (Pioneers)										
Alnus glutinosa (L) Gaertner Alder	100	3500	150	198.2	510	2	1.1	2-3	40	1
Betula pendula Roth Silver Birch	100	3000	120	214.6	610	1	0.11	1-2	30	1
Betula pubescens Ehrh Downy Birch	100	3000	120	214.6	610	1	0.12	2-3	30	1
Populus nigra L. Black Poplar	200	3000	150	174.7	410	2	–	–	25	–
Populus tremula L. Aspen	100	3500	100	297.2	450	1	0.12	1-2	25	1
Salix alba L. White Willow	130	3000	100	259.3	330	1	–	–	15	–
Salix caprea L. Goat Willow	80	1500	60	228.8	460	1	–	–	15	–
Competitors										
Carpinus betulus L. Hornbeam	100	3000	250	103.0	790	2	50	2-3	40	3
Fraxinus excelsior L. Ash	150	4000	300	113.3	650	2	80	2-3	40	3
Tilia cordata Miller Small-leaved Lime	200	4000	400	85.4	490	1	35	1-2	30	3
Tilia platyphyllos Scop. Large-leaved Lime	150	3500	350	85.7	490	1	110	2-3	40	3
Ulmus glabra Hudson Wych Elm	150	3700	400	79.0	640	3	15	1-2	50	2
Ulmus minor Miller Elm	120	3200	300	91.6	640	3	9	1-2	50	2
Stress Tolerators										
Juniperus communis L. Juniper	40	1500	400	65.0	600	4	9	1-2	15	3
Taxus baccata L. Yew	80	2000	500	35.4	640	5	60	2-3	70	3
Stress Tolerant Ruderals										
Acer campestre L. Field Maple	60	1500	100	135.4	610	2	80	1-2	30	2
Malus sylvestris Miller Crab Apple	40	1500	80	165.8	670	2	30	2-3	20	2
Prunus padus L. Bird Cherry	40	1500	80	165.8	–	2	50	2-3	20	2
Pyrus communis L. Pear (Common)	60	1800	100	159.1	700	2	25	2-3	20	2
Sorbus aria (L) Crantz Whitebeam	30	1500	100	130.4	710	2	440	–	20	–
Sorbus aucuparia L. Rowan	40	1700	60	247.2	730	2	250	2-3	20	2
Sorbus torminalis (L) Crantz Wild Service	70	2000	100	175.9	710	2	400	–	20	–
Competitive Stress Tolerators										
Fagus sylvatica L. Beech	150	4000	300	113.3	680	2	235	5-8	70	2
Quercus petraea (Matt) Liebl Durmast Sessile Oak	200	4000	500	68.3	650	4	3150	5-8	70	2
Quercus robur L. Common/Pedunculate Oak	230	4200	500	71.7	650	4	3850	3-8	70	2
Intermediate										
Pinus sylvestris L. Scots Pine	170	4500	450	84.5	490	3	6.1	3-4	40	1

Where to See Record Native Trees

The figure on the right is the Ordance Survey Map reference. The dimensions of the trees are given as follows: the tree's height x the tree's diameter — both in metres. The diameter reading was taken at 5ft from the ground and the date afterwards is the year when it was taken.

Abbotsbury, Dorset — SY5785
Oak, tall specimen: 42 x 1.47 (1986).

Abercynrig, Powys — SO0328
Alder, stoutest specimen: 15 x 1.32 (1988).
Ash, good specimen.

Achnagarry, Highland — NH3101
Cherry, record girth: 11 x 0.55 (1988).

Ardross Castle, Nr. Alness, Highland — NH6174
Goat Willow, record girth: 16 x 1.15 (1989).

Ashburnham Park, Sussex — TQ6914
Alder, tallest specimen: 32 x 0.75 (1983).

Aston on Clun, Shrops. — SO3982
Black Poplar, tree dressing ceremony.

Ballater, Grampian — NO3695
Juniper specimens.

Ballogie Estate, Ballater, Grampian — NO3695
Scots Pine, tallest specimen: 36 x 1.41 (1987).
Silver Birch, tallest specimen: 30 x 0.44 (1989).

Balmacaan, Drumnadrochit, Highland — NH5029
Grand Fir, record girth: 52 x 2.23 (1987).

Battersea Park, London — TQ2877
Whitebeam, tallest specimen: 14 x 0.63 (1987).

Belladrum, W. of Inverness, Highland — NH6345
Scots Pine, record girth: 33 x 1.69 (1987).

Bells Wood, Nr Bayford, Herts. — TZ3108
Bristlecone Pine: 12 x 0.28 (1985).

Belvoir Castle, Leics. — SK8133
Oak, tall specimen.
Yew, tallest specimen: 29 x 0.89 (1987).

Birnam, Dunkeld, Tayside — NO0242
Sycamore, record girth: 32 x 2.32 (1990).

Birr Castle, Co. Offaly — E32020
Box, tallest specimen: 12 x 0.19 (1985).

Bodnant Garden, Llanrwst, Gwynedd — SH7961
Coast Redwood: 47 x 1.59 (1984).

Bowthorpe, Lincs. — TF1709
Oak, record girth: 12 x 3.84 (1980).

Box Hill, Surrey — TQ1952
Box trees, Yew, Whitebeam and Wild Cherry.

Boxted Hall, Suffolk — TL8564
Walnut, record girth: 27 x 2.02 (1990).

Bradfield Woods, Suffolk — TL9206
Excellent coppice esp. ash, fine crab apple trees.

Brahan House, Highland — NX1434
Wych Elm, tallest specimen: 28 x 2.17 (1989).

Burnham Beeches, Berks. — SO9585
Ancient beech pollards.

Caledonian Pine Forest, Highland — NH9005
Spectacular ancient pine forest.

Canford School, Poole, Dorset — SZ0190
Sweet Chestnut, record girth: 36 x 1.84 (1984).

Castle Frazer, Aberdeen, Grampian — NJ7213
Holly, record girth: 9 x 0.97 (1988).

Castle Howard, Yorks. — SE7270
Wych Elm, record girth: 41 x 1.20 (1985).

Castle Leod, Highland — NO1043
Giant Redwood: 52 x 2.81 (1986).

Central Park, Bournemouth, Dorset — SZ0901
White Willow, tall specimen: 32 x 0.92 (1985).
Bay Willow, tall specimen: 18 x 0.57 (1985).
Dawn Redwood: 26 x 0.99 (1989).

Chilston Park, Nr Lenham, Kent — TQ8952
Field Maple, record girth: 21 x 1.34 (1990).

Chilworth, Hants. — SU4108
Rowan, record girth: 14 x 0.63 (1978).

Christ College, Brecon, Powys — SO0428
Fine Black Poplar.

Cirencester, Glos. — SV5195
Fine Black Poplar: 24 x 1.62.
Fine Black Poplar: 25 x 1.51.

Clapton Court, Som. — ST4106
Ash, tallest specimen: 38 x 0.91 (1985).

Claremont House, Esher, Surrey — TQ1464
Service Tree, tall specimen: 23 x 51 (1986).
Rowan, record girth: 23 x 0.51 (1986).

Cluny House, Aberfeldy, Tayside — NO1043
Giant Redwood: 36 x 3.45 (1988).

Corsham Courts, Nr. Calne, Wilts. — ST9971
Plane, record girth: 25 x 2.28 (1989).

Defynnoc Church, Powys — SN9227
Yew, record girth: 9 x 3.42 (1989).

Duntish House, Nr Dorchester, Dorset — ST6900
Plane, tallest specimen: 30 x 1.42 (1986).

East Carlton Park, Northampton, Northants. — SP7561
Common Lime, record girth: 29 x 2.13 (1979).

Easthampton, Snobdon, Herts. & Worcs. — SO3961
Sessile Oak, record girth: 25 x 3.18 (1989).

Epping Forest, Essex — TQ4197
Beech and other ancient pollards and woodland.

Felshamhall Wood, Suffolk — TL9366
Crab Apple: 10 x 1.03.

Florencecourt, Nr Enniskillen, Co. Fermanagh — E32233
Original Irish Yew Mother plant.

Forde Abbey, Chard, Dorset — ST3505
Small-leaved Lime, record girth: 24 x 1.65 (1988).

Gatton Park, Redhill, Surrey — TQ2850
Common Lime, tallest specimen: 44 x 1.59 (1979).

Glasnevin Botanic Gardens, Dublin — E33123
White Willow, record girth: 30 x 1.18 (1987).

Glenberrow, Nr Eastnor, Herts. & Worcs. — SO7636
Fine Black Poplar.

Gunnersbury Park, London — TQ1877
Box, record girth: 8 x 0.28 (1987).

Hall Place, Penshurst, Kent — TQ5243
Hawthorn, tallest specimen: 16 x 0.78 (1984).

Hallyburton House, Tayside — NO2438
Beech, tallest specimen: 46 x 1.51 (1986).

Hartlebury Castle, Herts. & Worcs. — SO8470
Common Osier, tall specimen: 8 x 0.16 (1988).

Hatfield Forest, Herts. & Worcs. — TL5421
Ancient Hornbeam and other pollards.
Hawthorn pollard, record girth: 16 x 1.16 (1989).

Hayley Wood, Cambs. — TL2953
Fine ancient wood.

Heron Court, Nr Christchurch, Dorset — SZ1593
Hornbeam, record girth: 20 x 1.46 (1985).

Hethel, Norwich, Norfolk — TG1402
Ancient Hawthorn planted by King John (Old Thorn).

Highnam Court, Over, Glos. — ST5882
Domestic Pear — Old Perry Pear, stoutest specimen:
17 x 0.83 (1988).

Honeywood Farm, Monkshall, Essex — TL8443
Wild Pear: 11 x 0.65 (1991)

Hurstbourne Priors, Andover, Hants. — SU4347
Horse Chestnut, record girth: 36 x 2.13 (1983).

Kew Gardens, Surrey — TQ1877
Fine Strawberry Tree.
Hornbeam, good group of trees.

Kinettles Castle, Glamis, Tayside — NO3846
Field Maple, tallest specimen: 27 x 0.81 (1986).

Kingly Vale, W. Sussex — SU8208
Yew woodland on the Downs.

Leicester University Botanic Gardens, Leics.   SK5904
Bristlecone Pine, good specimen: 12 x 0.25 (1985).

Leighton Hall, Shrops.   SJ6105
Black Poplar, record girth: 33 x 1.85 (1985).

Leith Hill, Surrey   TQ1342
Silver Birch, record girth: 26 x 1.33 (1987).

Lennoxlove, Lothian   NT4074
Sycamore, tallest specimen: 40 x 1.154 (1985).

Leonardslee Garden, Nr Lower Beeding, Sussex   TQ2227
Dawn Redwood: 30 x 0.58 (1989).

Lingholm, Keswick, Cumbria   NY2621
Norway Spruce, record girth: 43 x 1.47 (1983).

Loch Rannoch (Caledonian Pine Forest), Highland   NN5606
Scots Pine, good specimens.

Longnor Hall, Shrops.   SJ4800
Black Poplar, tallest specimen 38 x 1.63 (1985).

Markshall Avenue, Nr Chelmsford, Essex   TL8403
Wild Service: 26 x 1.24 (1991).

Markshall, Nr Chelmsford, Essex   TL8403
Hornbeam, good specimen: 20 x 0.72 (1990).

Megginch Castle, Tayside   NO4030
Whitebeam, tallest specimen: 12 x 0.83 (1986).

Meiklouer, Perthshire   NO1539
Planted Beech hedge 90ft high.

Moccas Park, Hereford, Herts. & Worcs.   SO3542
Ancient pollards (wood pasture).

Moniack Glen, Inverness, Highland   NH4754
Norway Spruce, tallest specimen: 52 x 0.8 (1986).

Moniack Castle, Highland   NH4754
Wineries where birch sap wine is produced.

Moniack Glen, Highland   NH4754
Goat Willow, tallest specimen: 21 x 0.49 (1987).

Moreton on Lugg, Herts. & Worcs.   SO5045
White Willow, record girth: 23 x 2.35 (1989).

Muckross Peninsula, Killarney, Co. Kerry   S49686
Yew wood and Hazel, good specimens.

Munches Estate, Dalbeattie, Dumfries & Gall.   NX8361
Aspen, record girth: 22 x 0.46 (1985).
Aspen, tallest specimen: 25 x 0.38 (1985).

Ochtertyre, by Crief, Tayside   NN8323
Hairy Birch, tallest specimen: 28 x 0.67 (1987).

Old Kiln, Frensham, Surrey   SU8441
Bird Cherry, tallest specimen: 14 x 0.33 (1988).

Ovington, Nr Winchester, Hants.   SU5633
Crack Willow, record girth: 21 x 1.29 (1980).

Oxford University Park, Oxon.   SP5305
Crack Willow, tallest specimen: 25 x 0.89 (1988).

Oxleas Wood, Falconwood, London   TQ4376
Ancient woodland.

Pinkney Park, Nr Westonbirt, Sherston, Glos.   ST8585
White Willow, tallest specimen: 31 x 0.90 (1981).

Pitchford Hall, Pitchford, Nr Condover, Shrops.   SJ5304
Large-leaved Lime, record girth: 14 x 2.36 (1984).

Priestwood, Great Kingshill, Bucks.   SU8899
Rowan, tallest specimen: 20 x 0.39 (1984).

Priors Mesne, Nr Coleford, Forest of Dean, Glos.   SO5711
Wild Cherry, tallest specimen: 31 x 0.71 (1976).

Rectory, Much Hadham, Herts.   TL4319
Horse Chestnut, tallest specimen: 37 x 1.81 (1984).

Rossies Priory, Tayside   NO2931
Ash, record girth: 12 x 2.81 (1988).

Scone Palace, Scone, Tayside   NO1125
Large-leaved Lime, tallest specimen: 37 x 1.43 (1981).

Silwood Park, Nr Ascot, Beds.   SU9168
Strawberry Tree, tallest specimen: 15 x 0.32 (1982).

St. Neots, Riverside Gardens, Cambs.   TL1796
Almond Willow: 18 x 1.08
Almond Willow: 23 x 0.87

Staverton Park, Suffolk   TM3551
Holly trees growing out of ancient oak pollards:
26 x 1.01 (1988).

Strone House, Nr Cairndow, Strathclyde   NN1810
Grand Fir, tallest tree in Britain: 63 x 1.84 (1989).

Studley Royal, Ripon, Yorks.   SE3070
Wild Cherry, record girth: 18 x 1.70 (1984).

The Lodge, Sandy, Beds.   TL1649
Strawberry Tree, record girth: 6 x 0.79 (1988).

Tickards Manor, Guildford, Surrey   TQ0049
Common Pear, tallest specimen: 21 x 0.73 (1986).

Tottenham House, Savernake Forest, Wilts.   SU2266
Small-leaved Lime, tallest specimen: 40 x 1.17 (1984).

Trebah, Mannansmith, Cornwall   SW7728
Hornbeam, tallest specimen: 30 x 0.86 (1985).

Tullynally Castle, Nr Castle Pollard, Co. Westmeath   E32427
Beech, record girth: 14 x 2.17 (1990).

Tyninghame, Hoddington, Lothian   NT6179
Sweet Chestnut, tallest specimen: 36 x 1.84 (1984).

Udimore, Sussex   TQ8718
Wild Service, tallest specimen: 20 x 1.34 (1989).

Ulcombe Church, Kent   TQ8449
Yew, record girth: 13 x 3.34 (1985).

West Felton, Shrewsbury, Shrops.   SJ3425
Original Dovaston Yew.

Westbury Court, W. of Gloucester, Glos.   SO7113
Holm Oak, record girth: 14 x 2.74 (1986).

Westonbirt Arboretum, Nr. Tetbury, Glos.   ST8993
Aspen, Hazel and Juniper — good specimens.

Whitfield House, Nr Thruxton, Herts. & Worcs.   SO4334
Sessile Oak, tallest specimen: 43 x 1.48 (1984).

Wicken Fen, Cambs.   TL5670
Bay Willow, tall specimen: 20 x 0.83.

Windsor Park, Berks.   SU9572
Ancient Oak woodland.

Woodstock, Nr Innistioge, Co. Kilkenny   E32613
Holm Oak, tallest specimen: 29 x 1.31 (1989).
Coast Redwood, record girth: 42 x 2.45 (1989).

Wotton House, Dorking, Surrey   TQ1649
Wild Service, record girth: 17 x 0.80 (1983).

Wyre Forest, Worcs.   SO7576
Beech, fine specimens. Whitty Pear tree.

Native Tree and Seed Suppliers

W = Wholesale, R = Retail

SCOTLAND

Banff & Buchanan Nurseries Ltd [W & R]
Baley Farm, Portsoy, Banff.

T. & W. Christie (Forres) Ltd [R]
The Nurseries, Forres, Moray.

Duartbeg Tree Nurseries [W & R]
by Scourie, Sutherland.

Ledaig Nursery [W & R]
Ledaig, Oban, Argyll.

Tilhill Nurseries [W]
Tillycorthie Nursery, Udny, Ellon, Aberdeenshire.

NORTHERN ENGLAND

Chiltern Seeds [R]
Bortree Stile, Ulverston, Cumbria.

Trees Please [W & R]
Low Urpeth Farm, Ouston, Chester-le-Street, Durham.

Weasdale Nurseries [W & R]
Newbiggin on Lune, Kirkby Stephen, Cumbria.

MIDDLE ENGLAND

Bernhard's Nurseries Ltd [W & R]

The Straight Mile, Rugby, Warwickshire.

Forestart [W]
Church Farm, Hadnell, Shrewsbury, Shropshire.

Merryweather Nursery [W & R]
Hallam Road, Southwell, Nottinghamshire.

EASTERN ENGLAND

Huverba UK Ltd [W]
Fairview Nurseries, Church Road, Emneth, Wisbech, Cambridgeshire.

Notcutts Nurseries Ltd [W]
Notcutts Garden Centre [R]
Woodbridge, Suffolk.

Read's Nurseries [R]
Hales Hall, Loddon, Norfolk.

Tacchi's Nurseries [W]
Tacchi's Garden World [R]
Wyton, Huntingdon, Cambridgeshire.

WESTERN ENGLAND

Trees and Wildflowers [W & R]
British Trust for Conservation Volunteers (BCTV)
The Old Estate Yard, Newton St Loe, Bath, Avon.

SOUTHERN ENGLAND

English Woodlands Ltd [W]
Burrow Nursery, Herrings Lane, Cross-in-Hand, Heathfield, Sussex.

Forestry Commission [W]
Research Station, Alice Holt Lodge, Wrecclesham, Farnham, Surrey.

Frilsham Nursery [W]
Frilsham, Yattendon, Newbury, Berkshire.

Oakover Nurseries [W]
Calehill Stables, The Leacon, Charing, Ashford, Kent.

Sandeman Seeds [W]
The Croft, Sutton, Pulborough, West Sussex.

Tilhill Nurseries [W]
Greenhills, Tilford, Farnham, Surrey.

WALES

Dingle Nurseries [W & R]
Welshpool, Powys.

Wild Seeds [R]
Branas, Llanderfel, Nr Bala, Gwynedd.

Woodlands Services and Supplies Ltd [W & R]
Brooklands, Mardy, Abergavenny, Gwent.

NORTHERN IRELAND AND EIRE

Ballard Products Ltd [W & R]
Ballard House, Kilbeggan, Co. Westmeath.

Baronscourt Nurseries [W & R]
Abercorn Estates, Newtonstewart, Co. Tyrone.

Coillte Nurseries [W & R]
Ballintemple Nursery, Ardattin, Co. Carlow.

Gurteen Agricultural College [W & R]
Ballingarry, Co. Tipperary.

Heather Noble [R]
Excelsior Trees, Clooneboney, Mohill, Co. Leitrim.

Rountree Nurseries [W & R]
Fivealley, Birr, Co. Offaly.

Ulster Native Trees [W]
67 Temple Rise, Temple Patrick, Ballyclare, Co. Antrim.

British and Irish Tree Organizations

Arboricultural Advisory & Information Service, Forestry Commission Research Station, Alice Holt Lodge, Wrecclesham, Farnham, Surrey.

Arboricultural Association, Ampfield House, Ampfield, Romsey, Hampshire.

Ashling Woodland Development (Co-operative Society), Mohill, Co. Leitrim, Eire.

Association of Professional Foresters, Brokerswood House, Brokerswood, Westbury, Wiltshire.

Bedgebury Pinetum, Bedgebury, Hawkhurst, West Sussex.

Bees and Trees Trust, c/o 36 Rock Lane, Ludlow, Shropshire.

Black Country Urban Forestry Unit, Red House, Hill Lane,

Great Barr, Sandwell, West Midlands.

Borders Community Woodlands, The Steading, Blainslie, Galashiels, Borders.

Botanic Gardens Conservation Secretariat, Descanso House, 199 Kew Road, Richmond, Surrey.

British Christmas Tree Growers Association, 12 Lauriston Road, Wimbledon, London SW19.

Brogdale Horticultural Trust (National Fruit Collections), Brogdale Road, Faversham, Kent.

C.A.B. International Forestry Bureau, Wallingford, Oxfordshire.

Capel Manor College, Bulsmoor Lane, Enfield, Middlesex.

Charlbury Tree Trust, Worm Wood Cottage, Pooles Lane, Charlbury, Oxfordshire.

Children's Tropical Forests UK,
The Old Rectory, Church Street, Market Deeping, Peterborough, Leicestershire.

Coed Cymru,
Stryd Frolic, Y Drenewydd, (Newtown) Powys.

Coillte (State Forestry Board),
Leeson Lane, Dublin 2, Eire.

Commonwealth Forestry Association,
Oxford Forestry Institute, South Parks Road, Oxford, Oxfordshire.

Commonwealth Forestry Bureau,
University of Oxford, South Parks Road, Oxfordshire.

Crann Sa Chathair (Woodland Management Trust),
23/25 Moss Street, Dublin 2, Eire.

Crann Sa Chathair (Woodland Management Trust),
Killegar, Co. Leitrim, via Cavan, Eire.

The Dendrologist,
Monksfield, Pednor Bottom, Chesham, Buckinghamshire.

Department of Agriculture, Forest Service, Public Relations and Education Branch, Dundonald House, Belfast, Northern Ireland.

Department of Energy, Forest Service, Leeson Lane, Dublin 2, Eire.

Devon Tree Bank,
c/o Devon Wildlife Trust, 35 Newbridge Street, Exeter, Devon.

Elms Across Europe,
Pitney Bowes Ltd, The Pinnacles, Elizabeth Way, Harlow, Essex.

English Woodlands Ltd,
Burrow Nursery, Cross-in-Hand, Heathfield, West Sussex.

English Woodlands Ltd,
Wealden Forest Park, Herne Common, Herne Bay, Kent.

English Woodlands Ltd,
18a High Street, Theale, Reading, Berkshire.

English Woodlands Ltd,
The Old Barn, Roke Lane, Witley, Godalming, Surrey.

Forestry Commission,
231 Corstorphine Road, Edinburgh, Lothian.
The addresses of other regional offices can be obtained by writing to the head office, above.

Forestry Commission Research Station,
Alice Holt, Wrecclesham, Farnham, Surrey.

Forestry Trust for Conservation and Education,
The Old Estate Office, Englefield Road, Theale, Reading, Berkshire.

Forests Forever Campaign,
4th Floor, Clareville House, 26/27 Oxendon Street, London SW1Y 4EL.

Friends of Westonbirt Arboretum,
Westonbirt Arboretum, Tetbury, Gloucestershire.

Fruit Identification Service,
c/o Royal Horticultural Society, Wisley Gardens, Wisley, Surrey.

Glasgow Tree Lovers' Society,
62 Kirkaldy Road, Maxwell Park, Glasgow, Strathclyde.

Green Wood Trust,
Rose Cottage, Dale Road, Coalbrookdale, Telford, Shropshire.

Green Wood Trust,
Coalbrookdale Station, Coach Road, Coalbrookdale, Telford, Shropshire.

Greenbelt Co., see Strathclyde Greenbelt Co.

Hardman Arboretum,
Dunham Road, Bowdon, Altringham, Manchester.

Hergest Croft Garden,
Kington, Hereford & Worcestershire.

Highland Wineries,
Moniack Castle, Kirkhill, Inverness.

Hillier Gardens and Arboretum,
Jermyns Lane, Ampfield, Nr Romsey, Hampshire.

Institute of Chartered Foresters of Great Britain,
22 Walker Street, Edinburgh, Lothian.

International Dendrology Society,
School House, Stannington, Morpeth, Northumberland.

International Forest Science Consultancy,
Woodhall Mill House, 10 Woodhall Mill Brae, Edinburgh, Lothian.

International Peace Forest,
PO Box 7, Stroud, Gloucestershire.

International Tree Crops Institute,
2 Convent Lane, Bocking, Braintree, Essex.

Lakeland Charcoal,
Devonshire House, Finsthwaite, Ulverston, Cumbria.

Loch Garry Tree Group,
Wester Balrobbie, Killiecrankie, Perthshire, Tayside.

London Tree Officers Association,
Front Office, Christchurch Avenue, Wealdstone, Middlesex.

Margaret Mee Amazon Trust,
c/o Herbarium, Royal Botanic Gardens, Kew, Richmond, Surrey.

Men of the Trees,
Sandy Lane, Crawley Down, West Sussex.

National Fruit Collections, see Brogdale Horticultural Trust.

National Small Woods Association,
c/o Tower House, North Street, Lewes, East Sussex.

Norfolk Forestry Club,
Norfolk College of Agriculture, Easton, Norwich, Norfolk.

Oak Glen
32 Upper Bagot Street, Dublin 4, Eire.

Oxford Forestry Institute,
University of Oxford, South Parks Road, Oxford, Oxfordshire.

Oxford Tree Club,
9 St Bernard's Road, Oxford, Oxfordshire.

Reading Tree Club,
38 New Road, Reading, Berkshire.

Reforest the Earth,
48 Bethel Street, Norwich, Norfolk.

Replanting Vietnam,
c/o EIB Ltd, PO Box 6, Diss, Norfolk.

Royal Botanic Gardens
Inverleith Row, Edinburgh.

Royal Botanic Gardens
Kew, Richmond, Surrey.

Royal Forestry Society of England, Wales and Northern Ireland,
102 High Street, Tring, Hertfordshire.

Royal Scottish Forestry Society,
11 Atholl Crescent, Edinburgh, Lothian.

Sacred Trees Trust,
31 Kings Avenue, Leeds, West Yorkshire.

Save Coolattin Woods,
Johnstown House, Carlow, Eire.

Save the Forests Save the Planet,
42 Windsor Road, London NW2.

School of Agriculture Arboretum,
University of Nottingham,
Sutton Bonnington,
Loughborough,
Leicestershire.

Scottish Arboricultural Society,
4 Knightsbridge Road,
Dechmont, West Lothian,
Lothian.

Scottish Community Woods Campaign,
3 Kenmore Street,
Aberfeldy, Tayside.

Scottish Forestry Trust,
5 Dublin Street Lane South,
Edinburgh, Lothian.

Scottish Tree Trust,
30 Edgemont Street,
Shawlands, Glasgow,
Strathclyde.

Scottish Woodland Owners Association,
6 Chester Street, Edinburgh,
Lothian.

Silvanus,
Unit 4, The National
School, St Thomas Road,
Launceston, Cornwall.

Society of Foresters of Great Britain,
see Institute of Chartered Foresters of Great Britain.

Society of Irish Foresters,
c/o Royal Dublin Society,
Ballsbridge, Dublin 4, Eire.

Society for the Preservation of Rain Forest Environment,
c/o Geography Department,
University of Hull, Kingston upon Hull, Humberside.

South Molton Woodland Projects,
The Mill, Bish Mill, South Molton, Devon.

Stevenage Woodlands Conservation Society,
7 Lodge Way, Stevenage,
Hertfordshire.

Strathclyde Greenbelt Co.,
61 Holland Street, Glasgow,
Strathclyde.

Task Force Trees,
4th Floor, 71 Kingsway,
London WC2B.

Timber Research and Development Association,
Stoding Lane, Hughenden Valley, High Wycombe,
Buckinghamshire.

Timber Trade Federation,
Clareville House,
26/27 Oxendon Street,
London SW1Y.

Tree Aid,
Mayfield, The Street,
Farmborough, Bath, Avon.

Tree Council,
35 Belgrave Square,
London SW1X.

Tree Council of Ireland,
33 Botanic Road, Glasnevin,
Dublin 9, Eire.

Tree Group,
11 Killin Avenue, Dundee,
Tayside.

Tree People,
89 Charlton Park, Midsomer Norton, Bath, Avon.

Tree Register of the British Isles,
Rosemead, 24 Lickfields Road, Rowledge, Farnham,
Surrey.

Tree Spirit,
Hawkbatch Farm, Arley,
Nr Bewdley, Hereford & Worcestershire.

Trees for Ireland,
22 Cabinteely Green,
Dublin 18,
Eire.

Trees for Life,
c/o Findhorn Foundation,
The Park, Forres, Grampian.

Trees for People,
141 London Road,
St Albans, Hertfordshire.

Trees for Survival,
7 Abbotsfield Crescent,
Tavistock, Devon.

Treesearch UK,
1 Meadow Cottages,
Springhill Farm, Cuddington Road, Dinton, Aylesbury,
Buckinghamshire.

Tubex Ltd,
Tannery House, Tannery Lane, Send, Woking,
Surrey.

Urban Forests,
7 Acacia Court, Brocket Road, Hoddesdon,
Hertfordshire.

Westonbirt Arboretum,
Westonbirt, Nr Tetbury,
Gloucestershire.

Winkworth Arboretum,
Hascombe Road,
Godalming, Surrey.

Winton Loan Woodland Trust,
1 Winton Loan, Edinburgh,
Lothian.

Woodland Heritage Museum,
Brokerswood House,
Brokerswood, Westbury,
Wiltshire.

Woodland Trust (Community Woodlands),
Autumn Park, Dysart Road,
Grantham, Lincolnshire.

Woodland Trust (Scotland),
54 Manor Place, Edinburgh,
Lothian.

Woodland Trust (Wales),
19 Maitland Place,
Grangetown, Cardiff, South Glamorgan.

World Forest Action,
6 Glebe Street, Oxford,
Oxfordshire.

World Rainforest Movement (UK Branch),
8 Chapel Row, Chadlington,

Further Reading

This reference list gives just a sample of the enormous number of published books, papers and articles on trees and tree topics. Sources used in the text are given here and I hope that readers interested in particular topics will find this list useful.

Identification

The best available field guides for identification of trees are the *Field Guide to the Trees of Britain and Northern Europe* by Alan Mitchell (1991) and *Trees in Britain, Europe and North America* by Alan Phillips (1988), which include many excellent drawings and photographs. Standard works produced by the Forestry Commission on native trees are now out of print: *Know Your Broadleaves* and *Know Your Conifers* are very informative — an expanded and updated version of these two books to be entitled *Forest and Woodland Trees in Britain* by John White will

be published by the Forestry Commission in the near future. More technical works giving botanical accounts of the trees and all other plants in these islands are *Flora of the British Isles*, third edition, by A. R. Clapham, A. G. Tutin and D. M. Moore (1987), and the excellent *New Flora of the British Isles* by Clive Stace (1991), which includes new keys, good photographs and drawings and many introduced species, hybrids and varieties. The nomenclature is also up to date. For cultivated trees and shrubs the Hillier guides, such as the latest edition of the Hilliers Manual, are the most comprehensive guides.

Distribution of Trees and Specific Species

Distribution maps of all British plants, including trees, are given by Walters & Perring (1962). There are handbooks on groups of particular interest such as *Willows and Poplars* by R. D. Meikle (1984) published by the Botanical Society of the British Isles (BSBI). Other trees, such as elms, have attracted specific books on all apsects of their natural and cultural history such as *Epitaph for the Elm* by G. Wilkinson (1978) and *Elm* by R. H. Richens (1983).

Champion Trees

Trees in these islands have been measured assiduously by Alan Mitchell, J. E. J. White and others; the most up-to-date version of *Champion Trees* was published in 1990.

Arboriculture

Many specialist handbooks and research reports on particular aspects of trees and arboriculture have been published by the Forestry Commission. A particularly useful series are the handbooks including, *No. 1 Forest Insects* by D. Bevan (1987), *Urban Forestry Practice* edited by B. G. Hibberd (1989) and *Treeshelters* by M. J. Potter (1991). All these publications as well as a complete list are available from HMSO. The properties of wood are discussed technically in the *Handbook of Hardwoods*, and the *Handbook of Softwoods* (HMSO).

Trees and Conservation

The role of trees in conservation is discussed by many authors; woodland conservation and management is the topic and also the title of Dr G. Peterken's standard work on the subject, which is about to be reprinted. There is no comprehensive inventory of the relationships of insects with trees, but one is in preparation by scientists at Imperial College, London.

A standard work on pollination, *The Pollination of Flowers*, is by M. Proctor and P. Yeo (1973). A. Darlington has written what is still the standard handbook on galls, *A Pocket Encyclopedia of Plant Galls* (1968). *Birds and Berries* by B. and D. Snow (1988) is a comprehensive study of that group of interactions. A good field guide to fungi is by Bon (1987).

History of Trees

The history of trees, woodland and tree cultivation in Britain has been thoroughly researched and admirably explained by O. Rackham in several definitive works, including *Trees and Woodland in the British Landscape* (1976), *History of the Countryside* (1986), and *Ancient Woodland* (1980). The earlier works on trees include John Evelyn's monumental *Sylva*, available in facsimile edition (1979), and J. C. Loudoun's *Arboretum et Fruticetum Britannicum* (1844), which also includes many accounts and drawings of individual trees. Famous trees were also drawn in great detail by J. G. Strutt in *Sylva Britannica* (1822). It would be most interesting if a contemporary artist were to follow his example with a similar book today. In Ireland, a recent book by E. Neeson entitled *A History of Irish Forestry* is an excellent history of trees as well as forestry.

Folklore of Trees

Literature on the folklore of trees is very scattered, but Geoffrey Grigson's *The Englishman's Flora* (1960) is perhaps the most important starting point; he also includes medicinal and culinary uses of trees and tree products. Old herbals, such as *Culpepper's Complete Herbal*, list medicinal and other uses. For tree-lore in Ireland, J. Lucas's article, 'The Sacred Trees of Ireland', though difficult to find, is essential. *The White Goddess* by Robert Graves (1990) is very informative on ancient folklore, which includes trees, the tree alphabet and what might be termed the mythology of trees.

Food From Trees

Richard Mabey in *Food for Free* (1972) and Roger Phillips in *Wild Food* (1983) have explored the culinary uses of wild plants, including trees, exhaustively and with imagination; both these books are strongly recommended.

Periodicals

Finally, there are a number of periodicals which concentrate on trees: *Tree News* is produced by the Tree Council, *The Dendrologist* by the International Dendrology Society and an excellent newer publication, *Reforesting Scotland* (lately *Tree-Planters' Guide to the Galaxy* is the journal of Reforesting Scotland. *Plant Lore: News and Notes* is a cyclostyled bulletin of folklore records circulated by Roy Vickery of the Natural History Museum.

General List of Publications

Allen, D., 'Alder in Folk Medicine' (*Plant-Lore: Notes and News*, **15**: 66, 1990).

American Forestry Association, *National Register of Big Trees* (1992).

Anon, *Chambers Practical Works of Robert Burns* (W. & R. Chambers Ltd, 1990).

Anon, *Handbook of Hardwoods* (HMSO, 1988).

Anon, *Handbook of Softwoods* (HMSO, 1986).

Anon, *Know Your Broadleaves* (Forestry Commission Booklet No. 20, HMSO, 1968).

Anon, *Penguin Dictionary of Botany* (Penguin Books, 1984).

Armstrong, L., *Woodcolliers and Charcoal Burning* (Coach Publishing House Ltd / Weald and Downland Open Air Museum, 1978).

Bailey, J., *The Westonbirt Arboretum Tree Heritage Trail* (Forestry Commission Research Division, 1985).

Baker, H., *The Fruit Garden Displayed* (Royal Horticultural Society, 1986).

Baker, Richard St Barbe, *My Life My Trees* (Findhorn Press, 1970).

Barratt, M., *Oak Swill Basket Making in The Lake District* (Barratt, 1983).

Bartholomew, B., Boufford, D. E. and Spongberg, S., *Metasequoia glyptostroboides — Its Present Status in Central China* (J. Arnold, *Arbor* **64**: 105-128).

Bellamy, D., *The Wild Boglands: Bellamy's Ireland* (Country House, 1990).

Bennett, K. D. and Birks, H. J. B., 'Postglacial History of Alder (*Alnus glutinosa* [L.] Gaertn.) in the British Isles (*Science*, **5**: 123-133, 1990).

Bevan, D., *Forest Insects : A Guide to Insects Feeding on Trees in Britain* (Forestry Commission Handbook No. 1, HMSO, 1987).

Birks, H. J. B., 'Holocene Isochrone Maps and Patterns of Tree-spreading in the British Isles' (J. Biogeograph., **16**: 503-540, 1989).

Bon, M., *The Mushrooms and Toadstools of Britain and Northwestern Europe* (Hodder & Stoughton, 1987).

Bown, D., *Westonbirt; the Forestry Commission's Finest Arboretum* (Forestry Commission / Julian Holland, 1990).

Brendall, T., *Willows of the British Isles* (Shire Natural History, 1985).

Briggs, T. R. A., *Annual Report in the Annals of the Botanical Exchange Club* (1870).

Brzeziecki, B. and Kienast, F., *Classifying the Life-history Strategies of Trees on the Basis of the Grimian Model* (in press).

Burdekin, D. A., *Common Decay Fungi in Broadleaved Trees* (HMSO Arboricultural Leaflet No. 5, 1979).

Clapham, A. R., Tutin A. G. and Moore D. M., *Flora of the British Isles* (Cambridge University Press, 1991).

Clifford, S. and King, A. (ed.), *Trees Be Company: An Anthology of Poetry* (Common Ground, Bristol Press, 1989).

Common Ground, *Orchards; A Guide to Local Conservation* (Common Ground, Bristol Press, 1989).

Colebourn, P., *Hampshire's Countryside Heritage: Ancient Woodland* (Hampshire County Council, 1983).

Corbet, S. A., 'Pollination and the Weather' (*Israel Journal of Botany*, 39: 13-30, 1990).

Corner, E. J. H., *The Life of Plants* (Master Books, 1968).

Cornish, V., *The Churchyard Yew and Immortality* (Frederick Muller, 1944).

Culpepper, N., *Culpepper's Complete Herbal* (Foulsham, London, facsimile edition, undated).

Darlington, A., *A Pocket Encyclopaedia of Plant Galls* (Blandford Press, 1968).

Dewitt, J. B., *Californian Redwoods Parks and Preserves* (Save the Redwoods League, 1985).

Dickson, J. H., *The Yew Tree (Taxus baccata L.) in Scotland: Native or Early Introduction or Both?* (in press).

Edlin, H. L., *Collins Guide to Tree Planting and Cultivation* (William Collins Sons and Co., 1970).

Edlin, H. L., *Trees, Woods and Man* (Collins New Naturalist Series, 1966).

Edlin, H. L., *Woodland Crafts of Britain* (David and Charles, 1973).

Elves, H. J. and Henry, A. H., *The Trees of Great Britain and Ireland* (Royal Forestry Society, 1969).

Evans, E. E., *Irish Folkways* (Routledge & Kegan Paul, 1959).

Evelyn, John, *Sylva* (Stobart and Son Ltd, facsimile edition, 1979).

Feehan, J., *Laois — An Environmental History* (Ballykilcavan Press, 1983).

Fife, Hugh, *The Lore of Highland Trees* (Famedram Publishers, undated).

Fitzrandolph, H. E. and Hay, M. D., *Rural Industries of England and Wales* (Vols 1 & 2, Oxford University Press, 1977).

Frazer J. G., *The Golden Bough — A Study in Magic and Religion* (Abridged Edition, Papermac Publishers, 1991).

Giles, A., 'The Grey Old Men of Moccas' (*Tree News*, September 1990).

Giorno, Jean, *The Man who Planted Trees* (Chelsea Green Publishing Co., 1985).

Godwin, H., *History of the British Flora — Phytogeography* (Cambridge University Press, 1984).

Graves, R., *The White Goddess* (Faber & Faber, 1990).

Greig, B. J. W., Gregory, S. C. and Strouts, R. G., *Honey Fungus* (Forestry Commission Booklet No. 100, HMSO, 1991).

Grigson, Geoffrey, *The Englishman's Flora* (Phoenix House Ltd, 1960).

Grime, J. P., *Plant Strategies and Vegetation Processes* (John Wiley and Sons Ltd, 1979).

Grime, J. P., Hodgson, J. G. and Hunt, R., *The Abridged Comparative Plant Ecology* (Unwin Hyman, 1990).

Harris, J. G. S., *Trees and the Law* (Arboricultural Association,

1989).

Hayes, S., *A Practical Treatise on Planting and Management of Woods and Coppices* (Dublin Society, 1794).

Hibberd, B. G. (ed), *Urban Forestry Practice* (Forestry Commission Handbook, No. 5).

Hicken, N. E., *The Natural History of an English Forest* (Nicholls, 1971).

Hobson, D. D., 'The Status of Populus nigra L. in the Republic of Ireland' (*Watsonia* 18: 303-305, 1991)

Hodge, S. A., *Urban Trees — A Survey of Street Trees in England* (Forestry Commission Bulletin No. 99, HMSO, 1991).

Hole, C., *A Dictionary of British Folk Customs* (Paladin, 1984).

Howard, A., *Countryways — The Four Seasons* (Countryside Books/TVS, 1987).

Howe, J., *Hazel Coppice; Past, Present and Future, the Hampshire Experience* (County Planning Dept, Hampshire County Council, 1991).

Innes, J. L., *Assessment of Tree Condition* (Forestry Commission Field Book No. 12, 1990).

Johns, Rev. C. A., *The Forest Trees of Britain* (SPCK, 1875).

Joyce, P. W., *The Origin and History of Irish Names of Places* (Longmans, Green & Co., seventh edition, 1901).

Kelly, F., 'The Old Irish Tree List' (*Celtica* 11: 107-124, 1976).

Kennedy, C. E. J. and Southwood, T. R. E., 'The Number of Species of Insect Associated with British Trees: A Re-analysis' (*Ecol.* 53: 455-478, 1984).

Kennelly, B., *Love of Ireland; Poems from the Irish* (The Mercier Press Ltd, 1989).

Kennelly, B., *A Time for Voices: Selected Poems 1960–1990* (Bloodaxe Books, 1990).

King, Angela and Clifford, Susan, *Trees Be Company* (The Bristol Press, 1989).

Kuser, J., 'Metasequoia Keeps on Growing' (*Arnoldia* 42: 130-138, 1982).

Ledig, F. T., 'The Conservation of Diversity in Forest Trees' (*Bioscience*, 38: 471-480, 1988).

Lewington, A., *Plants for People* (Natural History Museum, 1990).

Lipkis, A. and K., *The Simple Act of Planting a Tree* (Jeremy P. Tarcher, Los Angeles, 1990).

Loudoun, J. C., *Arboretum et Fruticetum Britannicum* (London, 1844).

Lucas, A. T., *The Sacred Trees of Ireland* (Hist. & Arch. Soc., 1962-3).

Lysaght, P., *Maytime Verdure Customs and Their Distribution in Ireland* (International Folklore Review, 1991).

Mabey, R., *Food for Free — A Guide to the Edible Wild Plants of Britain* (William Collins Sons & Co. Ltd, 1972).

Mather, A. S., *Global Forest Resources* (Belhaven Press, 1990).

Matthews, J. D., 'The Influence of the Weather on the Frequency of Beech Mast Years in England' (*Forestry* 28: 107-116, 1955).

McAllister, H. A., *The Rowan and its Relatives* (Ness Botanic Gardens, 1986).

Meikle, R. D., *Willows and Poplars of Great Britain and Ireland* (BSBI Handbook No. 4, 1984).

Mingay, G. E. (ed.), *The Agrarian History of England and Wales*

Vol. VI 1750–1850 (Cambridge University Press, 1989).

Mitchell, A., *A Field Guide to the Trees of Britain and Northern Europe* (Harper Collins, 1991).

Mitchell, A., Hallett, V. E. and White, J. E. J., *Champion Trees* (HMS0, third edition, 1990).

Mitchell, P. L., 'Repollarding Large Neglected Pollards : A Review of Current Practice and Results' (*Arboricult.*, **13**: 125-142, 1989).

Morton, A., *The Trees of Shropshire* (Airlife England, 1986).

Muir, J., *The Yosemite* (Sierra Club Books, 1988).

Neeson, E., *A History of Irish Forestry* (Lilliput Press, 1991).

Nelson, E. C., 'The Nomenclature and History in Cultivation of the Irish Yew, *Taxus baccata "fastigiata"*' (*Glasra*, **5**: 33-44, 1981).

O'Connor, F., *Kings, Lords and Commons* (Gill and Macmillan, 1991).

O'Heochaidh, S., NiNeill, M. and O'Cathain,˙ S., *Fairy Legends from Donegal* (University College Press, Dublin, 1977).

Opie and Opie, *Language and Lore of Schoolchildren* (Oxford University Press, 1959).

Perring, F. H. and Walters, S. M. (ed.), *Atlas of the British Flora* (Botanical Society of the British Isles, 1962).

Peterken, G., *Woodland Conservation and Management* (Chapman Hall, 1992).

Peters, C. M., Gentry, A. H. and Mendelsohn, R. O., Valuation of Amazonian Rainforest (*Nature*: **339**: 655-657, 1989).

Phillips, R., *Trees in Britain, Europe and North America* (Pan Books, 1988).

Phillips, R., *Wild Food* (Pan Books, 1983).

Pigott, C. D., 'Selective Damage to Tree Seedlings by Bank Voles' (*Oecologia*, **67**: 367-371, 1985).

Pigott, C. D. and Huntley, J. P., 'Factors Controlling the Distribution of *Tilia cordata* at the Northern Limits of its Geographical Range' (*New Phytol*. **81**: 429-441, 1987. *New Phytol*. **84**: 145-164, 1980. *New Phytol* **87**: 817-839, 1981. *New Phytol* **112**: 117-121, 1989).

Poore, D., *No Timber Without Trees* (Earthscan, 1989).

Potter M. J., *Treeshelters* (Forestry Commission Handbook No. 7, HMSO, 1991).

Powell, T. G. E., *Ancient Peoples & Places 6 — The Celts* (Thames and Hudson, 1958).

Proctor, M. and Yeo, P., *The Pollination of Flowers* (William Collins Sons and Co., 1973).

Rackham, O., *Ancient Woodland — Its History, Vegetation and Uses in England* (Edward Arnold, 1980).

Rackham, O., *The History of the British Countryside* (Dent, London, 1986).

Rackham, O., *Trees and Woodland in the British Landscape* (Dent, London, 1976).

Randolph, U. C., *Early Irish Satire and the Whitethorn* (Folklore, 1943).

Read, J. (ed.), *Pollard and Veteran Tree Management. Proceedings of a Meeting at Burnham Beeches* (Corp. of London, 1991).

Royal Horticultural Society, *Manual of Trees and Shrubs* (Hillier Press, 1981).

Richens, R. H., *Elm* (Cambridge University Press, 1983).

Roach, F. A., *Cultivated Fruits of Britain : Their Origin and History* (Basil Blackwell, 1985).

Rushforth, K., *Mitchell Beazley Pocket Guide to Trees* (Mitchell Beazley, 1987).

Savill, P. S., *The Silviculture of Trees used in British Forestry* (C. A. B. International, 1991).

Sealy, R. J., 'Arbutus unedo' (*J. Ecol*. **37**: 365-388, 1949).

Silverman, M., *Search for the Dawn Redwoods* (Silverman Publishers, 1990).

Sinden, Neil, *In a Nutshell: A Manifesto for Trees and A Guide to Growing and Planting Them* (Common Ground, Bristol Press, 1989).

Smith, A. H., *English Place-Name Elements* (English Place-Name Survey, Vols **25**, **26**, EPNS, University of Nottingham, 1970).

Snow, B. and D., *Birds and Berries* (T. and A. D. Poyser, 1988).

Spongberg, S. A., *A Reunion of Trees* (Harvard University Press, 1990).

Stace, C. A., *New Flora of the British Isles* (Cambridge University Press, 1991).

Step, E., *Wayside and Woodland Trees: A Guide to British Sylva* (Frederick Warne, 1948).

Stokoe, W. J., *The Caterpillars of the British Butterflies* (Frederick Warne, 1944).

Stokoe, W. J., *The Caterpillars of British Moths: 1st Series — Sphingidae to Brephidae* (Frederick Warne, 1948).

Stokoe, W. J., *The Caterpillars of British Moths: 2nd Series — Geometridae to Hepialidae* (Frederick Warne, 1948).

Strahm, W., *Plant Red Data Book for Rodrigues* (Koeltz Books for WWF and IUCN, 1989).

Strutt, J. G., *Sylva Britannica* (London, 1822).

Taplin, K., *Tongues in Trees: Studies in Literature & Ecology* (Green Books, 1989).

Thistleton-Dyer, T. F., *The Folklore of Plants* (London, 1889).

Thomas, K., *Man and the Natural World* (Penguin, 1983).

Thoreau, H. D., *Walden* (Bantam Books, 1982, first pub. 1854).

Toogood, A., *Garden Trees Handbook* (Harper Collins, 1990).

Vickery, R., *Holy Thorn of Glastonbury St Peter Port* (West Country Folklore, No. 12, 1979).

Vickery, R. (ed.), *Plant-Lore Studies* (Folklore Society, 1984).

Vickery, R. (ed.), *Unlucky Plants* (Folklore Society, 1985).

Watts, K., 'Scots Pine & Droveways' (Wiltshire Folklife, **19**: 3-6, 1989).

Webb, D. A., *Some Observations on the Arbutus in Ireland* (*The Irish Naturalists Journal*, **9**: 198-203 1948).

Whitbread, T., *When the Wind Blew* (Royal Society for Nature Conservation, 1991).

White, Gilbert, *A Natural History of Selbourne* (Penguin, 1990).

White, J. E. J., *Forest and Woodland Trees in Britain* (Forestry Commission, in press).

Wilkes, J. H., *Trees of the British Isles in History and Legend* (Frederick Muller, 1972).

Wilkinson, G., *Epitaph for the Elm* (Hutchinson, 1978).

Williamson, R., *The Great Yew Forest* (Macmillan, 1978).

Winter J. G., *The Catalogue of Phytophagous Insects and Mites on Trees in Great Britain* (Forestry Commission Booklet No. 53, 1983).

Glossary of Tree Terms

Agroforestry A method of land use based on the deliberate integration of trees and shrubs in crop and livestock production systems. Carefully selected and managed trees can increase soil fertility, control erosion, protect crops from livestock and adverse weather, as well as help conserve water.

Angiosperm See gymnosperm.

Anthers The apical part of a stem that produces pollen or microspores. (Male sex organ of the plant.)

Arboriculture The cultivation of trees in order to produce individual specimens of the greatest ornament, for shelter or any other primary purpose other than the production of timber.

Aril A fleshy or hairy outgrowth of a seed or ovule, i.e. not derived from the ovary which normally makes up the fruit. (The red fleshy cup surrounding the seed of the Yew is an aril.)

Carr Fen woodland usually dominated by alder.

Catkin A pendulous inflorescence modified for wind pollination (though sometimes insect pollinated).

Coppice/Coppicing A form of woodland management in which trees are cut back down to ground level regularly (every few years) to encourage growth of shoots from the base. The resulting thicket is termed a copse or a coppice.

Cotyledons Seeds in angiosperms have either one or two leaf-like parts that contain stored food. Flowering plant classification is based on distinguishing those with one cotyledon-like grasses (monocotyledons) — or two — as in beans or acorns (dicotyledons).

Dicotyledon See cotyledon.

Dioecious Plants in which the female and male reproductive organs are separated on different individuals (as opposed to monoecious where they are found on the same plant).

Dozed A term used by woodworkers to describe wood that has veins or patterns of darkened wood passing through it due to infection by fungi.

Fastigiate A tree with almost vertical branches close to stem, resulting in a pyramidal or conical form. e.g. Irish Yew or Lombardy Poplar.

Genus A rank in the taxonomic hierachy, meaning a group of similar species, denoted by a Latin name starting with a capital letter. The binomial naming system was originated in 1758 by a Swedish monk, Linnaeus, in his 'Species Plantarum'.

Grafting A horticultural method of plant propagation in which a segment (the scion) of the plant to be propagated is inserted into another plant (the stock) in such a way that their vascular tissues combine so allowing growth of the grafted segment.

Gymnosperm One of two important divisions of seed-bearing vascular plants, with seeds not enclosed in an ovary i.e. fruit and typically borne on cones e.g. conifers. The other division is angiosperm, in which seeds are enclosed in an ovary (fruit) e.g. apple, acorn, beech mast.

Heartwood The central wood of trees consisting of dead cells. The properties of this wood (darker colour, resistance to decay, greater density) make it more highly prized for furniture manufacture and other uses.

Inflorescence Any flowering structure consisting of more than one flower. Rowan or whitebeam flowers form an inflorescence, while a daffodil is a single flower.

Keys The common name given to the winged seeds found on some trees, e.g. ash, sycamore.

Krummholz The dwarfed and usually flattened trees that are found between rocks at high altitudes in mountains. They tend to grow along the ground and are thus able to withstand strong winds in these exposed regions, and also withstand snowfall.

Mast (years) The fruit of beech and some similar related trees. Some years trees produce large quantities of fruit and these are known as mast years.

Monocotyledon See cotyledon.

Monoecious Plants in which the female and male reproductive organs are found on the same plant (see dioecious).

Native tree A tree not originally introduced by human agency, growing on a site it occupies naturally.

Osier Species of willow used for basketmaking.

Ovule The female reproductive unit and its protective and nutritive tissue, which develops into the dispersal unit or seed after fertilization in plants.

Paleobotany Study of plantlife of the geological past.

Pollarding Method of tree-management in which the main trunk of a tree is cut at about 8-10 feet, and the resulting branches are then cropped on a regular rotation of a few years. Pollarding produces a characteristic tree shape of a short thick trunk with a mass of small branches at the top.

Pollen The male reproductive spores of seed plants which are produced in vast numbers usually in pollen sacks (anthers) borne on the stamens.

Pollination The transfer of pollen grains from the male reproductive organs, stamens, to the female reproductive organs, style and ovary, in seed plants.

Polygamous The condition of bearing male, female or hermaphrodite flowers on the same plant.

Ruderal Weed or pioneer species.

Silviculture The management and exploitation of forests.

Species A group of organisms which make up a single actual or potential successful breeding population. The main unit of biological classification of genus which is the second part in the Latin binomial naming system.

Spore Tiny reproductive cell of a plant.

Stamens Male part of flower that bears anthers which produce pollen.

Standard Tree grown to full height, usually for timber.

Stool Ground level base of a coppiced tree such as willow or hazel.

Stratification The practice of placing seeds between layers of moist sand or peat and exposing them to low temperature. This treatment is necessary for those seeds that need a period of chilling before germination can begin. Chilling in a refridgerator some weeks prior to sowing achieves the same objective with many kinds of seed.

Style Female part of flower that receives pollen.

Taxonomy The study of the principles and practice of classification, especially of living organisms.

Wildwood Prehistoric forest.

Withy One- or two-year-old willow shoots cut for basketwork.

Index

Illustration Acknowledgements

The Board of Trinity College Dublin: 84 below, 137. British Gall Society: 28, 42. By kind permission of Nancy Harrison: 109 below. Coates Willow Museum: 98 above. Crann: 160. EP Publishing: 85. The Forestry Commission: 26, 51, 52, 67, 78. From Moore, P.D., Webb, J.A. & Collinson, M. E. 1991 Pollen Analysis. 2nd edition, Blackwell Scientific Productions, Oxford: 74 above and below, 75 above. From J. Otis Williams, Mammoth Trees of California (Boston, 1871): 122. Gothic Image, Glastonbury: 141 above. Edward Green: 33, 56, 63, 89. Simon Hodge: 154. London Natural History Society: 88, 92. Mansell Collection: 144. Merryweather's Nursery: 108. Edward Milner: back cover, 22, 23, 24, 34, 40, 41, 49, 54, 55, 58, 59, 60 above, 61, 62, 76 below, 77, 80,82 above and below, 83, 84 above, 86, 87, 90 above, 95, 98 below, 99, 101 above and below, 104, 106, 109 above, 110, 111, 113 above and below, 114, 115, 116, 125 below, 130, 131, 133, 134, 136, 138 above and below, 139, 140 above and below, 141 below, 155. Natural History Museum: 75 below, 102. Oxford Scientific Films: 66, 70 below. Tim Page: 125 above. Edward Parker: 27, 70 above, 76 above, 79, 96, 97, 103, 105 above and below. Photographic Archives of Arnold Arboretum: 126. Royal Society for the Protection of Birds: 91, 117, 120. Stephen A. Spongberg: 128, 129. Larry Ulrich: 121, 124. University of Reading, Institute of Agricultural History and Museum of English Rural Life: 97 above, 100. Alan Watson: front cover, 2, 10, 11, 12, 14, 15, 16, 18, 19, 20, 30, 31, 36, 37, 38, 45, 48, 50, 60 below, 64 left, 71, 90 below, 123, 142, 146, 147. John White: 64 right. David Woodfall: 47.